Happiness Guaranteed
or
Your Misery Back

How to be Happy No Matter What!

J. Morton Davis
&
Ruki D. Renov

Copyright © 2018 J. Morton Davis & Ruki D. Renov
All rights reserved
First Edition

PAGE PUBLISHING, INC.
New York, NY

First originally published by Page Publishing, Inc. 2018

ISBN 978-1-64214-234-1 (Paperback)
ISBN 978-1-64214-236-5 (Hardcover)
ISBN 978-1-64214-235-8 (Digital)

Printed in the United States of America

To my gorgeous, vivacious, and brilliant wife, Rozi, with whom I made my greatest merger. She is the very definition—and the source—of more happiness than any one human being deserves.

—J. Morton Davis

> My Dear Friend,
> I wish you happiness every day of your life, in good health until you're 120, then we'll negotiate for more. Enjoy!
>
> Love, Morty

Acknowledgments
by J. Morton Davis

    I have written myself notes for a book on happiness for the last ten years. Then, my daughter Ruki Renov played a decisive role in bringing it to fruition. After so many years, publishing the Happiness Therapy Formula in the form of *Happiness Guaranteed or Your Misery Back* involved the dedicated cooperation and the contribution of many valuable friends and associates.

    I have been incredibly blessed to have received the assistance and editorial contributions from my devoted daughter, Ruki Renov, an accomplished author in her own right. Her brilliant and tireless efforts, as well as unique sense of humor and love of quotes, have informed this work with a magical warmth and spirit that exudes from every page.

    And of course whatever wisdom I've attained in the course of my now long life, I owe to all the great thinkers, philosophers and writers, to the biblical and Talmudic scholars' teachings and to some of the outstanding professors and teachers I've been lucky enough to have along the way who all taught me of the worthwhile and wonderful things in this world—the other stuff I discovered (or dreamed up) on my own.

    I must thank my wonderfully ingenious and dedicated colleagues, Leonard Katz and Marty Bell, and my truly phenomenal assistants, Ruth Robles, Alisa Flynn, Diane Vanderlinden, and Alison Brown, who helped track and organize my voluminous notes and ideas over the years.

    Finally, I would like to thank my entire family, starting with my exalted wife Rozi, and most especially my amazingly prolific daughters Esti Stahler, Ruki Renov, Rivki Rosenwald and Laya Perlysky, as well as my treasured sons-in-law Kal Renov, Alan Stahler, Dr. Lindsay Rosenwald and Dov Perlysky. Without their peristently encouraging me to keep writing, I might have been done with this book years ago!

I have been continuously motivated and inspired to write this book and present its ideas for my kids, grandkids and for all those I love, as well as for you, in the sincere hope that it, or even an idea or two in it, can influence your life positively and add a meaningful measure of happiness to you throughout your lifetime.

Foreword
by Ruki Renov

Two kids are talking to each other. One says, "I'm really worried. My dad works twelve hours a day to give me a nice home and good food. My mom works so hard all day cleaning, cooking and taking care of me. I'm worried sick." The other kid says, "What have you got to worry about? Sounds to me like you've got it made!" The first kid says, "What if they try to escape?"

"There, but for the grace of G-d, go I" (John Bradford).

One of the major themes of this book, which my father, J. Morton Davis, invested years of his life into, is to consciously choose to look at the bright side by appreciating all that you have and looking forward to all of life's wonders that lie ahead.

Two of the most precious things in life that can't be chosen, that I am blessed to have, and that I am beyond words in expressing my appreciation for, and look forward to having and enjoying for many years to come, are my amazing parents.

My father, J. Morton Davis, is well known for his brilliant career, his keen business acumen and his rise from poverty to success. My mother, Rozi Davis, though also brilliant, beautiful and talented, is better known for her role as a superb mother.

Both of them are authors, speakers, radio-show hosts and politically, community and religiously involved, as well as being extremely and most lovingly focused on and devoted to our family—their dynasty. Both my parents have outstanding writing ability and a spectacular sense of humor.

Yet, this book never seemed to get completed. I, therefore, lucky to have learned from the best, (them, of course) decided to try to make this happiness book a reality. After over two years of work, adding jokes, stories, psychological studies and quotes, to what I felt was already an amazing concept, containing brilliantly well thought out substance, current events, life lessons and superb relevancy, I believe I have finally brought my father's ideas to completion.

I know it will make my father exceedingly happy that it is finished. Most importantly, I hope reading and incorporating its lessons into your life makes you exuberantly happy.

Introduction

Just because you're miserable doesn't mean you can't enjoy your life.

If you can laugh, why cry?
If you can learn to cope, why lie around and mope?
If you can be productive, why laze around doing nothing?
If you can go out and find joy, why stay and sulk?
If you can bring gladness by helping others, why not find gladness by helping yourself?
If you can control your mind, why lose it?
If you can smile, why frown?
If you can feel good by being optimistic, why be sad by being a pessimist?
If you can make lemonade, why sit and stare at sour lemons?
If you can unburden yourself of anger and resentment, why carry the heavy load?
If you can love others, why not love yourself first?
If you can psychologically raise your spirits, why become dependent on dangerous drugs and spirits?
If you can conquer jealousy, why go around wanting someone else's greener grass?
If you can turn to people you love for help, why turn away from them?
If you can move on from tragedy, why let a death, deaden you as well. Why let a divorce, divorce you from living? Why let a financial loss cause you to lose more than your money? Why let life's struggles beat you down?

If you can believe that G-d loves you and is with you, why choose to feel lonely and unprotected?

If you can throw your problems up to G-d, why carry them yourself?

If you can take a busted balloon and blow it up, you're a miracle worker, but if you can take your shattered ego or your distraught soul and repair it, you are a student of *Happiness Guaranteed or Your Misery Back*.

Note: When quotes do not have author's name, author is unknown.

Day 1

G-d, wanting to hide the secret of happiness, called the angels together, asking them for suggestions where to hide it. The first angel said, "Hide it deep under the sea." The second angel said, "Hide it on the highest mountain in the world. Man will never find it there." The third angel said, "Hide it deep within the human soul. Human beings will never think to look there." And that's exactly what G-d did.

This book is a prescription for eliminating sadness and depression in order to produce a healthier, happier state of mind. Each individual must look deep within himself and decide that he wants to find genuine happiness.

The lessons presented herein can transform you, helping you perceive your life in a more positive way. This amazing conversion experience will develop through a healthier way of viewing your daily life and through the crystallization of a more fulfilling, upbeat attitude that can be self-implanted and sustained for the rest of your life.

This book stresses and explores the power of positive thinking and how it can change your personal and business life. It will show you that you have the power to control your mind in order to dramatically, advantageously change your life and achieve tremendous gratification and delight.

It will teach you to adopt and inculcate a second nature to perpetrate a positive, optimistic mind-set and an ever cheerful, hopeful outlook. As Hugh Downs so correctly said, "A happy person is not a person in a certain set of circumstances, but rather a person with a certain set of attitudes."

This book will guide you on how to develop a confluence of doing, thinking and feeling in harmony with your physiology, so that if you are not feeling good, you can change what you are doing, what you are thinking, how you view your situation and how you cope with it. You can consciously create a new outlook by altering your thinking and your state of mind, elevating yourself above all the noise and minutiae that attempt to impose an unpleasurable mind-set.

By incorporating the lessons of this book, you will learn to automatically, instinctively switch off depressing thoughts and switch on positive, uplifting ones as easily as you flick your bedroom lights on and off.

The book is divided into 365 days, so you can read a lesson a day or you can read ten a day and feel really accomplished by finishing your year's reading much sooner. Perhaps, the best way to begin altering your attitude is as a kind of short-term—one month or two months—personal fun experiment. The journey will be as meaningful and critically important as the destination. You will enjoy the process, savoring the emotional rewards and taking pleasure in each day. Once you get a spark of control, it will become a flame that lights the way for you and warms your very heart.

You may find repetition in the book. It's necessary because this is not a book to be read once and then hide on a library shelf; its lessons must be constantly repeated, restudied and practiced over and over again. Let the recommendations become an ingrained part of your nature.

The book also includes a spiritual component, based on our lifetime study of and influence by the Torah and other inspiring sources, which we believe can help you.

Start by telling yourself, "The happiest people don't have the best of everything, they just make the best of everything."

This book will teach you to take a new, beautiful view of all aspects of your life. "People are not disturbed by things but by the view they take of them" (Epictetus).

Day 2

When you feel stressed out, when everyone seems to be leaving you, when the world seems to be fading away in the mist, when your life feels like a big blur, when you have lost clarity, when you can't seem to retain focus, when you've lost your vision and perspective, please let me know; I will take you to an eye specialist for a check up.

Being happy is a conscious, logical decision. Life has unlimited potential for finding happiness, but you must accept that life isn't perfect. People aren't perfect. Circumstances aren't perfect.

You thought you'd be the best athlete, pull the best grades, land the best job, make the most money, marry the best spouse, have the most obedient kids, have a sympathetic boss, an understanding husband or wife and stay healthy and happy always—but some of this hasn't happened. Even if some of it has happened, it doesn't feel as marvelous as you had hoped it would. It's not as fulfilling, as rewarding, as ego boosting as you'd imagined.

This book will teach you how, despite life's imperfections, to train yourself to feel content, satisfied and appreciative. Being prepared and accepting of reality is a major step in limiting stress, coping with challenges and being able to enjoy life's magnificent benefits.

Studying the writings herein will help you stay cognizant of the fact that, everyone has fears and insecurities. We all have instances and areas in which we feel inadequate or incompetent. We often feel lonely, disrespected, unappreciated, unnoticed and insignificant. We all, to some degree, experience the feelings of helplessness and vulnerability. We all, at one time or another, have to conquer frustration and push through depression. We are all scared of hearing bad news or of being faced with challenging situations.

What if, sadly, you lost your job, got divorced, lost an arm or G-d forbid lost a loved one; should you lie down and go into permanent depression? This book will show you that life is good and that there is a happy, fulfilling life even after tragedy. Happiness is a choice and you have the power to choose it.

Viewing life from an optimistic perspective and learning to alter your thoughts and control your outlook will help you to reframe your disposition and increase your life enjoyment.

Perhaps, every day when you walk into your office your desk is piled high with paperwork, you have hundreds of e-mails to check and your boss always gives you a look of disappointment. What if you could learn to easily mange your e-mails, find a way of quickly going through your paperwork and learning to smile at your boss? Wouldn't this make your life more pleasant? With insight and direction, it's doable. Change is difficult but developing new habits is quite possible, especially when you have the will and the tools. This book will give you the instruction and the steps. You just have to contribute the desire to take those steps.

Wouldn't you love to learn to appreciate your job, your spouse, your children and your circumstances, despite how difficult they are, or learn to change your future to alter an unfixable situation?

This book will guide you on how to cultivate an outlook that will lower frustration and increase appreciation, as you manage your thought process to view your life and the world with positivity. It will teach you to control fear and anxiety.

You will come to understand and adjust your own thinking and master that thinking. You will learn to train yourself not to look at what others have, but rather to look and appreciate what you have; not to look at where you messed up, but rather to look at where you can improve; not to assign blame, but rather to take responsibility; not to look at what is upsetting you, but rather to look at how you might improve your circumstances; not to focus on regret, but rather to look forward and enthusiastically plan for the future. You will learn how to determine a path forward and start moving in that direction.

You will come to appreciate that it is inefficient to take on major changes that most often won't happen, but rather to take on tiny goals that add up; not to try to change your entire life, but rather to change one small act at a time.

You will acquire the ability not to try to force yourself to believe the world is beautiful, but rather to start noticing its beauty—the flowers, the butterflies, the caring people, the warm smiles…

This book will instruct you how to take on a small project that will help you like yourself and build your own self-esteem. You will learn to do for yourself, do for others, forgive yourself, forgive others, exercise, meditate, sing, love, laugh and thank G-d.

You will learn the value of talking to yourself, motivating yourself, encouraging yourself and truly liking yourself. It will instruct you on the benefits of finding time to stay goal oriented and focused and to find time to relax and chill.

You will find your life enriched by exploring the importance of being with the people who care about you; pushing yourself to smile, to laugh, to hold your head high, to put yourself in other people's positions viewing things through their eyes; learning to carry yourself with your shoulders erect in a stance of "I can," rather than "I can't;" taking the position of "I am worthy. I am capable;" and taking responsibility for who you are while recognizing much is out of your control, but how you react is in your control.

In essence, this book will teach you how to "stand up to your own obstacles and do something about them. You will find that they haven't half the strength that you think they have" (Norman Vincent Peale).

It will also reinforce the idea that you don't have to be the best you only have to be the best you can be. You don't have to like your circumstances but you do have to like yourself and you do have to work on developing the will, the confidence and the conviction to improve your circumstances.

Decide to be happy. Make others happy. Make yourself happy. "Happiness is like jam. You can't spread even a little without getting some on yourself."

Day 3

If everything seems to be going well, you have obviously overlooked something.

The *New York Post* (2014) published an article by positive psychologist Barbara Fredrickson who states that the "golden ratio" for one to thrive and be happy is to experience three positive emotions for one negative (3 to 1). Fredrickson concluded that less than 20 percent of individuals meet this ratio.

In 2005, Fredrickson and Marcel Losada outlined a "positivity calculus" theory drawn from fluid dynamics and a subfield of physics and found that flourishing is associated with a positivity ratio of about 2.9 and that a more common ratio of 2 to 1 could help people "get by" but not thrive.

The 3 to 1 ratio of positives to negatives, refers to overall happiness, but they believe that certain scenarios require different ratios, such as in order for a relationship to thrive, there needs to be a 5 to 1 ratio of positive to negative experiences.

A paper published in 2013 questioned these findings, claiming the study may not have much basis in psychological science because Fredrickson and Losanda never explained how an advanced mathematical formula could be applied to human emotion.

Nevertheless, all agree that to thrive, one must be happy. You have the power to make yourself happy. Psychologist Rick Hanson, author of *Hardwiring Happiness*, says, "We're surrounded by opportunities—ten seconds here or twenty seconds there—to just register positive experiences and learn from them. People don't do that when they could."

Whatever the happiness ratio may be, it is obvious that the more you instill happiness in your life by doing things you enjoy, whether it be working, travelling, eating, socializing, or by being with people you love, by liking yourself, by giving to or doing for others, by appreciating what you have, by accepting and facing life's flaws and challenges and by teaching your mind to focus on the positives, the happier and more productive you will be.

As Abraham Lincoln said, "People are as happy as they make up their mind to be."

Day 4

What do you get when you cross a thought and a light bulb? A bright idea!

"The greatest discovery of my generation is that a human being can alter his life by altering his attitudes" (William James). In the last two million years, the human brain has tripled in size due to the development of a new structure: the prefrontal cortex. According to psychologist Dan Gilbert, this part of the brain acts as an experience simulator. It helps us imagine how we would feel in a certain situation without our having to experience that situation. It helps us imagine that if we won the lottery we would be unbelievably happy. In the midst of unhappiness, we can envision happiness.

I used to think the brain was the most important organ. Then, I thought, look who's telling me that. Now, I continuously work on training my brain to think positive, upbeat thoughts, to see the world in a brighter light. You too have this awesome power to direct your thoughts to create your own happiness. Samuel Johnson taught, "Happiness is not a state to arrive at; rather, it's a manner of traveling." "The real voyage of discovery consists not in seeking new landscapes but in having new eyes" (Marcel Proust).

Day 5

My happiness depends on me, so you're off the hook.

Until 1998, scientists believed that after age three the brain doesn't change. Now, we know that the brain continually changes throughout life, called neuroplasticity. There are millions of neurons and pathways each thought is associated with one of many pathways. As we repeat a thought process, the pathway becomes wider allowing easier flow of thought. By fortifying a neural pathway, it attracts more and more similar thoughts.

Psychologists now believe we have to be aware what type of channels we are creating, such as hate and love channels, indifference and caring channels. If, for example, one is constantly selfish, this pathway widens and your response to a situation will most likely be selfish. Psychologists ask are you creating wider anger or compassion pathways? If one has cultivated compassion, his thoughts will be pulled into that channel. If the neural pathway for anger is larger, it pulls an anger response to the same trigger. If you strengthen your positive responses such as patience, caring and optimism, when a situation arises, you will have taught yourself to respond positively.

Throughout life, it is natural for all of us to feel pain, frustration, and anger. How we react to these feelings is up to us. You can cry, rant and rave, or you can respond with calm, thought-out logic. Learning to take time to deal effectively with these feelings will make you a more emotionally balanced and relaxed individual.

Practice being upbeat and happy, in order to widen your happiness pathways.

Day 6

"Some people think of the glass as half full. Some people think of the glass as half empty. I think of the glass as too big."—George Carlin

Mark Twain defined an optimist as "a person who travels on nothing from nowhere to happiness."

Elaine Fox, a psychologist at the University of Essex in England, author of a book on the science of optimism, *Rainy Brain, Sunny Brain*, maintains that you can constructively modify your brain circuits by strengthening what she refers to as the "sunny" brain and by weakening the "rainy" brain.

Ms. Fox wisely advises, "Take control over how you feel rather than letting feelings control you," which succinctly sums up the theme of this treatise on happiness. Ms. Fox fully endorses precisely what I am urging you to inculcate: if you learn to control how you feel, you control your own destiny. You will bounce back from setbacks and maximize your enjoyment in life!

If this concept can seemingly all be summarized in one sentence, why would I bother to author a book on this topic? I can only justify it by relating it to an example in my own life. I love playing tennis. I am very competitive, hopefully in a friendly and constructive way. I work hard, consistently, endlessly to improve my game. I've taken literally hundreds of lessons from innumerable professionals throughout the United States and the world. I've read any book that has been suggested to me which might give me an additional insight and enhance my game—my serve, my groundstrokes, my volleys, my overhand, my drop shot, my topspin, my underspin, even my sidespin, my footwork, my emotional attitude on the court, my physical stamina, etc. I listened to and watched the greatest tennis pros to see if I could pick up the slightest tip that might help make me more successful at this "simple" sport, which I consider a most exciting activity.

One would think that after a couple of lessons and reading a few books by successful players, I would consider this sufficient and decide that further investment in learning tennis techniques would be a waste of time, money and energy. But, the more and different ways I studied and learned to do this activity, the more fulfilling was the experience and the more successful I became. I cherish that investment, and to this day, I still work at it.

So, why wouldn't I, and why shouldn't you, do at least as much to improve your capacity to be a "winner" in the pursuit of a more fulfilling, happy life?

Work at being more optimistic in every situation and circumstance you are faced with. Consult as many different authors, books, articles, lecturers, professors, psychologists and caring friends that could help you learn to control your mind and its responses.

"Repetition of the same thought or physical action develops into a habit, which, repeated frequently enough, becomes an automatic reflex" (Norman Vincent Peale). Repeatedly, think of the positive side of every situation and every challenge.

To quote Donald Trump, "As you enjoy success you will be successful." Similarly, as you implement and practice the prescribed behavior in this book, you will find that you experience a more cheerful demeanor and an uplifting exuberant state of mind, which will encourage and inspire you to repeat and reinforce this happiness inducing behavior.

As fast as you can, turn each unhappy thought into a happy one.

Day 7

What's the definition of happiness? Getting up in the morning and seeing your mother-in-law's picture on a milk carton!

Does it make any sense that in the United States, where we have more advantages and greater prosperity than ever in history, the rates of depression are ten times higher than they were in 1960? Furthermore, where as in 1960 the average age for the onset of depression was twenty-nine and a half, today the average age is fourteen and a half. Studies show that 45 percent of college students are unable to function due to depression.

Sadly, our culture teaches and our minds falsely believe that only if we succeed in attaining our goal, will we be happy; if I pass the test, if I get the job, if I get the girl, then I will be happy. But, the happiness is often short lived. When we achieve our goal, we mistake the relief that we experience, for happiness. The harder one worked, the greater the suffering endured, to accomplish the goal, the greater the relief. Tal Ben Shahar, the brilliant author and Harvard professor, says this is negative happiness resulting from the relief. This is a feeling of release from pain, which is typical of members of society's rat race, which won't last.

Other individuals mistakenly seek happiness by avoiding pain and only seeking pleasure. They want happiness now and give no thought to future consequences. Tal Ben Shahar calls these individuals hedonists. They aimlessly do detrimental things, such as drinking and taking drugs with no thought of consequences. These people soon realize that life feels empty and meaningless.

Another unfortunate attitude belongs to individuals who feel only hopelessness and despair. Because of some event or experience in the past, they feel they have no control and therefore can't envision hope for the present or future. Shahar terms this "learned helplessness."

It is essential to realize that no one can be happy every moment of life, and expecting to be will just cause disappointment, frustration and unhappiness. Not everything we do can provide both present and future happiness. Sometimes, we must forego present pleasure to ensure greater future gains such as when we take exams, save for the future or practice piano. The goal, of course, is to spend as much time as you are able to immersed in activities, which provides you with both present and future benefits.

Unfortunately, if we only work towards the future, we miss out on enjoying the present. If we only live enjoying the present, we have no future and if we dwell in the disappointments of the past, we never create a future. Psychologists have consistently determined that in order to attain lasting happiness, one must enjoy the journey and be heading towards a fulfilling goal.

Day 8

Okay, who stopped the payment on my reality check?

Don't simply be complacent, as most people are, and accept the hopeless attitude that "it's out of my control, it just happens to me and I can't help it." Learn that you can be in charge. You can take control. Don't just let things happen to you. Make what you want to happen—especially when it comes to the state of your emotions. The people that actively develop the ability to mentally control their reactions are the happiest people in the world.

It's amazing; approximately 50 percent of our happiness is genetically determined. Up to an additional 40 percent comes from the things that recently occurred, but that happiness is short-lived. Even successes or victories you worked years to achieve lose their happiness impact after a few months. The remaining approximately 12 percent of our happiness has been shown to be in our power to control.

We each have a happiness baseline that we fluctuate around on a daily basis, but with effort, we can raise that baseline. Psychologists and neuroscientists have discovered that this 12 percent is quite significant in a person's perception of life.

As you develop the ability to master your attitude, it actually will modify your brain. Cutting-edge researchers have discovered that your brain will begin to display *unique* brainwave characteristics and higher states of consciousness. As you train your brain, your brain itself will change physically to incorporate this positive training. In due course, this alteration assists you to automatically, almost intuitively, introduce uplifting feelings without your having to think about or work at it.

Believe in your ability to command, direct and rule your own brain. You possess extraordinary, almost miraculous, power to design, chart and manage your own brain—to become the master of your brain, so that despite all circumstances, it adopts the most desirable mental state.

The reward for training your brain is an inner calmness, an ease of functioning, a gratifying emotional state and what we all are in perennial pursuit of—happiness. Take charge! Be the manager of your own brain and of the emotions it produces. Decide that life is to be enjoyed not just endured.

Day 9

Today may be the first day of the rest of your life, but on the other hand, it's also the last day of your life so far.

Two people can look at the exact same thing and see something different. One man loses his job and refuses to get out of bed. The other man loses his job and perceives it as an opportunity for a new start. One man breaks a leg and constantly complains about feeling like an invalid, while the other breaks his leg and thinks, "Wow, so many people willing to help me." One person fails a test and speaks of the horror of retaking it, and the other fails and speaks of the chance to learn the material much more thoroughly for the retest.

One man looks at old age and sees it as a privilege, the opportunity to enjoy his grandchildren, while the other rants and raves about the aches and pains of the aging process. One person suffers a terrible loss and thinks, "I will never be happy again." Another person suffers such a loss and thinks, "Eventually, when I live through this, I will have learned how to help others live through their sorrows."

Every negative has a potential positive. It is up to you to find it and to view the situation in that manner. One can surrender or take up the challenge. One can decide to be devastated by life's trials or to grow from them. "One person looks up at the sky and sees the darkness, the other looks up and sees the stars." "Happiness is not determined by what's happening around you but rather what's happening inside you." In order to achieve happiness, let go of what you think your life is supposed to look like and celebrate it for what it is.

Day 10

I'll have a café mocha vodka Valium latte to go please.

Rather than focusing on the little things that can make us happy, we tend to focus on the little things that don't really matter but rob us of our happiness. We can't be happy because we have become accustomed to living with worry and tension. We have made sorrow and grief part of our daily life. Sadly, you could pass the entire day without happiness but can't make it through a day without worrying.

We allow fears to dominate and ruin our lives, skew our perspective, deprive us of the chance to be better or do something we have never tried before. We do not focus on enjoying the present; rather, we allow little things to diminish our happiness throughout the day.

A cute story is told about Nasrudin, a 13th century philosopher, who was walking alone at night and saw a group of men approaching him. His imagination ran wild and he imagined they were going to rob him, murder him, and perhaps even leave him for dead. He worried what would happen to his family without him. He began to panic, to sweat, to shake and to become short of breath. He terrified himself to the point where he ran into a nearby cemetery and laid cowering inside an open grave awaiting his fate.

Meanwhile, the harmless strangers, worried by his behavior, approached and looked into his tomb. "What are you doing down there?" they asked with concern. Nasrudin, calmed down and said, "Well, put it this way: I am here because of you and you are here because of me."

We misuse our imagination allowing it to torment us. In case of anxiety, control your breathing, breathing out longer than you breathe in. This forces your body to calm down. Stop. Focus on your breathing. Take a breath in to the quick count of seven in your mind and then slowly breathe out to the quick count of eleven in your mind. Do this 7/11 breathing for about a minute. (This need not be exact, but breaths out have to be longer than the in-breaths.)

If you fear an upcoming event, the anticipation causes a physical response of anxiety such as a racing heart and sweats. This makes you even more anxious by the time the event occurs. To remain calm, do the 7/11 breathing while imagining the upcoming situation.

Anxiety clouds your thinking as the emotional part of the brain floods the thinking part. In times of fear, strengthen your thinking part. Rate your fear on a scale of 1 to 10. (10 being the most terrified.) Just "scaling," trying to figure out the number of your fear, kick-starts the thinking brain, calming you. You are taking control of your brain.

A bit of fear is useful in case there really is danger, but uncontrolled imagination is a nesting ground for anxiety and fear that can ruin your life. Calm your fears by imagining that things are going well and you are composed and relaxed in the dreaded situation.

Don't just allow fear and anxiety to happen to you. Take control. Use AWARE. *A*ccept that you are anxious. *W*atch for anxiety so that when you notice it, you can scale your level of fear and breathe longer on the out-breath. *A*ct normally as if nothing is wrong. This signals the unconscious mind that it is over reacting. *R*epeat the above steps in your mind if necessary. *E*xpect the best. Realizing that you are in control and can overcome your fear and anxiety will make you feel elated.

"The greatest weapon against stress is our ability to choose one thought over another" (William James).

Day 11

A woman told her friend, "Last year, we took a trip around the world. This year, we are going someplace else."

Every journey is planned ahead of time. On a directionless trip, one wanders aimlessly, arriving who knows where, after experiencing all manners of obstacles, misadventures and dangers.

This book is a guide as to the route to take, the method of conveyance, to reach the splendid destination of happiness. Don't go through the journey of life, surely the most meaningful and crucial journey any of us will ever take, without having a specific plan in your mind.

Those who want happiness without planning or working to achieve it are like those who want crops without plowing the ground.

Map out how to achieve the destination you are aiming for—to be constructive, to find contentment, to achieve happiness, not only in the end, but also all along the way. Realize that "the happiness of your life depends on the quality of your thoughts" (Marcus Aureleus). Decide to try a concept such as smiling through the pain or thinking of the benefit to be gained from every challenge, and work on that practice until it becomes automatic.

Decide that your happiness is the most worthwhile, propitious goal. How great your control can be is indeterminable. Just as athletes keep breaking records because the brain and body adjust to new levels, we don't know the limit to which our brainpower can expand to learn this new reaction. Our potential is unimaginable.

Your happiness is your decision.

Day 12

"I like life. It's something to do."—Ronnie Shakes

By now, you realize that *Happiness Guaranteed* presents an approach to life in which you focus only on the positive, today, tomorrow and next week. You accept life's challenges rather than succumb to them. You cry, you laugh, you move on.

Peysach Krohn tells of a seminar he attended in which a sales rep explained the sales experience as SW/3 N. "Some will, some won't, so what—next!" He realized this is the truth as it pertains to life. Some situations will work out, some won't, so what—next. Don't get stuck in the disappointing or painful now. Look back at all that's good. Look around at all the wonder that is. Look forward to all that can be. Think that life isn't good right now. It will get better. I haven't achieved what I hoped to, I will. My life is in pieces—so is a puzzle. I can put it back together. Turn every mistake into a lesson, every painful loss into a beautiful memory, every challenge into an opportunity for growth. Turn every frown into a smile, every tear into a stream of hope.

Dr. Rabbi Abraham Twerski explains that it is not the discovery of our defects that is frightening but the discovery of our strengths and skills. Being aware of our potential imposes the responsibility of accomplishing things. If we fear failure, we find it easy to think, "There is no use in my trying. I can't do it anyway." Remaining in a rut may be comfortable, while getting out of the rut is frightening. This fear of responsibility stems from a feeling of inadequacy. Even success frightens the insecure individual making him feel that he will be given more responsibility. Failure puts an end to this fear.

Each person, in order to make life's challenges manageable, must muster the courage to discover how great he really is, and that he has strengths and abilities he never imagined he possesses. "Too many of us are not living our dreams because we are living our fears" (Les Brown).

"Life is a series of daily problems interrupted by a catastrophe once in a while." Enjoy while it's calm. Savor the good times. Save your energy for when life gets rough. Build up your reserves of appreciation of faith and of self-worth.

Always seek the positive, and if it isn't immediately apparent, be positive that with effort, with stretching your mind's eye, you will find it. Some days will be good. Some won't. So what? Move on!

Day 13

Most people can't stand prosperity...but then again, most people don't have to.

If one ever required irrefutable evidence that what you think, how your mind works, and how your own attitude can play a major determining role in achieving a specific hoped for outcome, one needs only to look back to the enormously successful results so many people achieved by acquiring, digesting and practicing what Napoleon Hill conveyed in his 1932 book *Think and Get Rich*.

Hill effectively taught people to think their way to success. In like manner, you can think your way to happiness. By controlling and determining what thoughts you permit to occupy your mind, you can induce uplifting, encouraging, exhilarating feelings. This quintessential maneuver and all-powerful process will allow you to realize your incredible, tantalizing goal of lifelong happiness.

Similarly, T. Harv Eker recently wrote a best seller entitled *Secrets of the Millionaires Mind: Thinking Rich to get Rich*, explaining that how and what you think can actually make you a millionaire. If it can do that, clearly, how and what you think can surely serve to make you successful and happy too.

During the Crimean War in 1853-56, Leo Tolstoy described in *Sevastopol Sketches* how a Russian soldier whose leg had been amputated above the knee coped with agonizing pain. "The chief thing, your honor, is not to think," Tolstoy's amputee remarked. "If you don't think, it is nothing much. It mostly all comes from thinking." He trained his mind how to think or not think.

HAPPINESS GUARANTEED OR YOUR MISERY BACK

There are those misfortunate individuals who you surmise should be miserable, yet they are incredibly happy, and there are those extremely fortunate people, who you believe should be ecstatic, but are nevertheless miserable. Think yourself into a state of happiness. "Very often a change of self is more important than a change of scene" (Arthur Christopher Benson).

Day 14

Did Moses wander in the wilderness because G-d was testing him, or was it because, like most men, Moses refused to ask directions?

The very first humans resisted G-d's warnings in the Garden of Eden, disobeying and then lying as they ate the apple from the Tree of Knowledge, the only forbidden tree among the infinite number of magnificent trees there.

And with only two brothers, Cain and Abel, sharing the entire world, Cain murdered Abel out of jealousy. Abraham had to leave his father's home and land to begin a new life in a strange place. He then was tested and told to sacrifice his only son Isaac. Jacob had to endure the pain of losing a son when Joseph was sold into slavery. Moses was never allowed to enter the land of Israel. A whale swallowed Jonah and Delilah betrayed Samson. The most esteemed figures had to suffer life's challenges.

Tragedy, suffering, disappointments, disillusionments, frustration, aggravation, irritation, betrayal, physical and mental abuse, and finally death, are part of human existence. There is no escaping that reality.

This is not introduced to discourage or depress you. Obviously, that is not the purpose of a book intended to maximize the happiness in your life. However, even the greatest biblical figures, indeed everyone throughout the ages whom we most respect and admire, had to confront and overcome the anguish and ordeals that are an intrinsic part of the human existence.

HAPPINESS GUARANTEED OR YOUR MISERY BACK

Out of bad comes good. From the pain and suffering of the forefathers and prophets came the guidance and wisdom that directs us how to live better, more orderly and serene lives. They gave us Godliness as well as goodness. They taught us about sacrifice, charity and love.

While you can't run from trouble, you need not think about troubling things. The aim of this book is not trouble avoidance, which is impossible; rather, it is devising a plan of action to pre-program your thought processes, converting them into optimistic, inspiring, uplifting, happiness-generating notions.

Decide that "life may not be the party you hoped for, but while you are here, you might as well dance" (Jeanne C. Stein).

Day 15

If you're feeling good, don't worry…you'll get over it.

What makes one sad? Death, sickness, disabilities, financial difficulties, family issues, disappointment, indecision, failure, injustice, jealousy, anxiety, worry, fear, fights, defeat, loneliness, divorce, being baron, unfulfilled dreams, etc. Unfortunately, the list seems endless. From our great challenges to our simple frustrations, we must accept that they are unavoidable; but, it is said that, "G-d doesn't give us anything that we can't handle."

Perhaps, when we are first faced with these trials and tribulations, our reaction is that we can't deal with it, but G-d gives each of us the ability to summon strength we are not aware is within us. Just as one lowers a pail into a well in order to bring up water, G-d brings us down in order to lift us up, to allow us to reach way down within ourselves, to garner strength and draw up and bring forth potential. G-d gives us the ability to deal, to look for the positive and to be happy despite the negative experiences life throws our way. By practicing searching for the positive, when the challenges come our way, we are more prepared to shift into coping mode.

Train yourself to automatically think thoughts such as "a smile will make everything better," "this too shall pass," "this is for the best," "life is 10 percent what happens to me and 90 percent how I react to it," "G-d only gives me what I can handle," "every challenge is a chance for emotional, spiritual or financial strengthening."

As Napoleon said, "Most great people have attained their greatest success one step beyond their greatest failure."

HAPPINESS GUARANTEED OR YOUR MISERY BACK

Remind yourself, "I can be happy despite my situation; in a blink of an eye everything can change. Every lemon can be turned into lemonade." "Once you choose hope, anything is possible" (Christopher Reeves). Life has no limitations except the ones you make. "Rise above the storm and you will find the sunshine" (Mario Fernandez).

"The good life is a process, not a state of being. It is a direction not a destination" (Carl Rogers). Through all of life's challenges, in order to be happy, learn to see and appreciate the good and to retain a positive attitude. "No life is so hard that it can't be made easier by the way you take it." As Art Linkletter said, "Things turn out best for the people who make the best out of the way things turn out."

Day 16

I worry so much. I wonder what wine goes with fingernails!

Lucinda Basset, the leader of the Midwest Center for Stress Anxiety says, "Anxiety is worry gone out of control."

Worrying is carrying tomorrow's load with today's strength, carrying two days at once. It is moving into tomorrow ahead of time. "Worrying doesn't empty tomorrow of its sorrow; it empties today of its strength."

Epictetus wisely said, "Man is not worried by real problems so much as by his imagined anxieties about real problems." Mark Twain wrote, "I've had thousands of problems in my life, most of which never actually happened." We worry so much and build up so much fear and anxiety, and in reality, a very small percentage of the circumstances we fear ever come to be.

It seems most of us can't help worrying and worrying can't help us either. We must learn to stay in control. Focus on the issues at hand. We have that special power to control what we think and thereby eliminate, or at least substantially reduce, the amount of stress and anxiety we torture ourselves with.

By casting off anxiety, you will cultivate and enhance your state of "good feeling" and happiness.

Day 17

The worst time to have a heart attack is during a game of charades.

Studies show that worry is harmful both to one's mental health as well as physical health. A little worry spurs us to action but too much leads to anxiety, which negatively affects one's state of health and one's happiness level. You must decide not to let worrying get out of control. The problem with worrying is it becomes a self-perpetuating disorder.

Research shows that you can stop this cycle by setting aside a thirty-minute "worry time" per day. Penn State researchers in a 2011 study suggested a four-step program. Determine the issue you are worried about. If you find you are worrying about this problem at any other time, you must train your mind to switch to happier thoughts. Decide when and where you will worry about this issue. Don't try to totally avoid thinking about your issue because this will cause you to pay extra attention to the very thought you are trying to avoid. Finally, use your chosen worry time productively to come up with solutions to the worries.

Postponing worry is effective because it breaks the habit of dwelling on worries in the present moment, yet you are not trying to suppress the thought or judge it. You are simply training your brain to postpone your anxious thoughts, so that you feel more able to control your worries.

The most effective method to manage worrying, according to studies, may be ones based on mindfulness, which involves non-judgmental awareness of your own thoughts and emotions and implementing cognitive therapy strategies. In other words, train yourself to alter your thinking style, to do less emotional thinking and more constructive positive thinking.

A 2005 study in the *Journal of Behavior Research and Therapy* showed that people who try to suppress their worries induce heightened anxiety. University of Wisconsin-Milwaukee researchers found that accepting your worries lowers your worry level. Teach your mind to accept your worries, to write them down or speak them out, so that you can face them and deal with them. As you develop the ability to postpone your anxious thoughts, you'll start to realize that you have more control over worrying than you think. Less worrying will lead to a more relaxed, happier you.

Day 18

My friend said, "Smile, things could be worse." So, I smiled and sure enough, things got worse.

Interestingly, research shows that while you worry, you temporarily feel less anxious because you are distracted from your emotions and you foolishly believe you are accomplishing something. Once you stop worrying, the tension and anxiety returns, and no matter how much time you devoted to thinking of worse-case scenarios, you will be no better prepared to deal with them, should they actually arise.

Teach your mind to move from worrisome thoughts to problem solving. First, determine if it is possible to solve the worry at all by asking yourself is the problem something you are currently facing or an imaginary what-if? If it is an imaginary what-if issue, ask yourself whether this a realistic concern and how likely is it to happen? Finally, ask yourself whether there is anything you can do about the problem or to prepare for it or whether it is out of your control. If it is a solvable problem, one you can take action on right away, like needing cash, start to brainstorm by making a list of all possible solutions such as taking out a loan, speaking to your boss, borrowing from a friend, etc. Unproductive, unsolvable worries are those for which there is no productive corresponding action, such as what if my kid gets in an accident, what if I get cancer someday?

Concentrate on problems that you can affect. After evaluating your options, make a plan of action. Once you start doing something to solve your problem, you will start to feel better.

Oprah Winfrey said, "My philosophy is that not only are you responsible for your life, but doing the best at this moment puts you in the best place for the next moment."

Day 19

I can take reality in small doses but not as a lifestyle.

"Worry never robs tomorrow of its sorrow, it only saps today of its joy" (William Shakespeare).

Accept the worst-case scenario. All too often, things do not turn out for the best. Acknowledge this possibility. But, even when things go wrong, they will almost always go less wrong than you feared. Losing your job is unlikely to condemn you to starvation and death; losing a relative won't condemn you to a life of unrelenting misery. Those fears are based on irrational fears about the future.

By visualizing the worst, vividly imagining how wrong things can go, you'll often turn bottomless, nebulous fears into finite and manageable ones, which generates an acceptance and a calm.

Although your choices of action may be limited, you have the choice of thought. You can choose to stay calm and rational, which allows you to think straight and handle life's challenges.

"We could never learn to be brave and patient, if there were only joy in the world" (Helen Keller).

Day 20

Do you know what the death rate around here is? One per person.

Stop worrying. Can you think of a single thing that got better because you worried? Worrying only eats away at you, and if anything, it makes you weaker and less effective. The answer to any problem that is causing you worry, whether it is about money or about health, your child's behavior or whatever, is to figure out if there is any action you can take to help solve the problem. If there is, then devise and immediately implement a rational plan of action that will address that condition. Mobilizing your inner determination, your adrenaline, the very initiation of action itself can already go a long way to reducing that worrisome feeling if not, indeed, altogether clearing it up.

On the other hand, if you're worrying about the kind of problem over which you have little or no control, such as whether Iran will develop a nuclear bomb, the price of gasoline will skyrocket or the economy will suffer a serious recession, recognize that these are beyond your direct control to influence or resolve. Make up your mind that you're not going to waste your time, your energy or your healthy emotional feelings on concerns beyond your power to control. As a sage philosopher once said, when confronted with too overwhelming a problem, "that's beyond my pay scale!"

Briefly consider what you might do if that worrisome eventuality ever does arise and how you might properly prepare for it. Then, move on and have great day.

HAPPINESS GUARANTEED OR YOUR MISERY BACK

Abraham Lincoln expostulated, "The best thing about the future is that it comes one day at a time." Sometimes, we get overwhelmed by thinking about all of the problems and burdens we envision and which we see ourselves confronted with in the future, as if they all must be dealt with and overcome instantly, today. It's impossible. But, this state of mind will surely induce fearful dejection, despondence and inordinate depression. It is advisable to develop the following constructive approach. Count to ten, relax and realize that as you work to solve one problem at a time, you actually do have time. Realize that things will improve and so much that you worry about will resolve itself and disappear with just the passage of time. As the saying goes, "time cures all."

As the Bible says, "Do not worry about tomorrow, for tomorrow will worry about itself. Each day has enough trouble of its own." Don't worry, be happy—enjoy today!

Day 21

I hired a professional worrier to worry for me. He charges $5,000. I don't know how I'll pay him but I'll let him worry about it.

Are you busy worrying about things you can't affect? Wouldn't it be nice if we could be certain about everything in life? Is it logical that if we don't know the outcome, we tend to predict the worst, to view the world as more dangerous than it really is?

Many of us panic because we overestimate the possibility that things will turn out badly. We think of the worst-case scenario and treat it as if it were a reality. Then, too, most of us do not realize how capable we are of coping if, G-d forbid, the worst does happen.

Being anxious is debilitating. Don't just accept worry. Try to look more realistically at the situation and the chances of your fears actualizing. Think how great is the possibility that your worries will not actualize? Consider, what would you advise a friend who had your worries? Talk to yourself and tell yourself not to allow your unsubstantiated fears to take control of you. Speak to people who are likely to relax and reassure you. Accept that you are a worrier by nature and realize that chances are things will be fine just as they are the majority of times you needlessly worried. Focus on happier issues. Move your mind to calmer, more rational thinking. The more you are able to control your worries, the happier you will be.

"There is only one way to happiness and that is to cease worrying about things that are beyond the power of our will" (Epictetus).

Day 22

A plane is flying to Dallas. The pilot announces that the flight landing will be delayed one hour due to an engine. A few minutes later, the pilot announces the flight landing will be delayed four hours because of trouble with the second engine. Another few minutes pass and pilot again says, "I'm sorry to tell you, but we are going to be delayed by nine hours because the third engine is also having problems." One man turns to the other and says, "If the fourth engine goes bad, we will be up here all day."

  Millions of people have a fear of flying, wondering, "What keeps it up there? What if it crashes?" It's what you let your mind focus upon. If you tell yourself it's the safest place—safer than driving or crossing the street—then you can enjoy the flight. But, if you tell yourself it's going to hit a mountain, or it's going to have engine failure, or it is going to dive into the ground, then you will be nervous and scared and suffer through the flight. It is all in your perspective.

  A plane was experiencing terrible turbulence due to a storm. The winds were blowing and the rain crashed against the plane. The passengers were all in an uproar fearing the worst. The pilot came on the loud speaker and said, "The weather is dangerously bad. The rains are pounding and the wind gusts are horrendous. This plane is being hit very hard. Therefore, I ask each of you to do me a favor. When you are driving home from the airport, please remember to buckle your seat belt." For this the pilot received a commendation because his approach allayed the passengers fears by letting them see beyond the moment.

The trouble with worrying is that you can't envision the future positive outcome, which is the probability.

It is up to you to make your life a pleasant, relaxed flight.

Day 23

A young boy watched Michelangelo sculpt a large piece of marble, chipping and carving it for many days. One day the boy returned to see that the marble had become the statue of *David*. He asked Michelangelo, "How did you know there was a boy in there?"

Shape yourself. Sculpt your future and cause it to happen. A sculptor visualizes a finished piece and chips away the rest. Visualize yourself as you would be: effective and happy. Avoid fears, inhibitions, lack of confidence and self-criticism. Avoid focusing on your faults or shortcomings. Whatever you lack, in the way of talent or the "can't-dos" (can't lose weight, can't learn computer, can't be successful), get those thoughts out of your head.

Be quiet for several minutes and think positive thoughts about yourself and your life. Reawaken memories of the wonderful things that you have succeeded at, joyous things that happened in your past and contemplate the amazing things you can experience, attain or mold into your future. Go ahead, it's okay to smile. Use your powers to influence your thought process.

(Teach this exercise to your kids and they'll develop an appreciation of their abilities, accomplishments and all the positive things in life, instead of complaining about all the things that aren't going right.)

Re-educate yourself. Change the way you see yourself; focus on such things as your strengths, your talents, your capabilities and your inner goodness. Consider how you might meet your needs and how you might meet the needs of others. Think about the way you see others and the way you see the relationships between yourself and others and between your desired state and your actual state and how you can move from the former to the latter. Decide to use your positive view of life and of yourself to propel you to get up and do the things that will improve your state of well-being.

We weren't trained to have a positive state of mind. A positive attitude brings high energy, and thus greater productivity and self-satisfaction.

"Some people dream of great accomplishments while others stay awake and do them" (Anonymous). Look at the world through rose-colored glasses. See the good. See life's potential. See your own potential. It's within you—bring it out.

Day 24

If you want to test your memory, try to remember the things that worried you yesterday.

It is futile to worry about two days in every week: yesterday with its blunders, and tomorrow, which is beyond our control. That leaves us with today, during which we can do something to make yesterday's trials bearable or do nothing except dread what tomorrow will bring.

As Deepak Chopra, a great philosopher and outstanding spiritual leader, says, "The only time that exists for each of us is the present moment. Both the past and the future are only in our imaginations."

Each day happens as you enter into it. It is potentially the most important, most rewarding day of your life. It's up to you to exploit it and to work to make it so. Learn to appreciate that each day is special, precious and unique. It will never be again.

The whole world, with all its natural resources, the earth that grows our fruits, vegetables, plants and flowers, the light and heat of the sun, the incomparable beauty of the moon and the stars, the animals that provide our food, were made exclusively for man's pleasure. It was made for you, so take advantage! As the famous quote goes, "Yesterday is history. Tomorrow is a mystery. Today is a gift. That's why it is called the present." It is a gift we can fully enjoy right now.

Enjoy this moment. Enjoy your potential. You yourself will determine how the exciting journey of your life will play out.

Day 25

On the other hand, you have different fingers.

What do the following individuals have in common—a concert pianist, Liu Wei, an expert calligrapher, Shenzhen, an excellent pilot, Jessica Cox, a master guitarist, Tony Melendez, and a superb painter, Peter Longstaff? Would you believe they are each armless and each uses their feet to perform their skill?

These are but a handful of the countless disabled individuals who decided not to be defeated by circumstances, not to yield to their challenge, but rather to make up their minds to overcome their handicap and succeed. Rather than succumb to defeat and depression they decided to move forward and be happy.

Pilot Jessica says, "I never say 'I can't do that,' I just say 'I haven't worked it out yet.'" Though armless, she has even found a way of putting in her own contact lenses.

Armless, legless wrestler Kyle Maynard is a master at this sport as well as being a motivational speaker for the Washington Speaker's Bureau and author of the memoir *No Excuses*. If he hasn't been able to find a reason to despair, what right have we?

The renowned French Impressionist painter Claude Monet was not blind when he began his career but he was by the end of his career. Despite his worsening eyes, he continued to paint and didn't stop until he was almost completely blind. In his last decade of life, while he was nearly blind, he still painted a group of murals of water lilies.

Itzhak Perlman, considered the greatest violinist of all time, was a victim of Polio and was left paralyzed from the waist down. He enjoyed playing the violin from a young age and when he could no longer do much else due to the paralysis, he spent hours a day practicing violin. Perhaps the disease was what caused young Itzhak to become the great violinist he is today. Itzhak says, "The challenges he faces in life mold his life. By facing adversity you measure yourself."

Helen Keller, though blind and deaf, despite her condition, became a world famous author and speaker. Helen Keller said, "Although the world is full of suffering, it is full also of the overcoming of it. Character cannot be developed in ease and quiet. Only through experience of trial and suffering can the soul be strengthened, ambition inspired and success be achieved. Everything has its wonders, even darkness and I learn whatever state I am in, therein to be content."

How did these and so many other challenged individuals have the strength, the courage, the perseverance and most of all, the mindset and will to pursue and reach their dreams?

As Helen Keller wrote, "I am thankful that in a troubled world no calamity can prevent the return of spring." Train your mind to view the positives in life. See the potential. See the opportunity. See the beauty. "No matter how you feel get up, dress up, show up and never give up" (Regina Brett). As Eleanor Roosevelt so wisely said, "In the long run, we shape our lives, and we shape ourselves. The process never ends until we die. And the choices we make are ultimately our responsibility."

Day 26

A plane was in major trouble. The pilot came out of the cockpit fully dressed in a parachute. He said to the passengers, "Don't panic. I am going for help," and with that he jumped out the window.

"We may encounter many defeats but we must not be defeated" (Maya Angelou). One of life's greatest threats is the temptation to despair. The most effective way to overcome that temptation is to be physically active—doing things, preferably exciting, ultimately satisfying and rewarding things—and to control what you think and how you think about things.

Mr. Alain De Botton, author of *The Consolations of Philosophy*, offers Nietsche's advice: "Don't panic about panicking. Life is difficult, and angst is a normal human response." He describes his twenties as an anxious time and for him, reading great thinkers was the comfort.

I, myself, have always looked to figures from literature or history as sources of interesting ideas on how to live. People come up with all sorts of responses about what to do about anxiety, one of which is the quest for knowledge. I intellectualize things. That's my way of dealing with anxiety."

We all experience our share of sleepless nights and crippling self-doubt. Deal with that by thinking upbeat thoughts and staying busy. We must never despair and we must each find our personal way to deal with anxiety.

HAPPINESS GUARANTEED OR YOUR MISERY BACK

The power of positive thinking is arguably the most effective medicine available to mankind. Determine what area of focus will best aid you to control your thoughts and point them in a positive direction.

"The most glorious moments in your life are not the so-called days of success, but rather those days when out of dejection and despair you feel rise in you a challenge to life, and the promise of future accomplishments" (Gustave Flaubert).

Day 27

Progress may have been all right once but it is going on too long.

    Changing your thoughts, changing your behavior, even changing your walk can alter your state of mind. A recent study written up in the *New York Times*, found that deliberately walking like a happy person can lift one's spirits, while doting the gait of a depressed individual can bring on sadness. Other studies have shown that we can improve our mood by doing such things as talking to strangers, arranging matches between friends and even by abstaining from temptations such as pie à la mode. Not giving in to temptation seems a surprising way to increase one's happiness. Happiness in this case seems to be derived from the ability to feel in control as well as the added appreciation for whatever is refrained from. Refraining from fattening foods made one appreciate the ability to have it at another time.
    A 2014 study in the *Journal of Experimental Psychology*, found that commuters who struck up conversations with strangers on trains and buses, and in taxi cabs and waiting rooms, reported greater well-being than others instructed to commute in their normal disconnected manner. By smiling, making eye contact and striking up brief conversations, people increased their state of happiness.
    These studies confirm that actions can help boost our state of relative happiness by helping us appreciate experiences that are repeated in our everyday life.

HAPPINESS GUARANTEED OR YOUR MISERY BACK

Elizabeth Dunn, an associate psychology professor at the University of British Columbia, said that people are unaware that doses of social interactions that are available in our day, brighten our mood, and give us a sense of belonging.

Even sitting in a slumped posture, indicative of a depressed mood, causes one to become more depressed. Making things oneself, engaging in rituals around eating and drinking and going to religious services and the gym are all ways that were found to increase happiness.

All these findings prove that you are in control of your own happiness. Go out, speak to people, walk tall, sit straight, smile, abstain from things you believe you should and get involved in doing things that make you feel fulfilled. Bring on your own happiness.

Day 28

A philosopher once said, "People have more fun than anyone else."

Think happy thoughts if you want to be more creative and have more fun. That is the conclusion *Prevention Magazine* draws from a University of Toronto study that showed volunteers were better able to solve challenging puzzles after thinking happy thoughts and listening to upbeat music.

At any moment, you have the choice of choosing a positive or negative thought and mood. Suppose it's a rainy day, you can think, "Now I'm stuck bored at home," or you can think, "Now I can stay home and catch up on some of my work." You get backed up because of a car accident, you can be angry that you aren't moving or you can think how lucky you are that you aren't the one who is in the accident. You can notice how crowded the room is or you can notice the great people in the crowd. You can curse the thorns or admire the flowers.

Practice by yourself, with your children, with a friend. Make it a game. One person says something negative and the other retorts with a positive. Examples:

"I have nothing nice to wear."
"Luckily you look nice in anything."
"I hate to go to school."
"It's better than having to go to work for a living."
"I broke a leg."
"Lucky for you, you have another one."

"I'm so miserable because my friend passed away."

"Thank G-d he had a good life." or "It may be better than the miserable life he was suffering."

"I'm so lost and depressed."

"Now you have a marvelous opportunity to find a new direction and grow from the challenge."

"I don't like this color lollipop."

"How lucky you are to have a lollipop."

How often do we take our kids for a wonderful day out and rather than discussing all the fun things they did, they bring up the one thing they feel they missed out on? "But, I didn't get to go on the roller coaster." "But I didn't have ice cream." Pathetically, how often do we ourselves think this way? "But, I didn't get to travel this year." "But, I should've doubled my earnings rather than just increased them."

Get into the habit of, at the end of every day, saying all the things that you enjoyed and all the things that went right. Ask your children to enumerate and tell you about all the fun things they did on their outing and let them decide which activity or treat was the best one. Every week, find a time for family or friends to discuss the best thing that happened to each of you during the week.

Do these little exercises often enough and it will become second nature to think and look for the positive. Without realizing it, your whole attitude will be more positive and your spirit uplifted.

Katherine Mansfield writes, "Could we change our attitude, we should not only see life differently, but life itself would be different." If you think happy thoughts, you raise your spirits, whereas depressing thoughts lower them. Every thought is a seed. "If you plant crab apples, don't count on harvesting Golden Delicious" (Bill Meyer). Plant seeds of happiness. By changing your thoughts, you change your world.

Day 29

When everything is coming your way, you're in the wrong lane.

If you are driving along a busy highway and get hit by a speeding car and wind up with back trouble, how do you look at this event? Do you think, "Why me? Now I have to go for physical therapy." Or do you think, "Wow, that was a miracle. At the speed the car was going, I'm lucky to be alive?"

Psychologists have found that "every brain invents a 'counterfact'—an alternate scenario our brain creates to help us evaluate and make sense of what really happened." Those who saw their outcome as unlucky imagined an alternative scenario, such as not having been in an accident at all or a different car having been hit, so that their accident seemed very unfortunate. Those who viewed their outcome as lucky, thought of a scenario where they might have been maimed for life or even killed, so in comparison, they were fortunate.

Both counterparts are completely hypothetical. In any situation, our brain has the power to consciously select and invent a counterpart that makes us feel fortunate rather than unfortunate. By choosing a positive counterpart, we are consciously deciding to be relieved, appreciative and in a happy mindset, improving motivation and performance. If one chooses a negative counterpart, he is altering reality by allowing the event to exert even more control over him than it really should, making him more fearful of the event and feeling it was even worse than it actually was.

HAPPINESS GUARANTEED OR YOUR MISERY BACK

In my father's younger days, he sold vacuum cleaners door to door. My grandfather wisely advised him to remain optimistic, that 99 out of 100 customers will slam the door in his face, but 1 in 100 is waiting to buy. Every time someone slammed the door on him, he said he took the attitude, "I'm one customer closer to a sale."

Martin Seligman, who founded positive psychology, discovered that the majority of individuals feel distressed and helpless after facing continuous setbacks while a consistent minority, no matter what obstacle they faced, always chose the positive view and bounced right back. Seligman termed this way of interpreting adversity as optimistic "explanatory style."

One's explanatory style, the way one chooses to interpret past events, has a crucial impact on one's happiness and future success.

Someone with a positive explanatory style believes things are not that bad and will get better and therefore performs and achieves higher success. A person with a pessimistic explanatory style feels it's really bad and it's not going to get better. He therefore becomes helpless and stops trying.

Some people are born with an optimistic explanatory style but if you are not one of those, you can and should work to develop it.

"When something bad happens, you have three choices. You can either let it define you, let it destroy you, or let it strengthen you" (Anonymous).

Day 30

Pessimist: one who, when he has a choice of two evils, chooses both.

Thinking positively, seeing the bright side, interpreting setbacks as short-lived, envisioning possibilities rather than defeat, has been found to be a learnable skill. Practice the ABCD model of interpretation: Adversity, Belief, Consequence, and Disputation. Adversity is the event we can't change. Belief is how we view the event, why it happened, how we believe it will affect us, do we think it is solvable or do we feel defeated by it. If we view the adversity as having only a temporary effect, solvable and offering an opportunity for growth, then we maximize the chance of positive consequences arising from the adversity.

But if the belief has caused us to have a negative perception feeling vulnerable, helpless unable to progress then we need disputation, which is telling ourselves that our belief is just a belief and not reality. We have to challenge our feelings. We have to ask ourselves if our beliefs make sense. Can we interpret the event differently? If we can't undo our negative perception and fear of the event, can we at least convince ourselves that it was not as bad as we first believed, so that we can accept that even if it was bad it wasn't catastrophic?

It is important to realize that things are never as bad as we think. People are resilient. Following a terrible crisis, such as becoming paralyzed or losing a relative, after a period of hardship, most individuals return to their initial level of happiness.

HAPPINESS GUARANTEED OR YOUR MISERY BACK

This is the official ABCD model; I would try a simpler version: A—accept what happened, B—believe that it was for the best, C—concentrate and commit to seeing the event as an act of G-d for your benefit, D—decide that rather than being crushed by the adversity, you are going to become stronger.

To reach our happiest potential, when we have experienced an event that threatens to break our spirit and harm our ability to move forward, put the ABCD model into effect in order to bring on a more optimistic view. Every small degree to which you are able to control your thoughts and move them in a positive direction, makes you a happier, better-balanced individual.

Day 31

If ignorance is bliss, why aren't there more happy people?

Many people believe they should be happy every minute of every day and every night. During those inevitable periods when they don't feel that sense of happiness, they immediately consult a doctor or psychologist to prescribe an array of anti-depressant medications or mood-elevating drugs. There are times when it's not only admissible, but indeed appropriate to feel out of sorts and low. Life is not a perennial picnic. Disappointments and disasters that life periodically bestows on us will take the wind out of our sails and sadden us. These bleak, woeful, disheartening times are, regretfully, the realities that are a part of life.

Living with the unrealistic view that everybody else is happy all of the time, but you are victimized by "bad luck" will surely depress you. Develop realistic expectations. Nobody is happy all the time. Instead, with the power of positive thinking we can minimize the pain and unhappiness with which we are sometimes confronted to maximize our periods of happiness.

Develop and learn to command that empowering capability to control and induce your mind's thought processes to always be optimistic, to see the sunny side, the hopeful future, the successful realization of alluring dreams. Do this through the simple exercise of the "power of positive thinking."

Once you replace negative thoughts with positive ones, you'll start having positive results. Always be aware that "our greatest glory is not in never falling but in rising every time" (Confucius).

Day 32

Logic: A man said, "There is a new trend in our office. Everyone is putting names on their food. I saw it today, while I was eating a sandwich named Kevin."

Reality dictates that we fully appreciate and understand what is possible, what is achievable and what is, on the other hand, so tremendously challenging that it is practically beyond our capacity to manage or control.

Mr. Logic and Mr. Luck were taking a walk together. Mr. Logic said, "Let's stay on the side of the road so a car won't hit us." Mr. Luck shrugged and continued walking in the middle of the road while Mr. Logic moved onto the side of the road. A car came speeding down the road saw Mr. Luck in the center of the road and quickly swerved on to the curb to avoid hitting him, running over Mr. Logic.

Much that aggravates us is beyond our ability to control. Would that we could change everything that is undesirable, distressing and grievous, but unfortunately much as we'd like to, we just can't. Of course, we may change irritating externals, but it's easier to control how you react to what is happening in your life.

So, while you can't readily, or even with Herculean effort, change outside world events or the untoward, adverse conditions in your own life, you can, with a positive attitude and mindset, change from the inside out by transforming external negative predicaments into an intrinsically hopeful, encouraging and more pleasant mental state.

"The world is full of cactus, but we don't have to sit on it" (Will Foley).

Day 33

A suffering patient looked at his doctor and asked, "Are you certain I'll pull through?" I heard of a man who was treated for jaundice and died of diphtheria." "Don't be silly," said the doctor. "When I treat you for jaundice you die of jaundice."

One of the world's most renowned pharmaceutical companies ran a very touching advertisement on the lifesaving effectiveness of its drug by featuring a sweet little girl who is being treated by it, exuding the very thrill of being alive. The girl practices ice-skating and basketball, is improving her gymnastics and wants to be a doctor when she grows up so she can help others. Most of all, she values the fantastic gift of each new unfolding moment, feeling lucky just to be alive and appreciating all the experiences she might never have had.

This little girl is giving us a most incisive and enlightening lesson. Do we have to suffer the fear of cancer—the very imminence of death—before we appreciate, cherish and enjoy that incomparably precious gift that is given to us with each new moment? You can't help but lift your spirits and your capacity for happiness, if you keep focusing upon and constantly remind yourself how lucky you are. If you can just learn to feel lucky, you're well on your way to an ever-uplifted psyche and an immensely gratifying blissfulness.

Teach yourself to habitually summon up in your own mind, and to then continue to dwell upon whatever is good in your life, and

HAPPINESS GUARANTEED OR YOUR MISERY BACK

you will unequivocally generate and reap ongoing delightful, exuberantly pleasant feelings.

"Write your sad times in sand, write your good times in stone" (George Bernard Shaw).

Day 34

"My dad said, 'always leave them wanting more.' Ironically, that's how he lost his job in disaster relief."—Mark Watson

The belief that I will be happy when and only if I have…a bigger house, a better job, more respect, name brand clothing, etc. is a belief destined to cause frustration rather than happiness. Dr. Tal Ben Shahar terms this the "arrival fallacy." It's the belief that when you arrive at a certain destination or attain a specific goal, you will be happy. This is a compelling belief because it's partially true. But, is this happiness lasting?

Every new situation, even a happy event or an accomplishment, brings with it new responsibilities, new problems and new challenges. A bigger house means more space and more prestige but it also means more to take care of, more to clean, more to fix. A job promotion may mean more money but may mean a new boss to adjust to, more responsibility to handle and higher taxes.

Of course, goals are important. Working at each goal moves you forward, but be aware that you can be happy both before and after you achieve your goal. Do you need the bigger house or the promotion to make you happy? Don't wait for happiness. Don't postpone happiness. Be happy now!

Often people believe that if they don't get what they dreamed of they will never be happy. But, by believing there is no alternative way to find happiness, they stay stuck, unable to plan another strategy, form a new goal and move on to other means of achieving happiness.

Learn to be happy while working toward your goal and to remain happy whether or not you ever reach that goal.

Day 35

Change is inevitable, except for a vending machine.

You can't change an irreversible tragedy. You're entitled to wallow for a while. You can rest, go to bed, cry your heart out, but then you must find your way out. The serenity prayer says, "Give me the serenity to accept that which we cannot change, the courage to change that which we can, and the wisdom to know the difference."

Trying to make sense of everything will only frustrate you further because sometimes there are no logical answers. We deal with what is, not what we wish it were.

A successful philosophy of life worth cultivating is "It's not what happens to me, it's how I respond to what happens to me that will determine how resilient, zestful and pleasant my life will be."

Always keep hope alive! Hope is the restorative agent, the elixir for all our tragedies. Believe in a healthy resolution and you can win. It is in triumphing over adversity and vanquishing defeat that we rise to new heights and achieve personal growth. You win some, you lose some. Don't ever let defeat induce endless depression. Even the greatest athletes and most successful businessmen experience painful, distressing loss from time to time.

The greater the challenge, the more rewarding is the victory! Such an approach can often even lick cancer. Think positive and you will realize positive results. "You don't have the power to make life fair, but you do have the power to make life joyful" (Jonathan Lockwood Huie).

Day 36

Sorry, mind closed until further notice.

The ability to find happiness is deep inside of us. As I said, it is our job to search and dig deep down within our souls to find it.

Unfortunately, we can have all the money in the world and if one child is sick, we can't be happy. If we have married off ten children, but we have one unmarried child, we can't be happy. If we have fifty grandchildren but one of our children is baron, we walk around devastated. "A parent is only as happy as their least happy child."

If we make a wedding and a grandparent or parent is no longer with us, can we feel complete happiness? If we make six weddings in one year but have one funeral doesn't the loss overshadow all the wonderful events? Why can't we focus on and appreciate the positive? Sadly, pain and loss are much stronger emotions than happiness.

How, I wonder, does someone who has lost a precious child ever get himself to wake up and get out of bed? How does someone who lost a twenty-year-old daughter get herself to go and dance at her daughter's friends' weddings? How does someone who can't have children go to other people's baby showers? How does someone who is struggling to support his family hand another person who is hungry a dollar bill?

How did Holocaust survivors move on? How did people who lost their entire families, their homes, their dignity, and some, even their reproductive organs, forge on to lead a normal, productive life?

Alice Herz-Sommer, the oldest survivor of the Holocaust, recently died on February 23, 2014, at the age of 110. Alice's mother, father and brother were each murdered by the Nazis. Miraculously, she was able to survive that horrendous experience because she had been an outstanding concert pianist, whom the Nazi Gestapo found entertaining. She not only survived but also eventually thrived. She attributed her good health and long life to the fact that she always looked to see the best in everything.

How does Coby Robinson's mother write a book about her young son who was killed by Arabs? How do people plagued with cancer accept their death and strengthen others? How do people who suffer personal losses move on to form amazing organizations to help others?

One does this by building character, strengthening faith, finding something to work at that gives meaning to life, dedicating themselves to a cause and immersing themselves in people and things they enjoy in life.

How easy is it to just lie around and wallow in one's pain? Truthfully, it is probably not easy. It is probably even more painful than getting up and dealing with life.

When tragedy strikes, decide that you want to eventually be happy for yourself as well as for those around you. Find something or someone that gives your days' purpose or meaning and makes your life worth living.

"The mystery of human existence lies not in just staying alive, but in finding something to live for" (Fyodor Dostoyevsky).

Day 37

What do you call a man with no body and just a nose? Nobody knows!

Renowned storyteller Hanoch Teller said, "The only really happy people are the people I don't know well." Everyone has problems, anxieties, frustration, strife, fears and even terrible tragedies. The portfolio of reversals, misfortunes, disappointments, failures, and stresses, of people we don't know are not revealed to us, so we think they are luckier or happier.

There is a story of a man who goes to the doctor and tells him he's depressed, that life seems cruel and that he feels all alone in a threatening world. The doctor says that the treatment is simple. He tells his patient that the great clown Torrfini is in town tonight and that he should go see him. That, the doctor assured him, would pick him up. The man burst into tears. "But doctor," he said, "I am the Great Torrfini."

Everyone else's life looks amazing from the outside. But, in truth, we all have problems. It is said that if everyone threw their problems in a pile and then had to go choose one, we would each choose our own. Everyone you meet is fighting a battle you know nothing about.

There are two ways to recognize how blessed we are, either by looking around and taking notice of all that is good in our own life, or by looking around and seeing what other people are suffering and being grateful that their problems are not ours.

As a small child with a broken arm, I learned the lesson of appreciating all that I am fortunate to have. My family and I were on the beach and I began complaining about how itchy my cast was. My father showed me a little boy who had an arm amputated right above his elbow. He looked at me and said, "I cried because I had no shoes until I saw a boy who had no feet." In that one sentence, he put the whole world into perspective for me.

Appreciating what you have is one of life's most valuable lessons and possessions.

Day 38

I love life. I just wish I were better at it.

Set aside a few moments every day for thoughts and activities that give you joy. Think of something specific that makes you proud, happy, excited, and fulfilled. Do something that makes you feel productive, effective, inspired, and stimulated—like a winner.

It's what happens at the very margin of your mind that determines whether you are happy or sad. Very small adjustments by you can make a significant difference moving you from a depressed state of mind to one that produces the happy, optimistic feelings you want, and to which you are entitled. After all, the Old Testament tells us that G-d put us on this earth and gave us the gift of life—to be happy.

Make it routine. Start by play-acting. Pretend to be happy. If one pretends long enough, practicing consistently, incessantly, it becomes actualized. Even small "parts" can make a significant difference, changing you from a depressed person to a happy one. Soon, your play-acting will be real and produce the new, and more positive, happier you.

Studies show that if a marriage therapist instructs a husband to tell his wife every day that she looks beautiful, that he likes her hairdo or that her dress is pretty, and his wife is aware of her husband's assignment to say these compliments to her, nevertheless, his saying them makes him appreciate her more and her hearing them makes her feel more cared about. Our minds want to be happy and therefore after a short while we tend to forget the training and allow our emotions to accept happiness.

Which comes first, the chicken or the egg? Acting happy will cause happiness. Thinking happy causes happiness.

Research shows that the relationship between emotions and behavior is a two-way street. You feel happy so you smile. You smile and you feel happy. Frowning can make you sad. Clenching your jaw causes anger.

This applies to all aspects of your everyday. It's the "as if" principle. Act as if you are a certain type of person and you become that person.

Schedule a time every day during which you will think lovely thoughts and do things that will cause you to feel good. "Laugh when you can, apologize when you should, and let go of what you can't change. Life's too short to be anything…but happy" (Anonymous).

Day 39

Who says I have no willpower—I will get that pecan pie if it's the last thing I do!

In the late 1880s, William James taught that if we act as if something "is," then we create that reality.

What will make you happy? Are you frustrated by overweight? Do you want to develop willpower? Studies show that if you are tempted to eat fattening foods and you follow your mind's instruction to take the stance of resistance, such as making your hands into a fist or contracting your biceps, you are more likely to avoid the temptation of eating the forbidden foods. It's been proven, that if you use your less dominant hand to eat, thereby making yourself cognizant of the desire to resist, you will successfully resist the food.

You are controlling your mind. Perhaps, you want to have more confidence? You can focus on the positive things you've accomplished or you can visualize yourself being more assertive or possibly, an even more effective method is, to simply act as if you are more assertive. Sit yourself down at your desk. Put your feet up on the table, interlock your arms at the back of your head and put on the power pose. Unbelievably, you will begin to feel the power.

Studies show that these assertive actions will cause you to be much more successful than had you seated yourself on the floor, placed your hands in your lap and stared at the ground. Amazingly, even a moment of dominant posing has the capacity to boost your confidence.

Would you be happier if you could be more persistent? Studies found that when you feel like quitting, if you sit up straight and cross your arms, you are twice as likely to persevere in your task.

You can alter such acts as procrastination, just by acting as if you are interested in what you have to do and forcing yourself to begin the act you are avoiding; almost magically, the desire to complete the task will kick in.

The power of posing has been found not only to make you feel psychologically more confident and more competent, but also to raise the levels of your testosterone (which plays a role in sex drive, energy and behavior), confirming that shifting your pose changes the chemical makeup of your body.

Do you want to feel love for someone? Act in love. Treat someone as if you love him/her. Couples in love speak intimately to one another. But, the opposite also works. Talk intimately, confide in each other, ask personal questions and the intimate chats will build intimacy and cause the love.

Do you want to laugh more? Do you want to be more outgoing? Do you want to be more helpful? More accomplished? Just do it! Force yourself to laugh more, to say more, to help more, to push yourself more. It may be uncomfortable at first, but with time, you and only you can help yourself to grow.

My grandfather always said, "Do, do, do." Push yourself to do something, act like you can do it and it will get done.

Force yourself to do the things you wish to do and you will become the doer you'd like to be. Imitate the traits you want to incorporate and those traits will become a part of you. Think positively, you will act positively. Act positively and you will think positively.

Day 40

I wish there was a way to donate fat like you can donate blood!

An incisive, tremendously seductive advertisement headlined "Never Again" suggests that one can stop smoking, stop overeating, reduce stress, increase learning and memory, and much more through the power of suggestion—a form of mind management that it calls "hypnotherapy."

Hypnotherapy postulates that your mind works on your body to make desired physical and psychological changes while you relax on a reclining chair. It is a "powerful personal coaching," which induces behavior modification, successfully producing positive changes.

This is an effective approach to train your mind how to think, delivering extraordinary results in achieving transcendental happiness. Relax and allow your mind to control your physical feelings and emotions. Go to work on it—on yourself. Learn this new way to embark upon and successfully fulfill your auspicious voyage to consummate your very own personal happiness.

Lay back. Allow your body to undergo hypnotherapy. Let your mind take control. You can see a specialist or go on YouTube and experience hypnotherapy. It is a form of total relaxation, freeing your mind of weighty thoughts, doing deep breathing exercises and reaching deep down within yourself to a place of calm and serenity. Through music, visuals, and your imagination, you move your mind to a place of comfort. You work on attaining a sense of serenity, letting go of your burdensome thoughts and eventually softly allowing the inflow of positive, calming ones. Through positive suggestions, you implant within your subconscious, mind-control techniques, which allow you to cast off stress, anger, frustrations and fears and allow the inflow of calm, acceptance, rationalization, forgiveness, appreciation and happiness.

We have to calmly, smartly program our thinking. Ninety-five percent of all of our actions comes from our subconscious minds.

You cannot have a positive life dominated by a negative mind.

Day 41

Door open seven days a week and weekends too.

Your mind has the capacity to open doors. The only real opponent you have in this pursuit of happiness, in this battle to achieve a new higher state of positive attitude, self-control and happiness, is you yourself.

Once you make up your mind, once you mentally make the commitment and take the first step to be happy, amazingly, the psychodynamics that take over effectively propel you, almost effortlessly, to the fulfillment of your pursuit.

Just make up your mind and take the first step and you will be well on your way to the happiness you want to possess. "Happiness often sneaks in a door you didn't know you left open."

When you don't like the TV program you're watching, you wisely pick up your remote control and switch to something that makes you happier.

Similarly, when your mind suddenly focuses upon an aggravating thought, an experience, an eventuality that is irritating, aggravating or tormenting, don't just passively tolerate it! Change channels! Instantly, activate your own invaluable tool your "mental remote." Switch to a thought, or a dream that can excite you, making you feel good and happy.

From the very inception of retraining your mind, you have to know, absolutely, that it's up to you and only you which thoughts you choose to invite in and delve upon. If you choose joyful ones, you will be joyful. If you choose otherwise, you, and only you, are making your own hell on earth.

Reject negative thoughts! Invite and reinforce positive thoughts. "Sometimes, we are limited more by attitude than by opportunities" (Anonymous).

Day 42

The Israeli government announces that anyone who catches a terrorist will be rewarded $100,000 for each terrorist. Eleven terrorists pointing guns at them awaken two older citizens, camping out in the woods one night. Jacob turns to his compatriot with thrill and excitement "Joseph, we're rich!"

One man sees disaster and futility; another sees opportunity, even in the face of apparent adversity. One is totally discouraged; the other is inspired and uplifted.

The key is not to change others, to change the world or to change reality. It is to change you...It's attitudinal. It's how you decide to view and deal with the situation, as it exists—how to teach yourself to see things in their best light. It's a form of self-hypnosis that you can achieve.

It takes an active effort on your part. Like achieving anything worthwhile in life, you have to consciously work at it. You just can't be indifferent or passive. You have to make a personal determined commitment to achieve the goal—to be the boss of your own mind and the thoughts you allow to enter and remain there, at any given moment.

It's an effort, but an effort truly worth making because the payoff is in terms of the percentage of time you feel good. It's all in your hands—it's up to you.

The fact is there are very few things we are in a position to control in our lives but it is indeed possible, and enormously desirable, to control our own mind. Once you train yourself to do that, and with effort, it's truly achievable, and there is no more salutary investment that you can make in the pursuit of maximizing your happiness. Whatever effort it takes, force yourself to consciously do it. It's possible! It is the most important project you'll ever engage in.

This is arguably the ultimate freedom, for you are no longer just a victim of what happens to you or a slave to the "uncontrollable" thoughts that enter your head. Actually, the freedom you feel from the ability to do anything you want isn't necessarily the greatest freedom because we often do things that bring us problems. But, the ability to freely select what you will think is really the optimum, because thinking about anything, even the most ridiculous or perverse fantasies, so long as they are not acted out, can never get you into trouble and if you can develop the modus of always thinking uplifting, enjoyable thoughts, you will become the most blessed person and will have achieved a most enviable condition.

By the simple ploy, the incredible power to control and use the unbelievably amazing tool which your brain is, you can develop a spiritual and emotional freedom from the aggravation and constraints that extrinsic events and experiences impose and you can thereby attain new heights of fulfillment, success and emotional exhilaration and contentment.

Even the most trying and negative events, appropriately assimilated, managed and exploited can serve as a catalyst to catapult us to new inspirational heights and undertakings.

Either you control your attitude or it controls you.

Day 43

I know a man who didn't have a penny to his name. So, he changed his name!

Canyon Ranch, a world-class spa, offers the following counsel to encourage a better life: "Change your perspective. Change your life. It's the possibilities you choose that make all the difference. Simply take pleasure in being well."

You are the chairman, president and CEO of the most important project in this world: your life. Plan it, manage it, control it and direct it, so that you bring about maximum success.

Nothing is more important, more worthwhile or ultimately more rewarding than managing your own feelings and responses.

It's up to you. You are the one architect who can design and build this dream project. You are the playwright, the producer, the director and the main actor in a marvelous production. You may not get an Emmy or Oscar, but even more beneficiary, you will earn a full, wonderful and happy life.

Dedicate your head and your heart to producing your own inner serenity, joy and happiness. Seize the opportunity to focus on all the positive, beautiful, energizing phenomenon and the future adventures. Value the potentially magnificent relationships that lie ahead for you to experience and enjoy. Open your mind and your senses and train yourself to be aware of and appreciate all that is inspiring, alluring and exhilarating in this universe, but be cautious many people are so caught up with pursing pleasure that they don't take notice of the present joy and peace, and hurry right past the pleasure they are seeking.

H. Jackson Brown put it so perfectly: "Watch the sunrise at least once a year. Put a lot of marshmallows in your hot chocolate. Lie on your back and look at the stars. Never buy a coffee table you can't put your feet on. Never pass up a chance to jump on a trampoline. Don't overlook life's small joys while searching for the big one."

Teach yourself to stop and smell the roses.

Day 44

There are moments when everything goes well. Don't be frightened. It won't last.

With a powerful opening line, *A Tale of Two Cities* by Charles Dickens, describes human history: "It was the best of times, it was the worst of times." This is true for the macro condition of the world we live in, and for the micro condition of each individual.

Good and bad are part of our lives; they are there all the days we spend on this earth. When we get up in the morning, we can focus on all the things that are currently wrong—like nuclear bombs, our enemies, people dying in wars, terrible maladies like cancer and Alzheimer's, and contemplating these, become sad and depressed. Or, we can focus on all that is best in our lives—the blessings that we do have, the immeasurable wealth we do enjoy, our precious family, our invaluable friends, the potentially rewarding experiences that await us in the future, and become encouraged and joyful.

While all of these conditions are ever present, the good and the bad, if we can learn to see, and feel, that our glass is "half full" and then work to fill it the rest of the way, we will maximize our functionality, our effectiveness and our happiness. Alternatively, if we see, and feel, that our glass is "half empty" it will become a self-fulfilling prophecy and we will unnecessarily suffer dejection, distress, despondency and an overwhelming amount of torment and mental depression.

Clearly, your choice is obvious. Focus upon that which is best and it will help you feel uplifted, gratified and sunnily cheerful.

For me, no matter what, I always tell myself "it's the best of times" and then even if things are actually pretty terrible at that given moment, it inspires me to start to believe that good, pleasant, appealing experiences will surface shortly. Being positive and optimistic is self-fulfilling and expeditiously creates and, almost magically generates surprisingly desirable, pleasurable emotions.

Whenever things seem to be going wrong, I say to myself, "Life is good, life is an opportunity and life will be better." Almost instantly, I start to feel better.

Day 45

How many NCAA basketball players does it take to change a light bulb? Only one. But, he gets money, a car and three credit hours for it.

Jim Valvano, the famed basketball coach of the national champion North Carolina state team and tragic victim of a virulent life-threatening cancer, urged, "Don't give up. Don't ever give up!" He said, "I know I gotta go, I gotta go, and I have one last thing to say. I said it before and I'm gonna say it again: cancer can take away all my physical abilities but cannot touch my mind, it cannot touch my heart and it cannot touch my soul. And those three things are going to carry on forever."

Jim sagely counseled, "If you laugh, you think, and you cry, that's a full day. You do that seven days a week, you're going to have something special." Just one last thing I urge all of you, all of you, to enjoy your life, the precious moments you have; to spend each day with some laughter and some thought, so that will get your emotions going."

If Mr. Valvano could embrace this positive attitude in the face of his most devastating and depressing human malady, shouldn't you and I rejoice every moment of our lives? Finally, Jim Valvano said, "I will thank G-d for every day and every moment I have."

There are 86,400 seconds in a day. It's up to you to decide what to do with them.

Day 46

I looked at the obituaries the other day and I realized something—everybody dies in alphabetical order!

Believe in the future! Things indeed become better. Time does heal wounds. When you feel suicidal, "mend it, don't end it"!

A cancer victim suffering from apparently incurable cancer still managed to work effectively. When asked how long he expected to live, he answered, "I've realized it is possible to live with a sword of Damocles hanging above one. I prefer not to know how long I have left" (Anonymous).

Indeed, none of us actually knows when death will come. He also said, "By an act of will, one can control himself not to think about it." Furthermore, he added, "my major victory was that I don't think about death."

Gilda Radner, the comedian actress who died of cancer, counseled, "Some stories don't have a clear beginning, middle or end. Life is about not knowing—having to change, taking the moment and making the most of it without knowing what's going to happen next." Maybe it's that delicious ambiguity that makes life so interesting and exciting.

Another cancer survivor said, "The most important thing is keeping a sense of humor and hope, without indulging in gloom and doom. Don't invest your emotions in a reality you must accept. It's counterproductive and self-defeating to think the worst. To get the most out of life, focus on being productive; making the most of every minute of your life" (Anonymous).

Choose optimism! "Find a place inside where there is joy and the joy will burn out the pain" (Joseph Campbell).

Day 47

The survival of the fittest is going to make some man very lonesome some day.

Charles Darwin said, "It is not the strongest of species that survive, nor the most intelligent, but the ones most responsive to change." No matter what set of circumstances you are confronted with, no matter what the challenge you face, the most constructive adaptation is to retain a positive attitude and it will help you not only to most effectively survive but to ultimately achieve a sense of fulfillment, self-gratification, personal growth and a level of renewed happiness.

Mankind has recurrently demonstrated both the reality and the immensely rewarding effectiveness of this readily available, pragmatic adaptation.

In *Just Enough: Happiness, Significance, Achievement and Legacy*, Laura Nash and Howard Stevenson define happiness as "feelings of pleasure or contentment in and about your life." They define achievement as "accomplishments that compare favorably against similar goals others have strived for." Significance? "A positive impact on people you care about." And legacy is "establishing your values or accomplishments in ways that help others find future success."

The best selling author of *Who Moved My Cheese*, Spencer Johnson, describes the gift that makes you happy and successful at work and in life: "When you want to make the future better than the present, see what a wonderful future would look like. Make plans to help it happen. Put your plan into action in the present." First, visualize something wonderful you would like to achieve in the future then act to make it come to fruition. Make your own happiness come true.

A role model for Norman Vincent Pearle's classic *The Power of Positive Thinking* is Sir John Templeton, one of the world's outstanding and most successful investor and money managers. Templeton says he loves to turn every negative into a positive. Both his investment philosophy and his life have benefited enormously from this tremendously constructive way of thinking and have been so instrumental in his achieving the phenomenal success he has achieved. He, and his consistent adherence to positive thinking, is the kind of role model you should definitely learn to imitate and will inspire you on your own path to achieving a successful and happy life.

Jack Canfield, the co-creator of the *Chicken Soup* series, writes in *The Success Principles*, "If you want to be successful you have to take 100 percent responsibility for everything you experience in your life, doing everything with 100 percent commitment."

Achieving happiness is all up to you (and, of course, G-d). You are the one that can make it happen. You are the one responsible, and in the best sense, that's really great because it's all in your own hands. Make a 100 percent commitment to inculcate the habits and follow up with the actions that will insure your own happiness.

Day 48

Chicken soup is a traditional remedy for many people. One woman had two chickens. One became ill. She killed the second one to make chicken soup for the first one!

Medical science is adding years to our lives, but it is up to us to add life to our years. Rather than paying a doctor or psychologist, counsel your brain yourself, tell yourself, "I will advise you what to do and think" in order to always achieve a better state of mind and to thereby produce a happier sense of well-being forever hereafter."

It works and is cheap. You don't have to pay any doctor or psychologist. After all, who knows you better than you? Follow the program. You can and will become your best adviser and beneficiary of psychologically healthful growth and good feelings.

Consider this. If you don't allow yourself to be hurt, you won't feel hurt. If anything that can cause emotional hurt threatens to enter your mind, react as you would to any dangerous object, strengthen yourself and immediately avoid and reject it. Even when you seem headed for a mighty big fall, don't fall apart. Say to yourself, "One small crack doesn't mean you are broken. It means that you were put to the test and you didn't fall apart," and you won't fall apart.

Confront your problems! Deal with them! Believe you can and will overcome even the bleakest eventualities that arise in the course of your tenure here on this earth. Do not get upset with people and situations, both are powerless without your reaction.

Day 49

One blonde was on one side of the river and there was another blonde on the other side of the river. One blonde yells to the other blonde, "How do you get to the other side?" and the other blonde yells back, "You are on the other side!"

Attitude, attitude, attitude!

To each of us our own brain is the most valuable territory in the world. It is our mind more than any other factor in the universe that determines how happy or unhappy we will be. Yes, of course, external circumstances do play a major role, but it's our response to those circumstances, far more than the circumstance themselves, that determine our emotional state.

Two individuals experiencing the same circumstances can and often do experience diametrically opposed feelings. Some people who have become rich have experienced enormous joy as a consequence, while others have experienced anxiety, a perennial fear that they may lose what they have, and even a perverse sense of guilt. It caused them endless worry and, yes, unhappiness.

Obviously, it's not the actual circumstances, but rather one's response to those circumstances that in the last analysis determines one's state of happiness and that in turn is controlled by one's mind—the most vital, valuable territory in your world.

"An optimist is a person who sees a green light everywhere. The pessimist sees only the red light. But, the truly wise person is color blind" (Dr. Schwietzer). See the positive even in the negative.

Day 50

A prisoner was in jail for breaking into a dress shop three times. His cellmate asked, "Why did you go back to the same shop three times?" The prisoner said, "It was my wife's fault. She kept changing her mind."

Psychologists have discovered that prisoners and hostages can be brainwashed by their captors to act in ways that seem aberrant and counterproductive to their best interests. Indeed, through the subtle power of suggestion or via thought transforming propaganda, we can all be influenced to think and act in certain predetermined ways.

Brainwashing transforms thoughts, feelings and behavior. It can successfully design or redesign one's actions and one's emotions. Though we usually think of brainwashing as a negative, evil tool, the same process can be used constructively to inspire desirable positive attitudes and joy inducing emotion.

Enlist this tantalizing psychodynamic tool, and brainwash yourself to produce a positive state of mind that is positive, optimistic, hopeful and excited about the future, all of which will serve to generate a constantly gratifying emotional happiness.

Day 51

My mother is a typical Jewish mother. Once she was on jury duty. They sent her home. She insisted she was guilty.—Cathy Ladman

For many people, guilt causes feelings of hopelessness and depression; somehow, we feel we are to blame, and the guilt is devastating.

Even innocent victims of the Nazi Holocaust felt they were being punished for some unimaginable sin they must have committed.

Life subjects each of us to painful experiences. It is incumbent upon us to deal with them and resiliently regain our positive outlook.

Only you can make yourself feel like a victim; don't allow yourself to feel victimized. If you accept the burden of being a victim, for whatever reason, you are inflicting your own pain. If you believe that G-d is targeting you as the recipient of bad things, then you are a victim of your own thinking process. You cause yourself to feel defeated and hopeless. You are punishing yourself.

The holiest people, even during what one might regard as G-d's worst punishment, somehow put the best face on and believe the suffering to be purposeful. They believe they are experiencing an involvement with G-d that only G-d understands. They feel the pain will surely be worth the reward in this world and future joyous paradise in the next world. It is all in the way you look at something.

Conversely, some of us in the face of the greatest blessings and joy become depressed. We fear that this blessed state will pass or inordinately our imagination tends to generate a sense that we are in danger of losing this very blessed gift.

Regardless of any temporary discouraging reality, and in fact everything in the last analysis is temporary, imagine yourself, convince yourself, feel yourself "a winner." Believe that G-d is on your side and all that happens is for the best. "Sometimes, good things fall apart so that better things can fall together."

Day 52

I have a friend who needs psychological help. He treats golf as if it were a game!

Bobby Jones, a Hall of Fame golf legend who was considered one of the greatest golfers of all times, insisted, "Competitive golf is played in a five-inch course that resides between one's two ears."

In one short sentence, Jones captured a basic reality. It is your brain—the way you think, the attitude with which you confront life's experiences, the orientation and discipline by which you direct your mind—that can make you a "winner" in the most important competitive activity of all: the pursuit of success and happiness in the game of life.

Learn to effectively employ the five inches between your two ears, the most precious asset you possess, to see the good in every situation. Determine to find good in every circumstance, in every person, and in every challenge. Think, "I am capable. I am strong. If I believe in myself I can turn my dream into a winning plan, and my plan into my reality."

Day 53

My son spent twelve hundred dollars on a plane ticket to India, checked into a hotel at two hundred a day, hired a cab to take him a hundred and twenty miles at a cost of three hundred dollars to an ashram, and there he meditated on the simple life!

Mahatma Ghandi, pointing to the latent unused potential within each of us, postulated that "the difference between what we are doing and what we are capable of doing would solve most of the world's problems." You are much more than you think you are! Believe more in yourself and your own potential power to design your life. You will have more power and a real positive impact on your own life and on the life of others far beyond. It will help you fulfill and become fulfilled.

Learn to believe in yourself. Come to know that you are the most powerful person in the world with respect to what thoughts enter, inhabit or persist in your own mind. You are the lord and master of your own mind, controlling what you think, and therefore determining your emotional mood. If you learn to exercise that most potent, unmatched technique, that very practical ability, then you yourself activate and decide just how good you can feel. There is no greater strength than the power to control one's own mind.

It is up to you to find the strength in yourself to take control of your mind's thoughts and thought processes. Use your power to

HAPPINESS GUARANTEED OR YOUR MISERY BACK

produce an ongoing, everlasting "happiness" frame of mind—which, in fact, is the definition of and the very essence that is "happiness." Do this for yourself and you will admire and appreciate yourself for building your own character.

Day 54

Life is made up of the miserable and the horrible and if you're only miserable, you should be very happy.— Woody Allen

Solzhenitsyn, the Russian scientist and philosopher, asserted, "You can imprison my body but you can't ever imprison my mind."

The physical body is limited but your mind is boundless. You can control it, direct it, and channel it so that no matter what burden may confront you out there, you have the capacity to free your mind of that terrible situation, and by your own determination and will power, raise your spirits and bring about pleasant, desirable feelings.

Abraham Lincoln wisely observed, "Most folks are about as happy as they make up their minds to be."

He proclaimed, "You can do anything you set your mind to do." Lincoln was obviously successful in achieving his goals, and it's certainly worthwhile to his instruction. If we are to set our minds to do anything at all so as to bring any goal to fruition, then that of achieving success and "happiness" is the most valuable and rewarding of all (and, in fact, if we achieve happiness we have accomplished the ultimate success).

Follow Solzhenitsyn's advice to "direct your mind." Set your mind on happiness. "Write it on your heart that every day is the best day of the year" (Ralph Waldo Emerson).

Day 55

First Manager: "Say, what happened to all those 'Think' signs you used to have all over the office?"
Second Manager: "I had to take 'em down. Everyone was sitting around thinking and no work was getting done."

Albert Camus said, "Life is the sum of all your choices." Human beings have free will and willpower. Remember, if you will it, it can be. You have colossal power to design your own life's measure of happiness.

You are the engineer who designs your feelings. You are the builder who builds up your feelings of self-esteem. You are the pilot who guides your mental plane on a pleasant flight, across a safe, gratifying route that gets you where you want to go. Would you allow your plane to fly too low, or in a direction where it could run out of fuel over an ocean or before reaching a safe landing spot? No! Would you let it fly aimlessly into wind shear—causing you to crash and burn? Of course not!

Life is a series of challenges and how we handle them determine our level of humanity. A person, who is free of troubles, is usually free of growth as well. It doesn't matter what you can do, but what you will do. We rarely learn from pleasant experiences; it is the painful ones that usually teach us something. Unfortunately, most growth comes at the price of suffering.

Never allow your hope to evaporate. Your life is far too precious to squander on hopeless dismay. Take action. Instead of allowing yourself to remain immersed in your overactive sensitivity, find a way to force yourself to turn each frustrating, discouraging happening into inspiration for positive action. Become active, not just passive or reactive, in how you let your mind and your life go.

Thoughts and words can breed reality. Believe strongly enough and your dreams will come true. When the chips are down, it's our inner strength that bails us out, that revives and rejuvenates us. Failure is giving in to what seems inevitable. Success is overcoming, fighting back, winning!

Control the direction in which your mind takes you. Choose what thoughts you will allow and which ones you will not tolerate. Don't let others or external uncontrollable events do it. Manipulate your mind to serve you and your goal, achieving a better, fuller, healthier life that minimizes unhappiness and overwhelmingly maximizes happiness. When you sense dark thoughts, move instantly and decisively to reject them. Find a new, less dangerous, more fulfilling route that will bring you to a happy landing.

Day 56

I am great at multitasking. I can waste time, be unproductive all at once.

It is almost impossible to retain a feeling of happiness when we feel stressed, overwhelmed and out of control. We often wake up feeling that life is too hard. We have too much to do, too much to handle. We just have too many challenges on our plate. Our to-do list is pages long. Our unopened e-mails are uncountable. Our bills are piled high. We have shopping to do and carpools to drive.

At this point, you must get your brainpower to overcome your emotions. Rather than avoiding your challenges or going into a panic because of them, you need to problem solve. You must think how to tackle the daunting task ahead. First, choose a realistic goal. If you chose a goal that is unachievable, you end up being frustrated, discouraged and stressed. Next, write down your tasks and objectives and divide them into two lists—those you can control and those you can't. You will be amazed at how many things are out of your control.

Next, to regain control you must begin by tackling a small manageable challenge. Once you complete this task successfully, you will feel empowered to take on another. Each time you accomplish even the smallest task, allow your brain time to register that accomplishment and tell yourself you can take on a little more. Before you realize it, you will build the confidence and self-esteem to deal with the entire undertaking.

Accomplishing your mission is totally satisfying and rewarding. By taking it one step at a time, we train our minds that we can conquer a task, gaining the knowledge, resources and confidence to tackle another, even a bit more difficult one. Each small accomplishment strengthens your commitment to that project and gives you the resolve to do more.

A study showed that when a group of nursing home residents were put in charge of watering their own plants, not only did their happiness level substantially improve, their mortality rate dropped by 50 percent, because the feeling of being able to affect your life, by affecting an outcome, makes you joyful.

Day 57

Several elderly nuns were in their second floor convent when a fire broke out. They took their habits and tied them together and used them as a rope to climb out the window to safety. A newsman asked one of the nuns, "Weren't you afraid that the habits could have ripped and broken since they are so old?" The nun answered, "Nah. Don't yah know old habits are hard to break?"

For most of us, even though we are aware that exercising, taking walks and eating healthy will make us feel good, we don't bother to do it. In order to sustain positive change, positive psychologist William James suggested we turn each desired action into a habit. He said, "A tendency to act only becomes effectively ingrained in us in proportion to the uninterrupted frequency with which the actions actually occur, and the brain 'grows' to their use." Habits form because our brain actually changes in response to frequent practice. Our brains remain malleable even into our old age.

The problem is that even though most people resolve to do something, they don't stick to it. Eighty percent of New Year's resolutions are not kept. The major problem is that most of us rely on willpower, which deteriorates with use.

We would like to go swimming but changing into a swimsuit and going into a cold pool is just too tough compared to just pressing the remote control from your bed and enjoying an old movie.

Human beings do what is easiest, most convenient and a habit. In the end, we all turn to the path of least resistance.

To achieve our desired action, which will cause us increased satisfaction and happiness, we must first make the preferred action easier to do and then make it a habit.

To get yourself to swim, you could wear a bathing suit under your clothing, keep an extra change of clothing in your bag and keep the pool heated. At the same time, you could toss the remote control up on a very high shelf out of reach, making it easier to go to a warm pool than to find a ladder to go retrieve your remote. The rule, according to Shawn Anchor, is to lower the activation energy for habits you want to adopt and raise it for habits you want to avoid.

Amazingly, research shows that making a preferred activity twenty seconds easier or making a bad activity twenty seconds harder is enough to encourage you towards one activity and discourage you from the other. Simple ideas, like keeping healthy snacks in the refrigerator or hiding the junk food, helps you develop new habits. Researchers found that they can reduce cafeteria ice cream consumption by 50 percent just by closing the lid to the ice cream cooler. The less energy it takes to kick start a positive habit, the more likely that habit will stick.

Limiting choices also helps you form good habits. To do this, decide in advance when, where and how you are going to do the activity. If you know that exercise is good for you, rather than going to your shoe rack in the morning, leave your sneakers by the bed the night before, that way you've limited your choices and reduced your activation energy.

Shawn says that a weird phenomenon takes place in the human brain when you put your sneakers on—you start to think it is easier to go running now than to "take all this stuff off." In reality, it would be easier to take the sneakers off, but once your brain has tipped toward a habit, it will naturally keep rolling in that direction.

Next, set rules to limit your options, such as, "I will only eat three fruits a day" or "I will only check my e-mail every three hours." After the first few days, the rules can be relaxed, but to form a habit, rules should be followed stringently at first.

HAPPINESS GUARANTEED OR YOUR MISERY BACK

It is an accepted fact that it takes only twenty-one days of repeated practice until the action is ingrained in your brain's neural chemistry and becomes a habit.

When you work to form a habit that brings you satisfaction, appreciation of yourself and a fulfillment of your goal, you have instilled great happiness into your life.

Day 58

"Einstein explained his theory to me every day, and on my arrival, I was fully convinced that he understood it."—Chaim Weizman, President of Israel

The distance between depression and euphoria is miniscule. It's up to each of us to adjust the critical balance, so that it moves that tiny distance from misery to happiness—the space is infinitesimal but the difference is enormous.

Flip that switch in your brain. Devise a gateway to your brain. You decide what, at any given moment, gets in and what stays out. Most people believe the battle of life is external, but the real battle is within oneself. If we deal effectively and courageously with our inner battle, we will grow, succeed in life and achieve serene happiness.

You can make yourself better. You have self-healing power. When things upset you, immediately shift gears and think about things that make you happy.

Don't say, "It's easier said than done." "I'd like to, but it's impossible." "I can't get it out of my mind. It's ever-present. It just intrudes and stays in my thoughts." Don't accept that. Don't believe that. Your mind, indeed your brain is the most marvelous, most amazing, most phenomenal thing on the face of this earth. It is a miracle that can create miracles.

Think about it. Your brain can speak and understand languages. It can monitor all your bodily functions for eighty or more years, including food intake, waste disposal, orientation, walking, running, jumping, playing, driving, guiding your love making and educating

HAPPINESS GUARANTEED OR YOUR MISERY BACK

yourself and your offspring, innovating new ideas, managing a businesses and co-existing in the world around us. Why then can't it do a simple thing like choose what you will and will not think about? Why can't you decide to think about what makes you happy and avoid completely that which makes you sad and depressed?

How can your "miracle" brain choose what you want it to choose and exclude what inevitably brings about unpleasant feelings and real pain? The answer is simple. Your brain is like a file cabinet containing countless files of different thoughts, images, responses and feelings.

For some paradoxical reason—Murphy's Law—the most distasteful, objectionable, unpleasant, disturbing, aggravating and pain-producing files always seem to surface more often. This is not unlike business, where the biggest problems—the threatening lawsuit or the most destructive employee—force themselves on the boss's attention, dominating his business days as well as his non-business nights. The good things that are happening don't require his immediate attention, don't demand his urgent response and don't raise his "crisis" blood pressure. While it is true that a business's survival depends on resolving major crises, it is also true that a businessman overwhelmed by crises can become ineffective. The very survival of his business may be jeopardized. The key is to deal with the problem but keep control.

Calmly and effectively, deal with the frustrating files while you simultaneously train yourself to open the uplifting files that bring you joy and victory.

Day 59

I was going to kill myself today by taking one thousand aspirin, but after taking the first two, I felt better.

Gore Vidal, a truly brilliant author and modern day philosopher, incisively counseled, "It's of no consequence what others think of you, what matter is what you think of others." Too often, many of us get saddened and disheartened because we think we made a bad impression or that some people think less of us or don't like us. Try to remember life is not a popularity contest. If you make an effort and know you did or tried to do the best you can, you should feel good about yourself and not worry about what others may or may not think.

If it's your boss or your marriage partner, where the daily and ongoing relationship is critical to your own progress and happiness, if you are somehow responsible, it would be wise to recognize this and do all you can to improve your behavior. Do this for you, not because of what they may think of you, but what you think of yourself. If you feel good about what you do, then you will undoubtedly do well in every important relationship throughout your life. Even the President of the United States, who wins a majority in order to be elected to that position, is usually unpopular with almost half of all the people (in fact, possibly by even more than half) and may have only achieved that win because he is even less disliked than the opponent he ran against.

Win your own *self-satisfaction* in what you are. Get to like what you are and what you do and you will add not only to the totality of

HAPPINESS GUARANTEED OR YOUR MISERY BACK

your happiness, but the kind of inner comfort and confidence that will overwhelmingly help you succeed in life and win over all those who really matter.

Researchers have discovered that happiness, which includes being happy with how you perceive yourself, i.e. your looks, your personality, your intelligence, your personal niceness level, your sense of humor, your abilities, etc., determines your ability to succeed. A woman brought up to believe she is pretty will go after and be able to attract better-looking men. If a teacher is falsely told that his student has an above average IQ and, in turn, the teacher treats the student as if he were very bright, the student's feeling confident about his ability will to achieve greater success in his studies.

Don't see yourself through the eyes of those who don't value you. Know your worth even if others don't. Your personal vote of confidence will get you to where you want to be.

Day 60

I hope life isn't a joke because I don't get it.

To induce a feeling of well-being, minimize the time that negative events intrude upon your conscious mind and increase the time you think about your good fortune.

Life is often difficult and it takes an effort on your part to be happy. It doesn't just happen. Improving your capacity for producing a happy state takes an ongoing personal commitment

The road to improvement comes when we challenge our minds and push our bodies to do a little more than is comfortable. Pursuing any new mode of behavior is challenging but as every physical trainer will counsel you, "there is no gain without pain." Train yourself to look for something positive about this moment or this situation. Any fool can be happy when times are good. It takes a strong soul with real heart to develop smiles out of circumstances that make us cry."

You have to work hard to force yourself to develop the kind of new way to become the "boss" of your mind and be in control of its thoughts. But, the investment required to help make this your second nature—an automatic, ongoing, almost reflexive habit—will produce enormous rewards for you. Push away negative thoughts and think of the positives. Live by the motto—P.A.I.N.S.—positive attitude in negative situations.

Day 61

A magician had a terrible accident while sawing his assistant in half. The assistant left the act and moved to Dallas and Tulsa.

The great magician Harry Houdini proved that it's all mind over matter. He trained his mind to tolerate what for the rest of us would constitute some of the worst, most intense pain. As a consequence, he could stick a needle through his cheek or through his hand and not even wince, explaining that he was able to condition his mind, his thought processes, not to feel the pain.

He proved how powerful the control over our minds is and thereby the capacity to completely determine what we think and feel.

Why do people often do violent acts after watching violent movies? How come we walk around in better moods after being at a fun event? We act on the pattern we have been practicing. Our brains retain and control our feelings.

Take advantage of this capacity to control your mind. Employ this unbelievably immense power which you posses to avoid depression, to hold on to the upbeat feelings, which produce a happy state of being.

"Once you replace negative thoughts with positive ones, you'll start having positive results" (Willie Nelson).

Day 62

They said things wouldn't get better until we worked harder. So, we worked harder and they were right—things didn't get better!

"We convince ourselves that life will be better after we finish school, find a job, get married, have a baby, then another. Then, we are frustrated that the kids aren't old enough and we'll be more content when they are.

"After that we're frustrated that we have teenagers to deal with, we will certainly be happy when they are out of that stage.

"We tell ourselves that our life will be complete when our spouse gets his or her act together, when we get a nicer car, are able to go on a nice vacation, when we retire. The truth is there's no better time to be happy than right now." If not now, when?

Your life will always be filled with challenges. It's best to admit this to yourself and decide to be happy anyway. One of my favorite quotes comes from Alfred D. Souza. He said, "For a long time, it had seemed to me that life was about to begin—real life. But there was always some obstacle in the way, something to be gotten through first, some unfinished business, time still to be served, a debt to be paid. Then, life would begin. At last it dawned on me that these obstacles were my life."

This perspective has helped me to see that there is no way to happiness. Happiness is the way, so treasure every moment that you have. And treasure it more because you shared it with someone special, special enough to spend your time...and remember that time waits for no one.

So stop waiting until you finish school, until you go back to school, until you lose ten pounds, until you gain ten pounds, until you have kids, until your kids leave the house, until you start work, until you retire, until you get married, until you get divorced, until Friday night, until Sunday morning, until you get a new car or home, until your car or home is paid off, until spring, until summer, until fall, until winter, until you are off welfare, until the first or fifteenth, until your song comes on, until you've had a drink, until you've sobered up, until you die, until you are born again to decide that there is no better time than right now to be happy...happiness is a journey, not a destination.

So, "Work like you don't need money. Love like you've never been hurt and dance like no one's watching" (Anonymous).

Day 63

***The Daily Globe* is short of staff today. Two of the editorial writers are out with a good mood.**

My wife, Rozi, worries about her family's problems, her friend's problems, and the problems of the world that she reads about in *The New York Times*.

Reading about and seeing the pictures of young American military personnel killed and maimed during the wars in Afghanistan and Iraq caused her such agitation that she developed painful migraine headaches.

Rozi also loves doing crossword puzzles in *The New York Times*. It's a healthy distraction that gives her hours of joy, especially when she concludes successfully. She really enjoys solving the challenging word problems. However, she began to dread retrieving the crossword puzzle from *The New York Times,* confronted as she was by the endless distressing front-page articles.

When her good friend suggested that someone else give her the crossword puzzles so she need not see the news stories, the migraines disappeared. Rozi and I learned that you do what works to avoid focusing on the negative.

Some years ago, there was a best-selling song, "Look away, look away, look away!" That is a useful lesson. Look away from the bad. Focus your eyes and mind on positive things.

Anne Frank wrote in her diary, "I don't think of all the misery but of the beauty that still remains." If Anne Frank, living in a tiny, crowded hideout, with no sunlight, starved, and in fear of being dis-

HAPPINESS GUARANTEED OR YOUR MISERY BACK

covered by the Nazis, could retain such a beautifully upbeat attitude, cannot we, living in great comfort, achieve the same magnificent sunny outlook?

Day 64

As my mother used to say, "You'll get unconditional love from me when you've earned it."—Drew Hastings

Studies reveal that social relationships are the best path to well-being and lowered stress. It's considered the best antidote to depression and a prescription for high performance. Yet, sadly in the midst of stress, rather than turning to friends, family and social interaction, when people are down, they tend to turn away from social contact. The most successful individuals, rather than turning away from social contact, hold tighter to their social support system, which helps them remain more productive, energetic and resilient.

When people are disappointed, embarrassed, are suffering losses or feel like failures, rather than holding their heads high and facing their issues, they often hide. They lie in bed. They lock themselves in their offices. They refuse invitations. They don't realize that they are not only running from the embarrassment, they are running toward deeper depression.

Scientific studies have proven that the most crucial contribution to causing a person to be happy is love. Only one characteristic was found to distinguish the happiest 10 percent from other people, the strength of their social relationships. Shawn Anchor's study of over 1,600 Harvard undergraduates found that social support was a far greater predictor of happiness than factors such as GPA, SAT scores, family income, age, gender and race. He found the correlation between social support and happiness was .7, which for researchers is considered huge. (Psychology findings are significant at .3).

HAPPINESS GUARANTEED OR YOUR MISERY BACK

It is the being with those you love, respect and enjoy who are able to help pull you through your down mood, put life into perspective, help you concentrate on other more joyful matters and allow happiness to re-enter your life. "Without a family, man, alone in the world, trembles with the cold" (Andre Maurois). As Michael J. Fox so beautifully said, "Family is not an important thing, it's everything."

To be happy and upbeat, keep family and friends close. "The only rock I know that stays steady, the only institution I know that works, is the family" (Lee Iococca).

Day 65

"I never knew what happiness was until I got married… and then it was too late."

It is our minds that have the ability to decide how we want to view and react to different aspects of our lives, how we choose to interpret conversations, actions and events.

In *Seven Principles of Marriage,* world-renowned therapist John Gottman explains how, in a marriage, the husband and wife are each in a state of either positive or negative-sentiment override, where they choose to judge their spouse in a positive or negative light. For a marriage to survive, the ratio of positive to negative emotion in a given encounter has to be at least five to one.

A wife, who wants to look at her marriage in a positive light, can say to herself, "My husband is screaming at me, not because he is mean, but rather because he is going through a tough time at work." A husband who wants a happy marriage will think, "My wife may not be as beautiful as she was when she was young, but she knows me better than anyone else."

If either one of the couple is in negative sentiment override, they continually view the act of the other, no matter how good or how innocent, as having been done with bad intentions, which leads to criticism, contempt, stonewalling and defensiveness, all of which are detrimental to a marriage.

By learning to think in a positive light, by giving your spouse the benefit of the doubt, by deciding to be more understanding, more giving, less judgmental, by training your mind to decide, "I want to be happy in this marriage and therefore I will take steps to think positively," you can achieve this happy state of marriage.

Couples counselors no longer ask the couple what their problems are. What are the deficiencies? They ask, "What is going well in your life? What's good about your relationship?" We are able to build a better relationship by focusing on the strengths.

By accepting this principal, acknowledging that it is up to you to determine how you choose to perceive the world, in all circumstances and relationships, you will have the power to choose the beautiful and uplifting view of positivity.

Day 66

A woman telephoned the airline and asked, "How long does it take to fly to Miami?" The clerk said, "Just a minute." The woman said, "Thank you," and happily hung up.

Small attitudinal alterations can change your life. Suppose, every night you return home to find your wife overwhelmed by household chores and screaming children. The moment you walk through the door, she hands you a textbook and tells you to help your son finish his homework. Does this make you want to come home?

Perhaps, you can start keeping a running list of all the wonderful things your wife does for you, and before you entered your home at night, you review this list. Do you think this would help you walk through the door feeling more understanding, more forgiving, more accepting and overall more prepared for the chaos?

Suppose you and your wife made up that despite the insanity, every night by 9 p.m., when the kids are in bed, you would find an hour to relax and just talk? Or perhaps you might makeup that one night every couple of weeks, you would let a babysitter deal with the hectic-ness and the two of you would go out for dinner or even just a walk. Would these actions and plans make the rough times more tolerable? Of course, they would. As long as we accept and are willing to psychologically work through the rocky times and are armed with the tools to plan for and look forward to the good times, we can be happy.

HAPPINESS GUARANTEED OR YOUR MISERY BACK

What if you and your spouse decided that arguments are alright, that you can "agree to disagree," or that you will break arguments with timeouts or jokes, wouldn't you have changed your attitude and create a less stressful, happier environment? Changing how you perceive a person, be it, a friend, relative, your boss or your child, will help you create an entirely favorably different relationship.

What about learning to alter your expectations concerning your children? Suppose you accept that your child may not be top of his class or may not be the school superstar? By lowering your expectations, not only do you lower your frustration and disappointment, you will find that you are proud of your child for what he does achieve. By taking pride in your child's accomplishments, whatever they might be, you will raise his self-esteem, causing him to rise to an even higher level and bringing you unimagined pride.

There are countless ways of training your mind to view, and thereby deal, differently with people, so that you appreciate them more, and in so doing, make your life more pleasant.

Day 67

Wife: "How would you describe me?"
Husband: "ABCDEFGHIJK."
Wife: "What does that mean?"
Husband: "adorable, beautiful, cute, delightful, elegant, fashionable, gorgeous, and hot."
Wife: "Aw, thank you, but what about IJK?"
Husband: "I'm just kidding!"

Sometimes we expect more from others because we ourselves would be willing to do more for them.

Elizabeth Wurtzel, author of *Prozac Nation*, wrote, "Some friends don't understand this [depression]. They don't understand how desperate I am to have someone say, 'I love you and I support you just the way you are because you're wonderful just the way you are.' They don't understand that I can't remember anyone ever saying that to me. I am so demanding and difficult for my friends because I want to crumble and fall apart before them, so that they will love me even though I am no fun, lying in bed, crying all the time, not moving. Depression is all about 'if you loved me you would...'"

Fiona Apple wrote, "When you're surrounded by all these people, it can be lonelier than when you're by yourself. You can be in a huge crowd, but if you don't feel like you can trust anyone or talk to anybody, you feel like you're really alone."

It's important to be aware that "there are wounds that never show on the body that are deeper and more hurtful than anything that bleeds." You may not see another's pain just as others often can't see yours. Only you know your pain and, therefore, you have to learn to turn to others or learn the art of overcoming that pain.

When you are down, sometimes all you need is a hug, a word of encouragement, and an understanding heart. When others are down, be cognizant of their need to be cared about. When you are down, hopefully someone will take notice of your suffering.

Try to understand the blackness, lethargy, hopelessness, and loneliness they're going through. Be there for them when they come through the other side. "It's hard to be a friend to someone who's depressed, but it is one of the kindest, noblest, and best things you will ever do" (Stephen Fry).

Give love, get love—this is the road to happiness. Encourage a person to see that there is a light at the end of the tunnel and help point them in the positive direction. Hopefully, when you are down, others will do this for you.

By realizing that life will have these challenges, that sometimes you will be down and depressed, you will have strengthened yourself to the point of knowing, on your own, that troubles are temporary and the light is not that far away.

Day 68

A patient went to his doctor because he had walking pneumonia. The doctor gave him a prescription and said, "Take one every few miles."

In numerous trials of new drugs, the scientific research data presented to the FDA finds that placebos (fake drugs, like plain sugar pills) produce positive improvements in patients that are almost equal to and, remarkably, in some cases even greater than, that of the actual medicinal treatment being tested. In every one of these studies, although the participants are receiving placebos that only provide them with the belief that they are actually receiving a medical treatment, a significant number of patients remarkably report improvement.

If for any reason you have retained the slightest doubt of the power of one's thoughts and the positive impact it is capable of producing, the positive impact of placebos, which are merely suggestions to a person's mind, is proof of the power of positive thinking to deliver salutary, actually uplifting, physical relief and even good health.

If ingesting a placebo can make you feel better, you yourself by the power of controlling what you choose to think and feel can surely make yourself feel better. Choose to feel good. It really works to effectively reduce depression, anxiety and other serious maladies. Eventually, it will engender a beneficent state of happiness.

It's absolutely a kind of transcendental miracle that G-d has given each of us the unilateral power to cure ourselves through thinking uplifting, happy thoughts. I have come to realize that the most important aspect of being a self-made man is being a man who has the ability to make himself happy.

Day 69

"Do the right thing. It will gratify some people and astonish the rest."—Mark Twain

"Dear Lord,

"So far today, I'm doing all right. I have not gossiped, lost my temper, nor been greedy, grumpy, nasty, selfish, or self-indulgent. I have not whined, complained, cursed or eaten any chocolate. I have charged nothing on my credit card.

"But I will be getting out of bed in a minute, and I think that I will really need your help then."

Being a good person, a giving person, and a caring person has been proven to make a person feel good about themself. Controlling your temper, sharing with others, making someone feel good, are all effective ways to make you feel better about yourself and happier with yourself.

Work on developing your character. Being a better person will make you a happier person. One day your life will flash before your eyes. Make sure it's worth watching and smiling about.

Day 70

Some people are so poor all they have is money.

The kiss of someone you love can make you feel better and happier than any material fortune. It has the power to lift your spirits. It improves your outlook, your feelings and your sense of being loved and inspired. Real, enjoyable, fulfilling happiness comes from love and the incomparable emotional, ongoing high it produces, not from some collection of designer price tags.

Helen Keller said, "The best and most beautiful things in the world cannot be seen or even touched. They must be felt with the heart." Friendship, empathy, understanding, gratitude, love—these are the most luscious ingredients for happiness.

Love may not fix all your problems but at least you don't have to face them alone. Give love and earn love in return. You will earn the most enviable fortune this world of ours can produce—"happiness."

Day 71

If a job's worth doing, make sure you delegate it to the right person.

By pursing four basic values of faith, family, community and work, you are most likely to achieve happiness. The first three make sense since no dying person ever regretted devoting too much time to any of them, but work is a surprising one.

Yet, rewarding work, unrelated to income, is a major component of happiness.

Relieving poverty causes great increases in happiness, but once someone earns above a middle-class income, happiness is affected only slightly or not at all. But, if someone lacks a job, the rate of suicide, divorce and severe disease dramatically increases. Work can bring happiness by marrying our passions to our skills, empowering us to create value in our lives and in the lives of others. "Happiness," said Franklin D. Roosevelt, "lies not in the mere possession of money; it lies in the joy of achievement, in the thrill of creative effort." Data proves that people who feel they are successful at work are twice as likely to say they are overall happy as those who don't feel successful.

Michael Bloomberg claims that he found the greatest high is staying busy, that working hard at something you can be excited by, is more than satisfying—it's fun, it's even thrilling and it can be, perhaps, the most important contributor to a person's happiness.

Today, it is fully recognized by psychologists and neuroscientists that rather than success bringing happiness, as we become happier and more positive, we are more likely to achieve success.

HAPPINESS GUARANTEED OR YOUR MISERY BACK

"Do not educate your child to be rich. Educate him to be happy." Give him the right focus, so that when he grows up, he'll know the value of things, not the price. In this way, you are passing on the secret of happiness."

Learn from the last words of Steve Jobs, founder and CEO of Apple. "I have come to the pinnacle of success in business. In the eyes of others, my life has been the symbol of success. However, apart from work, I have little joy. Finally, my wealth is simply a fact to which I am accustomed. At this time, lying on the hospital bed and remembering all my life, I realize that all the accolades and riches, of which I was once so proud, have become insignificant with my imminent death. In the dark, which I look at green lights, of the equipment for artificial respiration and feel the buzz of their mechanical sounds I can feel the breath of my approaching death looming over me.

"Only now do I understand that once you accumulate enough money for the rest of your life you have to pursue objectives that are not related to wealth. It should be something more important. For example, stories of love, art, dreams of my childhood. No, stop pursuing wealth; it can only make a person into a twisted being, just like me. G-d had made us one way, we can feel the love in the heart of each of us and not illusions built by fame or money, like I made in my life, I cannot take them with me. I can only take with me the memories that were strengthened by love. This is the true wealth that will follow you, will accompany you; he will give strength and light to go ahead.

"Love can travel thousands of miles and so life has no limits. Move to where you want to go. Strive to reach the goals you want to achieve. Everything is in your heart and in your hands. What is the world's most expensive bed? The hospital bed.

"You, if you have money, can hire someone to drive your car, but you cannot hire someone to take your illness that is killing you. Material things lost can be found. But, one thing you can never find when you lose: life. Whatever stage of life where we are right now, at the end we will have to face the day when the curtain falls. Please treasure your family love, love for your spouse, love for your friends…Treat everyone well and stay friendly with your neighbors."

"The hardest thing to find in life is happiness—money is only hard to find because it gets wasted trying to find happiness."

Day 72

"Life is too important to be taken seriously."—Oscar Wilde

An idealistic young man sought the advice of an elderly sage. "I want to change the world," he said. "I want to make it a better place. Where should I concentrate my efforts?"

The sage smiled. "You remind me of myself," he said. "As an idealistic young man, I resolved to change the world for the better, but before long I discovered that it was impossible. The world is too big. So, I decided to change my city for the better, but after a while, I discovered that was also beyond my grasp. As the years progressed, I wanted to inspire my immediate circle of family and friends, but that too was beyond my ability. Finally, in my old age, I realized that I should try to change myself. Had I originally focused inwards and started with trying to change myself, I might have been able to do something for my family, community, and ultimately perhaps even for the world as well." (the Parsha Odyssey).

Working on your own self-improvement and positive attitude will empower you to help others. "No matter the situation, don't let your emotions overpower your intelligence" (Anonymous).

Day 73

When you start a diet, the first thing you lose is your patience.

We diet to attain a healthier body, by controlling what we eat as well as how much we eat. If we diet properly over the course of a lifetime, we tend to live a longer, illness free, vigorous life.

In the same way we need to control our eating to attain a healthier body, we must control what we think in order to attain a healthier mind. "You've got to train your mind, your body and your emotions," an inspirational motivator, Anthony Robbins, urged in an interview. "Most people who are committed to making their life better may train their body and diet and exercise, but they aren't happy. They have a two-legged stool. I'm going to give them the third: emotional fitness." One must be equally committed to train his mind to achieve quality happiness.

Fashion your life after Frank Sinatra's hit song "I Did It My Way." Choose the thoughts that enter your brain just as you choose the food that enters your mouth. You wouldn't allow unpleasant, irritant causing, polluted or poisonous food in your mouth; in like fashion, resist unpleasant, debilitating, tormenting thoughts.

Be the master of your own mind. Then, you too, will be able to sing, "I did it my way," with the emphasis on "I did it" because it will be you that has indeed done it. "Don't let your emotions distract you from what has to be done. Control your emotions or your emotions will control you" (Anonymous).

Day 74

Laugh and the whole world laughs with you, snore and you sleep alone.

Radical Remission, a book by Dr. Kelly Turner, looks at cases of people who have made seemingly miraculous recoveries from cancer when medical science suggested there was no ground for hope. Dr. Turner interviewed over a thousand individuals who survived cancer against the odds and found that they had nine factors in common: radically changing your diet, taking control of your health, following your intuition, using herbs and supplements, releasing suppressed emotions, increasing positive emotions, embracing social support, deepening your spiritual connection and having strong reasons for living.

Laughing is one of the best ways of increasing positive emotions. When we feel happy and relaxed, our bodies release immune-boosting hormones, which enables our body to produce more immune cells and become healthier.

Pioneering doctors, such as Patch Adams, have recognized the importance of humor in caring for patients of all kinds. Doctors today realize the importance of positive emotions and often use humor or music to calm their patients and create positive feelings.

A good laugh is good for your body and your mind. Which comes first, the laughter or the cure? If laughter can help you to heal, control your mind, control your emotions, think happy, and think funny. Laugh away your problems.

One of Benjamin Franklin's incisive proverbs was, "Trouble knocked at the door, but, hearing laughter, hurried away."

Day 75

We really live in a world of medical specialists. Today, four out of five doctors recommend another doctor.

In early 2007, Sharon Begley authored a book entitled *Train Your Mind, Change Your Brain: How a New Science Reveals our Extraordinary Power to Transform Ourselves*. It describes an emerging new science called neuroplasticity, which asserts that the brain can actually change its structure and function in response to the experiential input it receives.

The Wall Street Journal review of the book marvels at how "something as intangible and insubstantial as a thought would rewire the brain." This science, and this book as well, emanate from the insights of the great and brilliant Dalai Lama, the Tibetan Buddhist leader, who discerned how "thinking"—the power of the mind—can change the brain. He said, "The basic thing is that everyone wants happiness, no one wants suffering. And happiness mainly comes from our own attitude, rather than from external factors. If your own mental attitude is correct, even if you remain in a hostile atmosphere, you feel happy."

This is yet another proof that controlling your thoughts can change your mood and, yes, even change your physical brain to produce a state of emotional happiness. The smallest change in your perspective can alter your brain and transform your life. Think, what tiny attitude adjustment can turn your world around? "When you have control over your thoughts, you have control over your mind" (Anonymous).

Day 76

"A person will sometimes devote all of his life to the development of one part of his body—the wishbone."— Robert Frost

Benjamin Disraeli said, "Action may not always bring happiness, but there is no happiness without action." So many individuals suffer from depression, obsessive-compulsive disorder and low self-esteem, making it hard for such people to act. They are stunted by their thoughts and fears. Many people suffer from procrastination and anxiety.

The road to finding happiness begins with taking responsibility to make your life happy. Happiness doesn't come to you. You have to create it. Amy Closver says, "It's frightening leaving the comfort of misery." People enjoy wallowing in their misery. It makes them feel alive albeit that they are feeling horrible. But, think, is that what you really want? People really do want to be happy and you are no different. But, if you want your life to change, you have to change it and you can. You will have to start taking action to think and act differently and create a new reality. When you work for happiness, when you invest energy in making yourself happy, you appreciate it and consequently you work to hold on to that happiness.

By working towards this happiness, you are telling yourself that the quality of your life is worth fighting for. You are taking responsibility, strengthening your confidence and building up your self-worth by showing yourself you are in charge. You are not a victim.

You must make the first move, take the first step while accepting the challenge and realize it will not be easy. Anything worth getting is worth fighting for. You are fighting for your very life. Commit to do the work. To do this, first examine your life. Think about your relationships, your health, your work, your activities and your involvements and determine how you feel about each aspect. Consider which areas of your life are making you unhappy and which you are satisfied with? Now, honestly, write down for your self-awareness, why these things leave you lacking. Only by understanding what makes you unhappy can you institute change.

Now look at these areas of your life and try to figure out what would make you happy. Take each area. In the social arena, are you lonely? Could you ask friends to invite you out? Could you ask them to set you up with someone to date? Could you try to work on your relationship with your spouse? If you are unhappy at work, could you change your job? Could you return to school to study for a different career?

By asking yourself these questions, you explore new options and you analyze whether choosing those options would really make you happy. Often you realize, that the things you think would make you happy truly wouldn't.

Once you find options that you believe appeal to you, resolve to try them, even if you are anxious. Fear is healthy. It means you are stretching. You are stepping outside of your comfort zone but this shows you are perhaps doing something really worth doing.

Sit down with a pen and paper and start taking stock of your life, friends, involvements, and determine what you can change to make yourself stretch and grow into a happier individual.

"To thrive in life, you need three bones: a wishbone, a backbone and a funny bone."

Day 77

If at first you don't succeed, failure may be your thing.

In his sermon on September 18, 2005, Dr. Arthur Caliandro said, "Giving up is not an option." When Thomas Edison invented the light bulb, he tried over two thousand experiments before he got it right. A young reporter asked him how it felt to have failed so many times. Edison replied, "I never failed once; I invented the light bulb. It just happened to be a two-thousand-step process."

In 1952, Edmund Hillary attempted but failed to climb Mount Everest, the world's tallest mountain. Sometime after that, he was asked to address a group of people in England. He began his talk by pointing to a picture of Mount Everest, saying, "You beat me the first time, but I'll beat you the next time because you've grown all that you're going to grow and I'm still growing." Within the year, Hillary conquered the mountain. Afterwards, he said, "You don't conquer the mountain, you conquer yourself."

The first time comedian Jerry Seinfeld performed on stage at a comedy club, he looked at his audience, froze and was booed off stage. Seinfeld didn't give up. He went back and tried again the following night. This time he completed his set to laughter and applause that set him on his successful career.

Outstanding leading man, actor, singer, dancer Fred Astaire, as a reminder of where he came from, kept the note that he received from the MGM testing director after his first screen test. It said, "Can't act. Can't sing. Slightly bald. Can dance a little." Today, Astaire is considered one of the best dancers of all time.

HAPPINESS GUARANTEED OR YOUR MISERY BACK

Sidney Poitier, Oscar winner and one of the best regarded actors in the business, after his first audition was told by the casting director, "Why don't you stop wasting people's time and go out and become a dishwasher or something."

The iconic Charlie Chaplin, star of silent screen, was initially rejected by Hollywood studio chiefs who felt his act was a little too nonsensical to ever sell.

Before starring in her own show, *I Love Lucy*, Lucille Ball was considered a failed actress and a B-movie star. Her drama instructor advised her to try a different position. She went on to win thirteen Emmy nominations, four Emmys and a Lifetime Achievement Award from the Kennedy Center.

Harrison Ford, actor par excellence, was originally told by the movie execs that he simply didn't have what it takes to be a star.

Author of the classic novel Little Women, Louisa May Alcott, unable to get her works published, was encouraged to find work as a servant by her family to help make ends meet.

Famed poet Emily Dickenson, in her lifetime, was all but ignored, having fewer than a dozen poems published out of almost 1,800 completed works.

Jack London, author of *The Call of The Wild*, had his first story rejected 600 times before being accepted.

Charles Schultz, writer of the *Peanuts* comic strip, had his cartoons rejected by his high school yearbook staff and later was rejected for a position working with Walt Disney.

Vice President Dick Cheney flunked out of Yale twice. President Harry S. Truman originally owned a shirt store that went bankrupt.

Amazingly, one out of four United States presidents lost their first run for president.

Who is better known than Winston Churchill? Yet, before becoming Prime Minister of the United Kingdom at age sixty-two, he struggled in school, failed out of sixth grade and suffered many political defeats.

Forge on through failure and rejection. Turn your failures into fountains of inspiration. "Shoot for the moon. Even if you miss, you'll land among the stars."

Day 78

My bank sent back a check with a note saying, "insufficient funds." Them or me?

Janet Yellen, the Chairwoman of the Federal Reserve and one of the most accomplished and powerful women of her generation, told New York University graduates to "expect failure and learn from it." She sagely advised these graduating students, "finding the right path in life involves missteps. Even Yankees legend Babe Ruth (probably the greatest baseball player of all time) failed most of the time when stepping up to bat. "I learned the lesson," Yellen continued, "that one's response to the inevitable setbacks matters as much as the balance of victories and defeats." She urged them to "show grit and an abiding commitment to work hard toward long-range goals and persevere through the setbacks that come along the way."

Remain courageous, fight for what you believe in, be persistent, stay focused, and you will overcome all the difficulties and challenges and go on to successfully achieve your envisioned dreams.

Keep trying and "every day, ask yourself if what you are doing today is getting you closer to where you want to be tomorrow." As Michael Jordan said, "I can accept failure, everyone fails at something. But, I can't accept not trying."

Day 79

Did you hear about the "Dial-A-Prayer" telephone service for agnostics? You dial the number and no one answers.

Psalm 121, recited by Jews and Gentiles alike, says, "I lift up my eyes to the mountains. From where does my help come? My help comes from the Lord, who made heaven and Earth."

The question is asked, why not just say, "My help comes from the Lord;" why the need to clarify that this is the Lord who made the heavens and Earth? This is a lesson not only in faith but also in remaining optimistic. One day, the world was a void and empty place and then in an instant, G-d made a heaven and Earth. One day, life can be empty and hopeless and then, in an instant, life can be full, rich and superb. The Hebrew word, which is used as "from where," is "may ein." Ein has two other meanings: "from nothing" and "from eyes." Depending on how you view things, you can see nothingness or, with a positive perspective, you can see happiness right in front of you.

The Hebrew word for mountains, "harim," also has another meaning. It means "parents." In times of trouble, when life feels hopeless, look up to your parents, turn to those who love you and care about you. Furthermore, as parents, realize that your children look to you for both love and direction. Teach them to view life with a beautiful, positive perspective.

A man was on an airplane that was passing through a storm. The pilot came on the loud speaker and announced that no food or beverages would be served because of the severity of the storm. The passengers began to panic a bit. The pilot then announced, "Everyone fasten your seat belts and do not leave your seats." The plane began to shake side to side then up and down. Passengers began to cry and scream. The man noticed one little girl who in the midst of all the turmoil remained calm and unfazed. She sat reading her book totally oblivious to the shaking plane. When the plane finally touched down safely, the man waited for the little girl to disembark, curious as to why she had remained so calm.

"Why," he inquired of her, "were you not worried?" "Because," she answered, "the pilot is my father and he told me he was going to take me home. I never doubted he would."

Have faith that G-d, our father, will see you safely through the storm.

Day 80

If at first you don't succeed, hide all evidence that you tried.

Things happen by default, so if you don't plan, you cannot be in charge of what happens to you. You have no control. Though your plans may not always achieve the desired result, you have a better chance of reaching your objective if you decide on a plan of action and then work towards fulfilling that goal.

Accomplishment results from a commitment to achieve, intelligent planning, focused effort and, often, hard work. You can spend a lifetime planning and preparing or you can get yourself up and start doing. Of course, as the well-known statement goes, "Man plans and G-d laughs." In the end, G-d determines whether you succeed or fail, whether things go well or go poorly, whether life goes smoothly or you are challenged.

Morris, in desperate need of funds, begged G-d, "Please let me win the lottery. I promise I will give a tenth of my winnings to charity." The next week, Morris was even more desperate so he begged G-d, "Please, G-d, let me win the lottery. I promise I will give half of my winnings to charity. Finally, in utter desperation, Morris turned to G-d and said, "Please, G-d, let me win the lottery. I swear I will give 90 percent of my winnings to charity." Suddenly, the booming voice of G-d called out, "Morris, do me a favor. Buy a lottery ticket."

Don't just wait for life to happen to you, be an active participant. "Some people pursue opportunities others create them." If an opportunity presents itself, move on it. If no opportunities come your way, it's a greater challenge, but with the will, you can make your own opportunities.

It is up to G-d, but we must do our part. Plan to move forward with faith and determination. Remember, none of us plans to fail, but so many of us fail to plan.

Day 81

People are making end-of-the-world jokes like there is no tomorrow.

When we suffer, when we are in pain, as much as others care and may wish to help, no one can fully comprehend your pain and no one has the ability to completely pull you through this period, except you. When you, G-d forbid, lose a loved one, or break up with someone, or experience a trauma, or are just feeling lousy, you will look at the world and see it going on as usual. You will feel, as the song so aptly goes, "Why does the sun go on shining? Why does the sea rush to shore? Don't they know it's the end of the world ('cause you don't love me anymore)." As much as you feel, "Stop the world, I want to get off," it is up to you to rejoin the world.

Tragically, I have a few close friends who have lost children. I doubt there is any pain as great as this. Yet, I was at the funeral of one of these children, standing beside a woman who had lost a child the previous year. She said to me, "I wish I could turn the clock ahead one year for these parents, so that they can realize that they can survive, accept and even grow from this pain."

We have the ability to make peace with tragedy. We lose someone old and we realize we are lucky he passed away before losing his faculties. We lose someone young and decide at least this child didn't have to live in this harsh world. We break up with someone and realize he wasn't right for me in a certain aspect. Our mind has the ability to find a way to make even painful occurrences acceptable to us, so that we can go on. It's a survival mechanism.

By being cognizant of this gift that we all possess, we can and should allow our minds to decide that we choose to mourn, retain the beautiful memories and then hold our pain within us and move on to return to a state of happiness. We choose to rejoin the world that is still functioning and awaiting our return.

Day 82

If only we'd try to stop being happy, we could have a pretty good time.

Bruce Kramer who was an ALS (Lou Gehrig's disease) patient said in a radio show interview that his fatal disease "cured him of planning." Planning is wise, even essential, but way too often we foolishly spend far too much of our precious, limited, time contemplating our future. But, in the process, we somehow fail to avail ourselves of the enormous exciting opportunities and joys immediately at hand

While Mr. Kramer's statement, that his "disease cured him of planning," sounds kind of silly, what he was saying has a great deal of merit. If you are set free, released from that ongoing compulsion to design your future, you can better begin to enjoy today and all of the days leading up to that future that may never come or that we can really ever plan. We can't spend time regretting yesterday or fearing tomorrow. You have to live and enjoy today.

"In life there will never be the same yesterday. Enjoy today, in order to have some wonderful yesterdays, to talk about tomorrow" (Mitta Xinindu).

Day 83

No, I don't need anger management. You need to stop making me angry.

Best-selling author Arthur Brooks wrote that, throughout his career, President Dwight Eisenhower, because he had a bad temper and tended to feel angry, would deal effectively with that problem by writing down on a piece of paper whatever was upsetting him. He would then throw away that paper along with his anger. It helped him rein in his disturbing, hostile emotions and helped him to feel and act better.

A good friend of mine, who did very well in life, told me that when he was very young, his father gave him this same advice. Write down what bothers you then toss it away. He said this act had always helped him rid himself of troubling issues.

A successful author once said that writing a book that included his own negative personal experiences he had lived through seemed to work as well in dealing with his psychological malaise. It served as a sort of therapy that helped relieve his neurotic anxieties and psychosomatic neurosis.

If you are going through a difficult period and become depressed by the prevailing agitating circumstances that you are experiencing, write down on a piece of paper just what's distressing you. Look at it for a brief moment, then throw it away and see if it doesn't help you get over it and move on.

It's an intriguing secret strategic maneuver that seems to work for many who have tried it. And, of course, to the extent you can avoid or minimize the amount of time you endure or suffer negative, sad, tormenting emotions you do improve your mental state, and quality of life.

So, keep a trashcan handy.

Day 84

You can't buy happiness. But, you can buy donuts. And that's kind of the same thing.

People have so many problems. What's yours? Perhaps you feel unfulfilled. Perhaps life feels hopeless. Perhaps you can't find anyone to love. You feel like you have so much love to give. You look at others and say, "Why not me? Why them?" Envy won't get you anywhere. Self-pity is self-defeating. Think, how can I make myself happy? Try telling yourself, it may not be perfect, but for now, perhaps, I have to channel my "giving-energy" somewhere else.

Are you miserable because you can't conceive? Are you thinking why does everyone else get pregnant? You can stay and be miserable or you can look into specialists who might help you conceive. You can speak to people who have adopted. You can join a support group with other people in your unfortunate position. It's not easy. It may be gut-wrenching pain, but decide to get past the challenge and find a path that may not have been your first choice, but will make you happy.

Is your problem that you are dealing with a devastating loss? Being miserable won't undo it. Think, would the deceased person want you to be suffering because of them? Of course, you must give yourself time to grieve. But, wouldn't they want you to go on functioning and even delighting in life? Would they want you to establish or give to a worthy cause in their memory? Would they want you to help others who are in the same situation as you are?

HAPPINESS GUARANTEED OR YOUR MISERY BACK

Is your problem that you are paralyzed by an uncontrollable baseless fear? Are you afraid of failure? Are you afraid to take responsibility? Are you afraid of the future? Consider the worst scenario. Consider the best scenario. Take a chance. Take a step one step at a time.

Everyone has problems, financial worries, health issues, aging worries, loneliness issues, and problems with their children, their spouse or their in-laws. Some dwell on it. Some move past it. We can't turn the clock back. We can only shape the future.

Ultimately, only you can pull yourself out of depression. No one can be helped who doesn't want to be helped. Only you can make up your mind and figure out what steps to take to move into the happiness realm. You don't have to see the whole staircase, just take the first step. "When you are in the valley, keep your goal firmly in view and you will get the renewed energy to continue the climb" (Dennis Waitley).

Day 85

I just had a near-life experience.

Rabbi Pesach Krohn, a world-class lecturer, scholar and highly esteemed religious leader who helps countless individuals deal with life-challenging difficulties, adversities and devastating tragedies, tells of a righteous woman he had the privilege of working with over a number of years,

He says that he learned she was hospitalized with a fatal form of cancer and, therefore, promptly went to visit this woman he so respected and admired. She was in far worse shape than he even anticipated. He further learned from her doctors that she had been living and dealing with this horrific malady for more than a decade, all the time working with him, courageously, helping so many others.

When he tried to commiserate with her, she insisted that really there was no need and that she was a very lucky individual. She protested saying how blessed she was with healthy, accomplished children and wonderful, loving grandchildren. Instead of moping and feeling sorry for herself, she inspired him to feel uplifted and exalted.

How magnificent that a mere mortal human being could, in the face of such catastrophic affliction, such overwhelming cataclysmic misfortune, not only be uncomplaining but also be so positive, appreciative and thankful. He found it incredible and just amazing. Instead of depression, she manifested the most astonishing, awesome and transcendent exhilaration.

Rabbi Krohn's admiration for this remarkable woman, whom he had already venerated for her lifelong selfless dedication to helping

HAPPINESS GUARANTEED OR YOUR MISERY BACK

so many, soared. He disclosed that this experience had a profound, inexpressible impact on him personally. He had a new respect for the spectacular power and, indeed, mysterious miracle of each human being. He marveled at the remarkably transcendental epiphany that can be realized, if and when one focuses upon his or her blessings, rather than their deprivations, and how someone can resolutely train one's mind to reflect upon, envisage and truly appreciate the (too often taken for granted) immeasurably priceless possessions we do have.

It's this kind of lesson we all need to fully assimilate, soak in and master, so as to endow ourselves with the salutary attitude than will so enhance our "happiness" capacity.

Tap into your unique ability to minimize your hardships and focus on your blessings. "You don't get to choose how you are going to die, or when. You can only decide how you're going to live now" (Jaon Baez).

Day 86

Aging seems to be the only way to live a long life.

There is a terribly sad story about a woman who gives birth to a child. As the new mother cradles her baby in her arms, the doctor gives her and her husband the horrible news that the baby is going to die. They are broken-hearted. As tears roll down their cheeks, they ask the doctor, "How long will the baby will live." The doctor says, "The baby will live a normal life but he could die at any moment or he could live until 120."

Every child who is born is destined to die. Each person can endlessly stay and worry about their doom or they can make something of their life. It's what you do with your life that counts.

Be aware that you have a limited time in this world. You are in danger of dying at any moment. Appreciate every moment and make each one count by living a happy, productive life. Don't be frightened and saddened by the fact that the sand in the hourglass is falling, be uplifted and productive by thinking, "How can I gather that sand to build my dreamed of castle?"

Day 87

Tourist: What beautiful scenery! Lived here all your life?
Farmer: Not yet.

Placing yourself in the right environment affects one's mood. Don't you feel better sitting on a hill looking down at the landscape where you experience joy and harmony? Don't you enjoy looking at a source of water, such as a river or a stream, where you see beauty and are protected from thirst, or sitting under a low canopy tree which offers protection and shade? People love being where there are animals, which provides proof of habitation. Studies prove this to be true.

Nancy Etcoff, an evolutionary psychologist and author of *The Survival of the Prettiest*, explains that building windowless, nature-less isolated offices full of cubicles ignores what people actually want.

A study of patients hospitalized for gallbladder surgery compared those whose rooms looked out on a park with those facing a brick wall. The park-view patients used less pain medication, had shorter stays, and complained less to their nurses. In darkness, one tends to feel dark and gloomy while in light one feels alive and hopeful.

You have the power to control your happiness. Place yourself in an environment that elicits a happy state of mind. "It takes but one positive thought when given a chance to survive and thrive to overpower an entire army of negative thoughts" (Robert Schuller).

Day 88

"I want to live till I die. No more no less."—Eddie Izzard

"Every man dies, but not every man really lives" (Braveheart).

Bob Clyatt, the chief executive of HorizonLive.com, said, "When I was ten, my sister Sally, died in a car crash. She was sixteen, the third in line of us five kids; I was the fourth. She taught me to read when I was four. After her death, I had the notion that I had to fill my life with as many experiences as possible because every day is a gift that can be snatched away from you at any moment."

When Elizabeth Taylor was seventy-six, she was interviewed by Larry King, who asked her about media reports that characterized her as suffering from Alzheimer's and practically dead. She responded that although doctors had believed her life ended on four different occasions, she was not suffering from Alzheimer's; indeed, she was very much alive and reinvigorated by her new creative venture of jewelry designing.

Bob Dylan said, "If you get up in the morning looking forward to what you are doing, spend the day doing what you like, and then go to sleep at night after that kind of day, you are a success."

Being involved with and surrounded by people you care about, makes for a successful and happy life. If you pursue a goal that excites you, you too will become energized and elated.

"Happiness is a small and unworthy goal for something as big and fancy as a whole lifetime, and should be taken in small doses" (Russell Baker). Every minute of your life is precious and fleeting. Make the most of it. Pursue your passions. Do the things you enjoy, surrounded by the people you love.

Day 89

"My friends tell me I have an intimacy problem. But, they don't really know me."—Gary Shandling

Now and then, it's good to pause in our pursuit of happiness and just be happy. Feeling love for someone and being loved by someone keeps you happy.

You know it is love when you're not thinking about your own happiness any more…you're thinking about his/hers. Whether it's love for a friend, a spouse or a child, love makes you feel fulfilled. Loving someone makes you feel good about yourself.

It is the giving to another person that makes you love and care about this individual even more than the receiving.

Are you in love? On the average, 30,000 people fall in love per day (Waters, Preston, Daily, 4/27/12). Imagine how many more are enjoying the blissful state of being in love. Studies show that people fall in love only four times over a lifetime (Huffpost.com). Eight out of ten fall madly in love with one person while in their twenties, four out of ten in their thirties and three out of ten after reaching their forties. Yet, at all times, many are still "in love" or enjoying being in a relationship. Many have spouses, partners, children, close friends and relatives and even pets to love throughout a lifetime.

When you choose to love others, to give to others, to be there for others, you are making a conscious decision to bring happiness into your life.

Day 90

**Yahoo.com: "World's oldest man dies!"
Why does this keep happening?**

Eighty-nine thousand people die in their sleep in the USA daily, so if you woke up today, be ecstatic. If you think about it, you should be the happiest and most appreciative person in the world, just because you are alive. The worldwide average of deaths per day is 154,138 (Answers.com). Thank G-d there are 363,554 births per day in the universe with a population of seven billion, so it is a happy world. The average life expectancy in 2011, which is rising constantly, was 66.12, or 24,150 days. Even if some of those days are depressing or even devastating, you have loads more on which to enjoy happy thoughts and events.

In the US, there are 27,000 car accidents per day. If you weren't a victim of one of them, think how wonderful life is. Frighteningly, 1,660,990 are diagnosed with some sort of cancer. Men have slightly less than a one out of two lifetime risk of developing cancer. For women, the risk is a little more than one in three, so if you don't have cancer or you are alive to fight the disease in an age when every new day brings miraculous medical breakthroughs, keep on smiling.

Six million people break bones per year. If you are in tact, tell yourself, "I'm lucky."

"Life is so ironic. It takes sadness to know happiness, noise to appreciate silence, and absence to value presence." We all can chose to look at the negative and cry or at the beautiful positive side and rejoice. Choose to rejoice!

Day 91

When life is going wrong, when stress engulfs you, when tears flow down your eyes, just give me a call: I sell tissues.

When you get introspective and feel down and depressed thinking you're not as successful, well off or as lucky as others are, or as you would wish to be, think of Oliver Burkeman, author of *The Antidote: Happiness for People Who Can't Stand Positive Thinking*, who tells us that the stoic ancient philosophers recommended "deliberately visualizing the worst-case scenario." Burkeman explains, "This action tends to reduce anxiety about the future. By soberly picturing how badly things could be in reality....These incisive philosophers noted, that, imagining that you might lose the relationships and possessions you currently enjoy increases your gratitude for having them now."

While such a seemingly negative, or frightening, thought-process approach may seem a strange way to overcome a depressed mood, it's a great strategy—certainly worth trying. I've tried it and it's worked for me. Imagining the worst, I suddenly appreciate and realized how lucky I am to have achieved what I have (despite that I do hope for more) and then feel very blessed to possess all that I do.

Unfortunately, there must be some principle of nature, which states that we never know the quality of what we have until it is gone? By envisioning the bad possibilities, it helps turn a negative state into a positive one, that helps you see things favorably and thereby emotionally uplifts your mindset and mood.

Try this technique of considering the negative alternatives that might exist but thankfully don't, in order to appreciate the positive reality.

Day 92

"Attitudes are contagious. Are yours worth catching?"
—Dennis and Wendy Mannering

Beth Agnew, a writer, educator, laughter-leader, and business consultant in writing about how to help people deal with adversity through hard times, clearly shares the philosophy and the teachings I counsel, encourage and champion in this book. She concisely and brilliantly imparts the following salient wisdom: The old adage in the holy book says, "As you think so shall you be." In the book of Proverbs, it is written, "As a man thinketh in his heart, so is he." The power of our thoughts determines our reality. The gurus tell us "change your thoughts." Think positively. To change our circumstances we need to think positively.

Further, taking some literary license and paraphrasing her superbly consequential insights and advice, she goes on to suggest that people should move on to the act of mentally (and emotionally) considering, and meditating about workable solutions to their problems. This will help trigger the creative, problem-solving part of your subconscious. It will also help you feel better and give you more peace.

Decide that you don't want to stay and sulk, be worried and anxious. Facing your issues, dealing with your problems is the best way to put your problems behind you. "A day of worry is more exhausting than a week of work" (John Lubbock). As Winston Churchill said, "I never worry about action, only inaction." Fear is immobilizing. Force yourself to move forward.

No magic potions…no fairy dust…no one to push you…no one to do it for you, just one determined foot in front of the other…

Day 93

I was an optimist when I installed the VCR by myself. Now, I get movies on my electric can opener.

Mayor Rudy Giuliani wisely counsels, "You never solve any problems with pessimism. You solve them most effectively and expeditiously with optimism." He attributes much of his life's outstanding success to that pragmatically rewarding attitude. And it does indeed make for a much more joyous existence.

Winston Churchill said, "A pessimist sees the difficulty in every opportunity, an optimist sees the opportunity in every difficulty."

It is much more enjoyable to face life with optimism. It may not be tonight, tomorrow or the next day…but everything is going to be okay. Look at life with a positive attitude. A positive attitude helps you cope with the daily affairs of life by making you feel more hopeful and less anxious or worried.

Developing an optimistic way of thinking brings constructive changes, such as facilitating motivation and energy to accomplish your goals. It will make you feel personally inspired and enable you to inspire others. It will give you the strength not to give up despite the many obstacles you may encounter. You will feel energized and propelled to do things. You will be able to move ahead because you will expect success rather than failure. You will regard failure and problems as blessings in disguise. You will develop self-confidence, believing in your abilities. Instead of dwelling on problems, you will look for solutions and see and recognize opportunities. You will earn

HAPPINESS GUARANTEED OR YOUR MISERY BACK

the love and respect of others and people will want to be around you. Life will seem altogether more bright and cheerful.

If you expect the worst, the worst will come. You bring on your own stress, your own frustration, your own jealousy, your own anger and your own sadness. Alternatively, by being optimistic you can bring on your own happiness.

"Optimists enrich the present, enhance the future, challenge the improbable and attain the impossible" (William Arthur).

Day 94

"I don't believe television and computers are going to merge. You go to your TV when you want to turn your brain off. You go to your computer when you want to turn your brain on."—Steve Jobs, Apple Computer

Catholicos Karekin said he regarded public fascination with modern technology and contemporary society's emphasis on speed and efficiency as a challenge to religious faith, with its emphasis on ritual and tradition. Technology, he said, "does not give full satisfaction to the inner person."

Life is complex. We are confronted with too many, often-conflicting choices. There's too much data. We would like to, but unfortunately cannot, control our environment.

Steve Jobs, the genius techy entrepreneur who created the super successful Apple computer and iPhone, and Malcolm Gladwell, who wrote the best selling book *Blink: The Power of Thinking Without Thinking*, both argue that we can make better decisions than those arrived at by long contemplation and extensive research. Gladwell introduced the slogan "Blink, don't think," which insists that our instant, sort of instinctive decisions are the best way to go. Steven Jobs agreed, saying, "Life is random."

A *New York Times* article explains that these men are not saying "Don't worry, just be happy." Rather, they are advising people to relax; life is random but you can enjoy the ride.

It is up to you to make the ride through life a relaxed and enjoyable one.

Day 95

The patient said to the psychiatrist, "Nobody takes me seriously." The psychiatrist said, "You're kidding!"

    A growing number of therapists have found success using positive psychology. This treatment focuses on the affirmative aspects of a patient's life with the goal of helping him feel more optimistic and fulfilled. The positive approach is being used with everyone from depressed patients and anorexics to disaster victims and veterans returning from war with post-traumatic stress disorder. Increasingly, people with no mental illness or disorder who function well but want to function better are giving the upbeat method a try.

    When Margaret felt worried or sad, she did what many people do. She took antidepressants or talked to a therapist about the issues bothering her: her divorce, her shyness, and how her mother was depressed when she was growing up. But, neither the drugs nor the sessions made her feel much better. Deciding to try a different approach, she met with a psychologist to talk about the good things in her life.

    She said, "I thought it would be better to focus on my strengths, rather than the same old stuff of how I or my family was inadequate." The therapy session focusing on the positive helped her control her emotions, and she has fewer bad moods. "If you focus on what makes you feel good or things you're good at, it's logical you'll feel better."

    "It's great if you can increase people's positive emotions, but this doesn't get rid of their negative ones," says Julie Norem, professor of psychology at Wellesley College. "The important thing is that people learn to manage them."

The field of positive psychology was created in 1998 when Martin Seligman, a psychology professor at the University of Pennsylvania, became president of the American Psychological Association. He made it his goal to persuade others in his profession to focus on the conditions that help people feel happy. He founded the Positive Psychology Center at the University of Pennsylvania and organized conferences in this nascent field. At Harvard, positive psychology has been the most popular elective course.

Positive psychology has taken off as an academic discipline. A few years ago, University of Pennsylvania created a master's program in applied positive psychology, and in the first year, received one hundred applications for thirty-five slots.

"The main thing is to teach people to put more positive experiences in their day, to appreciate and notice these experiences," says Carol Kauffman, a positive therapist and assistant clinical professor at Harvard Medical School. After patients identify themselves and their disorder, Dr. Kauffman has them name something positive about their lives. She explains, "It makes them feel empowered. Positive therapy is not about candy and chocolates and vacations. It's about working on your strengths, and there are no shortcuts."

"Our beliefs about what we are and what we can be precisely determine what we can be."

Day 96

I told my psychiatrist I keep thinking I'm ugly and he told me to lie on the couch...face down!

The *Comprehensive Textbook of Psychiatry*, the clinical "bible" of psychiatry and clinical psychology, has thousands of lines on anxiety and depression, hundreds of lines on terror, shame and guilt. But, it contains only five lines on hope, one line on joy, and not a single line on compassion, forgiveness, or love. The focus used to be only on the painful emotions and suggested that denial was the appropriate form of relief.

Positive psychology places it's focus on such topics as hope and optimism, personal growth, gratitude and wisdom, love of learning, friendship and harmonious marriage, the mind-body relationship, courage, resilience, and happiness. We are each a mixture of strengths and weaknesses. No one has it all and no one lacks it all.

It is now believed that the best opportunity for achieving happiness comes from deciding that you want to be happy and that you yourself, through directing your thoughts and determining actions, can make yourself happy.

"Happiness is an ongoing process of fresh challenges, and...it takes the right attitudes and activities to continue to be happy" (Ed Diener). We each have the right to choose our own attitude in any given situation—why not choose happiness?

Day 97

"I know that there are people who hate their fellow man, and I hate people like that!"—Tom Lehrer

Heidi Hall turned to a positive psychologist to learn to be a better manager at work and to be happier. One exercise had her writing a letter expressing forgiveness to someone who had wronged her. She chose her landlord, who had charged her five hundred dollars for damage she says wasn't her fault. "I had a lot of anger and a sense of injustice," says Ms. Hall, thirty-six years old. The letter helped her realize that you are only hurting yourself when you hold onto anger.

"Forgiving isn't something you do for someone else. It's something you do for yourself. It's saying you're not important enough to have a stranglehold on me; it's saying you don't get to trap me in the past. I am worthy of a future" (Jodi Picoult).

Being angry is like holding on to a hot coal with the intention of throwing it at someone else but meanwhile you are the one getting burned. Aristotle said, "Anybody can become angry—that is easy, but to be angry with the right person and to the right degree and at the right time and for the right purpose, and in the right way—that is not easy." Think, who is your anger hurting? Don't allow the person who caused your anger to also control your ability to be happy. It is impossible to be angry and happy at the same time.

Choose to let go of your anger for your own well-being.

Day 98

A man goes into a diner. He says to the waitress, "I'd like a cup of coffee but *no cream* please." The waitress comes back and says to him, "I'm sorry but we're out of cream but I can give it to you with *no milk*."

Focusing on the positive has proven to be an amazing technique for finding happiness.

Positive coach/psychologist Paul Lloyd coaches on such topics as how to frame bad events in a positive context. He identified an experience he savors—his Saturday morning ritual of making coffee and biscuits—and wrote a short essay about its positives.

Even the American Red Cross is utilizing some positive psychology techniques. It encourages psychologists and other mental-health experts who volunteer to work with victims of a disaster to help people focus on how they survived, as opposed to reliving the trauma that occurred. "You are reinforcing the coping skills rather than the horror of the experience," says Susan Allstetter Neufeldt, a retired psychologist who volunteered with the Red Cross in Dallas and New Orleans after Hurricane Katrina.

Whenever your mind is thinking of negative issues, whether it be an experience, a fear or a worry, quickly switch and think of enjoying your steaming cup of coffee or of spending a day with your beautiful children. Put your mind on any enjoyable experience you have had or you plan to have. Thinking of good things will make you feel good.

"If we try to see something positive in everything we do, life won't necessarily become easier but it becomes more valuable" (Anonymous).

Day 99

When I die, I want to die like my grandfather who died peacefully in his sleep. Not screaming like all the passengers in his car.

If ever a time comes when you feel so overwhelmed, intimidated, and even panicked by a situation or set of unfolding circumstances that almost, literally, paralyzes you with anxiety and fear, just step back for a moment and tell yourself, "I'll deal with it." Just that reassurance to yourself that you'll deal with it, will help to relax you and rescue you from the emotional frenzy and generally exaggerated apprehension of what, at such times of terror-driven alarm, you envision as imminently occurring.

Whatever you do, don't punish yourself and become your own worst enemy by constantly focusing upon and envisioning the most harrowing, terrible outcomes and thereby unduly torturing yourself.

In most cases, in fact almost always, your worst fears are just that—tremendously and inordinately exaggerated. Almost nothing is so daunting that with the passage of time and with reasonable effort cannot be solved, resolved and effectively dealt with.

Once you tell yourself, "I'll deal with it," it stops being so instantaneously urgent, momentous, stressful or all-encompassing. It will stimulate in you a more rational, far more peaceful sense that in due time you will both address this fear-inspiring, threatening situation and effectively counteract and solve this troubling vexation.

At times when I myself faced this kind of terribly frightening predicament and told myself, "I'll deal with it," that declaration itself helped me immediately return to a more normally composed and cool-headed emotional state. I was able to put the fear aside and start to enjoy a more salutary, constructive ongoing existence. Ultimately things do work out. If you just relax, you can calmly and levelheadedly deal with the challenges that confront you no matter how intimidating and frightening they may seem at first blush.

After all, like it or not, for better or worse, problems and working on their solutions are very basic to the game of life. Effectively solving the challenges you face is one of the truly gratifying rewards that you will experience, which serves to enhance your state of overall happiness.

"The greater the obstacle, the more glory in overcoming it" (Moliere).

Day 100

"When you reach the end of your rope, tie a knot and hang on."—Thomas Jefferson

"Life always offers you a second chance. It's called tomorrow."

Are you feeling down, depressed? Don't deal in the now. Ask yourself what would your life look like if you were happy?

What's your problem? Are you lonely? Are you single? Think, would you be happy if you were married, if you had a family? Yes, you believe you would. Okay, think, what do I have to do to create that reality? I have to find a good wife/husband. Will I then be happy? No, because I don't have a job and can't support a family. Okay, now think further. What kind of job could you find that could support a family and make you happy? Consider what are you good at: a musician, a coach, a therapist or maybe a businessman? Fine, what are you qualified to be?

All right, think, I want to be a therapist, a teacher, a businessman, but it's complicated. I have to return to school but I don't have the patience to apply or the will to study for years. All right, don't give up. Think what are my alternatives. Can I do an online course or are there private seminars? Who can I ask?

Keep focusing on your goal. You want to be happy. To do that, you've determined that you need a spouse and children. To have a family, you realize you have to find a job and for a job, you realize you need to get an education. So, get moving, figure out how to get that education.

Find a way to bypass each obstacle. You can stay stuck in the mud or you can work to dig yourself out and to get your feet firmly on dry ground and even, eventually build your sand castle.

Choose a goal and determine the steps you must start taking to achieve that goal and forge forward. Remember, a river cuts through rock not because of its power but its persistence.

Day 101

"I think I've discovered the secret of life. You just hang around until you get used to it."—Sally Brown

Your life hasn't gone the way you planned—it isn't over yet. Today is the first day of the rest of your life. Change it. You may not be able to make it perfect, but you may be able to make it better.

You write a book one word at a time. You compose a song one note at a time. You dance one step at a time. The same holds true for anything you take on. Progress starts with the first small step.

"Failure is not fatal and success is not final; it is the courage to continue that counts" (Winston Churchill). "Never let success get to your head and never let failure get to your heart" (Dark Angel). Keep on going. Keep on doing. Each step gets you one step closer to success. "The number one reason why people give up so fast is because they tend to look at how far they still have to go instead of how far they have gotten" (Anonymous). Pat yourself on the back for every bit of effort and encourage yourself to forge ahead. Failure is only postponed success as long as you continue to work towards your goal. You may not reach perfection but you will go far.

Day 102

When you don't know where you are going, you won't know when you get there.

Obstacles to reaching your goals will continually arise. Treat them like bowling pins. Set up each scenario and its obstacle then find a way to knock each down. Don't stay pinned down. Work your way through each challenge, so that you can reach a happy place. Determine what change will make you happy?

Am I in a bad relationship? What can I do to improve it? Should I get out of it or work at it? Am I stuck in a horrible job? Should I stick with it or quit? Am I overwhelmed by how many courses I am taking or am I just not allotting my time efficiently? Am I just drifting, with no goals? Am I finding myself always angry and frustrated? Let me explore my reasons for being down? Let me consider my options. Let me speak to a guidance counselor, friends, therapists, someone who can give me direction, someone who can be there as a support.

Know yourself, recognize your needs, determine your strengths and weaknesses then find a way to plot a new direction. Recognize that there are always obstacles to success but those obstacles are there to force you to adjust, to change and to grow, not to stop you. "It is not in the still calm of life, or the repose of a pacific station, that great characters are formed. The habits of a vigorous mind are formed in contending with difficulties" (Abigail Adams).

Day 103

"I've got my faults but living in the past is not one of them. There's no future in it."—Sparky Anderson

Albert Einstein said, "Learn from yesterday, live for today, hope for tomorrow."

Eight hundred years ago, in the *Guide to The Perplexed* (Volume 1, chapter 60), Moses Maimonides advised us to stay in the present. Concentrate on the prayer you are saying or on that which you are learning. Focus on what you are listening to and block out other thoughts. Direct your mind only to what you are doing. Today, psychologists recommend mindfulness training, which is learning to stay focused in the present. Scientific evidence proves that this reduces harmful emotions like anger and fear and also strengthens the body by lowering blood pressure and heart rate.

I read a proverb which goes, "Don't look where you fell but where you slipped," meaning find the cause for your fall. That may be important but I believe, "Don't look where you fell. Look where you landed" would be a more important message. Don't keep analyzing why this happened to you. Accept it. Figure out where you stand and how you can productively move forward from there. "Success is getting up one more time than you've been knocked down" (Anonymous).

Deal in the present. Regretting yesterday only holds you back. Fearing tomorrow doesn't let you move forward.

Day 104

**Why do people always send flowers when someone passes on?
What would you suggest dear...fruit?**

Nobel Prize-winning psychologist and behavioral economist Daniel Kahneman of Princeton had thousands of subjects keep diaries of their day including activities, feelings, companions and places and then identified some correlates of happiness. He found that people are in a terrible mood while commuting. TV watching was just all right. If people had a better night's sleep, they were in a better mood. People were actually not in a great mood when spending time with their children. Having intimate relations received the highest positive rating followed by socializing, which highlights how important the "need to belong" is for human satisfaction.

Nancy Etcoff, an evolutionary psychologist, then conducted a study and found that an intervention as simple as a gift of flowers that stayed in one's home for a few days could affect a variety of emotions, such as decreasing anxiety and depression and enhanced relaxation, energy and compassion at home.

Decide to be happy. Decide to make others happy. Get out there and connect to people. Send someone you love flowers. Hopefully, they will do the same for you.

Day 105

Life: a play with a lousy third act

David Menachem Gordon, a lone soldier from the US, twenty-one years old, in the Gavati Division of the Israeli Army, recently found dead, wrote this in his inspirational blog before his death:

"Today Is a New Day, but this is not my time to go, grace has brought us another day but if tomorrow were to bring my turn;

"What would I leave unsaid?

"What would I leave undone?

"What would I leave behind?

"String cheese,

"Today is a new day with new opportunities:

"To Think, To speak, To face my fears, To act, To create, To exercise, To laugh, To be free, To be me, To believe in myself, To love myself, To care for myself, To have faith, To give thanks, To connect with friends and family, To connect with a community, a unit, To develop a lifestyle, To achieve or at least pursue my goals, To try new things, To express myself, To be happy and experience pleasure, To grow and feel good in the process, To love—to hope, To hope to love, To see what I am capable of, To pursue knowledge, clarity and understanding, To better myself, To face reality, To break barriers, To love—to give, To give to love, To contribute in conversation, To pray, To meditate, To break bad habits, To make good habits, To use my imagination, To reach out, To get involved, To be a leader, To change the world, To realize who I am, To recognize who I am not, To identify with who I want to become, To find rhythm, To ask, To listen,

To learn To be aware, To pursue my dreams, goals and ambitions, To be responsible, To be positive, To give it one more shot, To make one more effort, To live life."

David added: "This is a timeless piece—for today and every day."

David's tragic passing brings his message home: appreciate all the opportunities for growth we are given each day and begin to accomplish each day.

Day 106

If G-d is watching us, the least we can do is be entertaining.

There are five levels of happiness according to Rabbi Noach Weinberger, founder of Aish Hatorah, the lowest being physical pleasure, which should be for survival not for selfishness. A higher level of happiness is love, which is the essence of giving. The next level of deriving pleasure is meaning, which is fighting for a cause you believe in. An even higher level of pleasure comes from power and creativity, which is being productive, causing positive change and growth for bettering oneself. The highest level of pleasure is a relationship with G-d, which is knowing that we are not living for ourselves, and we have the ability to connect with G-d.

Polls have demonstrated that people who connect with G-d are happier than others.

"When I'm worried, it's usually because I'm trying to do everything by myself. When I'm at peace, it's usually because I remember G-d is in control" (Dave Willis). Be aware that "man's way leads to a hopeless end, while G-d's way leads to an endless hope" (Anonymous).

Day 107

Most men want to serve G-d, but only in an advisory position.

One night I dreamed I was walking along the beach with the Lord. Many scenes from my life flashed across the sky. In each scene, I noticed footprints in the sand. Sometimes, there were two sets of footprints; other times there was one set of footprints.

This bothered me because I noticed that during the low periods of my life, when I was suffering from anguish, sorrow or defeat, I could see only one set of footprints.

So I said to the Lord, "You promised me, Lord, that if I followed You, You would walk with me always. But, I have noticed that during the most trying periods of my life there has only been one set of footprints in the sand. Why when I needed you most, have you not been there for me?"

The Lord replied, "The times when you have seen only one set of footprints is when I carried you." (Mary Stevenson)

By staying aware that G-d is not only with us in times of pain, but that G-d carries us through these difficult times, it is easier to handle and enjoy the challenges of life.

When people are told to relax and meditate, they often think of things that occurred in their past because they know how it turned out. A lack of relaxation may be due to uncertainty. If we put our faith in G-d and believe whatever happens is in His hands and is for our best, we can alleviate much of our anxiety.

When you can't sleep at night, throw your problems up to G-d. He is up all night anyway.

Day 108

I have faith. I just need proof.

"When the solution is simple, G-d is answering" (Albert Einstien).

I asked for strength, and G-d gave me difficulties to make me strong.
I asked for wisdom, and G-d gave me problems to solve.
I asked for prosperity, and G-d gave me brawn and brain to work.
I asked for courage, and G-d gave me dangers to overcome.
I asked for love, and G-d gave me troubled people to help.
I asked for favors, and G-d gave me opportunities.
I received nothing I wanted. I received everything I needed.
My prayers were answered (Anonymous)

It is unreasonable and unrealistic to pray that we never have any troubles, because that's not human. Pray that all that happens to you, though you can't comprehend the logic, is for the best and that G-d grant you the energy, wisdom, and courage to deal effectively with whatever torment you encounter.

"As I look back on my life, I realize that every time I thought I was being rejected from something good, I was actually being redirected to something better" (Steve Maraboli).

Day 109

I intend to live forever—so far, so good.

I have lost close relatives and dear friends whose absences have left a big void in my life. I have had major disappointments in business.

One former co-worker, whom I had brought into my business, cheated me in a hurtful way. I had trusted and mentored him since he was a child, yet I was forced to write a check for millions of dollars to extricate myself from a mess of his doing. The deceit pained me to the core, and it was coupled with the fact that I was unable to take advantage of a pharmaceutical business deal. In addition, at the time, The *New York Post* was up for sale. Had I not lost so much money, I could have done that deal, which was something I really wanted to do. In fact, then Governor Hugh Carey had approached my friend, Jerry Finklestein, to request of me that I bail that newspaper out.

It was a crushing disappointment but I kept my perspective. I had not lost an arm or a leg, or an eye. Thank G-d no one in my family had passed away. Indeed, people who have lost arms or legs or eyes have gone on to set ambitious goals for themselves; many people who have lost fortunes continue to live good lives.

"Sometimes, G-d doesn't give you what you want, not because you don't deserve it, but because you deserve better." We must believe that G-d knows what is best for us, and although we can't fathom his plan for us, we must trust that He loves us and is doing what is best for us. As a child often doesn't understand why a father slaps him for running into traffic, so we don't understand G-d's slaps, but we are

HAPPINESS GUARANTEED OR YOUR MISERY BACK

far better off and it's certainly more agreeable to accept that they are for our good.

Accept G-d's plan but know G-d wants you to be happy. Don't let the downs get you down. Pick yourself up and you will feel "up."

Day 110

Seven days without prayer makes one weak.

"In a mighty gesture, G-d reminds us of his provisional power in a wondrous way. In the midst of a rainstorm—yet another form of sustenance—a lightning bolt illuminates the sky." This was in a blog by David Menachem Gordon, a lone American soldier in the elitist division of the Israeli army, who was found dead not far from his army base.

Build your inner strength by emphasizing the concept of faith and hope. Through the storms and troubles of life try to see the positive.

Realize that when G-d closes a door, somewhere he opens a window. It is up to you to open your eyes and find the window to happiness.

"There are souls in this world which have the gift of finding joy everywhere and of leaving it behind when they leave" (Fredrick Faber). Such seems to be how David Menachem Gordon was. Learn a lesson from the way he lived.

Look for the good in every situation, and if it isn't evident, believe it to be present anyway. G-d's plan is hidden from us. Consider a man who grew up in the forest and was never exposed to civilization. He leaves the forest and comes to a farm. He sees a farmer throwing seeds all over the ground. "Why are you throwing stuff all over?" he asks. "Just wait, you'll see," says the farmer. Then, the farmer tills the earth and the man questions, "Why are you ripping up the ground?" And the farmer says, "Just wait, you'll see." Then the wheat grows and the farmer pulls it all out of the ground and the man says, "Why are you pulling up all the things you planted?" Once again, the farmer replies, "You'll see." Finally, the farmer takes his harvest and makes dough and puts it in the oven. The man thinks this makes no sense. Of course, when the delicious bread is baked and tasted, the man will understand this process that looked so negative to him. So, too, in the next world when we understand the results of all our trials and tribulations, we will comprehend G-d's plan and realize how perfect it was for our benefit. We will then see, what we should know now, all negative-seeming experiences have a positive purpose.

Day 111

The other day someone asked me if I play Trivial Pursuit. I said, "Every day of my life."

You can react to tragedy in a constructive manner because this is a form of self-hypnosis that we all know, at some level, "how to do." For example, have you ever told yourself you had to wake up at a given time and then woke up at exactly that time without an alarm going off—just some inner magical alarm that we have somehow trained our unconscious mind to respond to? Or haven't you just as remarkably, unexplainably, set the alarm for say 7:00 a.m. and then awakened just a moment, or even just a few seconds, before the alarm went off? That's self-hypnosis. So, realize you are capable of self-hypnosis.

Self-hypnotize yourself to think only positively, never negatively, and you'll be amazed and thrilled at both your ability to do this and at the phenomenally unbelievable, desirable results.

Take time to make your soul happy. Just as meditation and yoga lift up your spinal column and helps you become more erect, let self-hypnosis and the positive attitude help uplift and inspire you to stand up to the world and its challenges.

Day 112

Stress is when you wake up screaming and you realize you haven't fallen asleep yet.

"Anywhere is paradise. It's up to you." Many counselors have described visualization as the ultimate consciousness tool. Since the dawn of human awareness, our innate powers of "picture making" have been the central inspiration for the arts, spiritual awakenings and holistic healing rituals that have been practiced by Shamanic cultures world wide as well as many healing modalities today.

An explosion of research and interest in alternative medicine approaches to health/wellness invites us to develop a greater awareness of, and appreciation for, the workings of the brains' right hemisphere and imagery processes, because "what we envision we become!"

A behavioral therapist at Canyon Ranch explains the concept of using imagery for relaxation and stress reduction. Since the mind and body are inextricably bound, the ability to relax and quiet our mind is as important as relaxing our musculature. Imagery training improves with practice.

Here is an outline to help develop the relaxation skill known as imaging or visualization:

The Basic Technique

1. Take a minute or two to get settled and relaxed. Loosen any tight clothing and sit or lie down comfortably.

2. Close your eyes and put your body at ease with several slow, deep breaths. Continue to relax with regular, rhythmic deep breathing. Provide yourself with suggestions of the sensation of warmth and heaviness in the body and limbs. This will intensify your feeling of relaxation.
3. Call up your relaxation image. Imagine a peaceful, serene natural scene.
4. With as much detail as possible, respond to your image with all of your senses by asking yourself some of the following, very slowly:
Sights—What can I see around me? (clouds, surf, sky, sun)
Smells—What smells do I notice? (ocean, grass, flowers)
Sounds—What do I hear? (birds, wind, water)
Tastes—What can I taste? (salt air, salt water, chocolate, food)
Touches—What textures do I notice around me? (soft, rough, slippery)

Some relaxation imagery suggestions include a deserted island; a cool mountaintop; a sandy, warm beach; an autumn day in the park; sailing on a calm lake; or a cozy study with a warming fire. Be creative but personal in choosing a peaceful scene to frequently envision and practice relaxing in this way. Find a time and place of solitude.

"Look into the distance, into the future and visualize the tomorrow you are going to build—and begin to build that tomorrow today" (Jonathan Lockwood Huie).

Day 113

Either Heaven or Hell will have continuous orchestra music. Which one you think it will be tells a lot about you.

Benjamin Zander, conductor of the Boston Philharmonic Orchestra and an inspirational speaker and author, likes to tell stories about musicians who are blocked. He described a young woman in the Israel Philharmonic, once an energetic player, who was now "completely demolished." She had just gone through a divorce because her husband hated music and she was so scared of the war that she carried her gas mask everywhere. She had put duct tape on the windows and eventually moved into the home of her overprotective, demanding, having been driven to distraction by air-raid sirens.

Mr. Zander phoned his wife and asked if there was anything he could do for this unfortunate young woman while visiting Israel. His wife said, "No," adding, "you'll never have the strength or the power to fight against the parents, the war and the divorce." Instead, his wife suggested her husband should say that he was Merlin, the magic person who lived his life backward, so he knows what's going to happen.

Mr. Zander told the young woman, "I am Merlin the famous magician. Because I live my life backward, I know the future. During the five days that I'm here, I am certain that nothing can happen to you, so go back to your house and open the windows. Take out your violin. I know that you will remarry and your future husband loves the violin."

Though suspicious at first, she listened to him and moved back to her house. She played with all her heart at the rehearsal the next day, remarking at the end, "Ben, you know in that second movement I think the tempo's too slow." When he heard that remark Mr. Zander thought, "She's back!"

At the end of the concert, Zander told her, "Merlin's leaving—you know that." And she said, "I know." Then he said, "But, you know his power goes on," and she answered, "I know."

Sometime later, the Israel Philharmonic came to Boston, and Mr. Zander went to see them. At the interval she came running toward Mr. Zander with her arms outstretched, "Merlin!"

It's all in the mind! Positive belief and positive expectation leads to positive results.

Day 114

Can you do me a favor? Take a picture of yourself and send it to me. I am playing cards and seem to be missing a joker.

A man had done a tremendous favor for a friend. Years later, he needed help with a small loan. He called his friend a number of times leaving messages to which he never received a response. He became furious feeling that he had done so much for this friend and now when he himself needed a small favor, his friend just ignored him. One day he bumped into his friend and began uncontrollably shouting at him. His friend softly apologized, stating that his daughter had been deathly ill overseas and he had not been in the country for the past six months and had not gotten any messages. Of course, he would be only too happy to extend the loan.

Think positively before jumping to conclusions. When you view others favorably, you will like people more, making life more pleasant.

There is a beautiful true story of an elderly man, Yisroel Nosson Bruckstein, who was walking with his grandson in the park. Suddenly, they passed another elderly man and the two men shook their heads in acknowledgement at one another and each continued on his way. The grandson asked his grandfather who that man was. Mr. Bruckstein said, "He and I were best friends back in Germany." "How come if you were best friends you just sort of smiled at one another but didn't stop to hug and talk?" asked his grandson. "Mr. Bruckstein said, "I will tell you. When we were in Germany at the beginning of the rise of the Nazi regime, it was nearly impossible to get visas to leave the country. I managed to get visas for my family and hid them to use when the time came that we could get away.

"I told no one about these visas or where they were hidden except for my best friend, the man we just passed. The night I went to get my visas, I found they were no longer where I had hid them and soon discovered that my best friend and his family had fled Germany. I immediately knew what had happened.

"Except for me, my entire family was wiped out in the concentration camps." The grandson was aghast, "Why do you even acknowledge him and smile at him anymore after he did such a horribly atrocious thing to you?" "Because," said Mr. Bruckstein, "I understand that he did it not to hurt me but in desperation to save his own family. Who am I to judge how any one acts in a dire situation like that? So, I don't speak to him but I acknowledge him to show him I don't judge what he did."

Always put yourself in the other person's place. Think the best of each other, especially of those you love. Assume the good. Doubt the bad. If you look at people with a positive eye, your entire inner being will feel that positive sort of uplifting karma.

Day 115

"One of the strangest things about life is that the poor, who need the money the most, are the ones who never have it."—Finley Peter Dunne

"We can only be said to be alive in those moments when our hearts are conscious of our treasures" (Thornton Wilder).

To be happy, you must appreciate what you have, be satisfied and avoid being jealous. Learn to look at what you have, not at what you are missing. Don't envy what others have rather appreciate what you have.

We have to notice all that we are grateful for. We have to shift our focus to appreciation of the positives rather than being frustrated by the negatives. We have to realize what is good in our lives and our relationships. We have to notice our talents, our appearance, our bodily functions, our education, our work and our ability to think and feel and we must appreciate and use these wisely. "We should certainly count our blessings, but we should also make our blessings count" (Neal A. Maxwell).

There will always be more things to wish for. There will always exist people who seem, at least on the outside, to have a better life, more possessions, a more prestigious job or a more fulfilling relationship. But, it is all in your attitude. Surprisingly, people with less are often happier than those who have more.

If you value all you have, you will find you have the happiness you seek.

Day 116

The first commandment was when Eve told Adam to eat the apple.

A lovely little girl was holding two apples with both hands. Her mom came in and softly asked her little daughter with a smile: "My sweetie, could you give your mom one of your two apples?"

The girl looked up at her mom for some seconds, then she suddenly took a quick bite of one apple, and then quickly of the other. The mom felt the smile on her face freeze. She tried hard not to reveal her disappointment.

Then the little girl handed one of her bitten apples to her mom and said: "Mommy, here you are. This is the sweeter one."

No matter who you are, how experienced you are, and how knowledgeable you think you are, always delay judgment. Give others the privilege to explain themselves. What you see may not be the reality.

Day 117

I used to be indecisive but now I am not quite sure.

It is very difficult to be happy when you are stuck trying to make a decision. Fear of making the wrong decision is a reason many people hesitate. They are immobilized by a fear of making a mistake, or failing, or even succeeding, or what other people may think, or afraid to look dumb, or not making the perfect decision. Often indecision is due to a lack of confidence. "No decision" is itself a decision, but it's one that causes much anxiety and leads to missing out on opportunities.

Learning to make a decision is a valuable tool. First, determine what you are afraid of and the worst possible outcome of your decision and how you would deal with it if that happened. Then, set the fear aside and make the decision that sounds best to you. Avoid paralysis by analysis. Set a time limit then decide which you feel will do the most good for you and follow your gut.

Malcolm Gladwell, author of *Blink*, explains that mistrusting emotion-driven decisions may be dangerous. What you refer to as "your gut" is actually a wealth of knowledge marbled with empirically validated facts that you weren't in touch with at critical crossroads. Set up your gut as a straw man, primed for criticism, and blame a poor choice on it, so that you protect your analytic self (your cortex) from blame.

Realize that people generally know what the right choice is, but they allow themselves to consider a lower path and then get caught in the conflict. Learn to trust yourself and not second-guess yourself.

Ask yourself, will this matter in ten years? Most decisions are reversible or adjustable, so don't take the decision so seriously. "If you don't make the right decision, make the decision right."

Be aware that some things are beyond your control, so the right decision may go wrong despite perfect analysis. Act, examine your results, make adjustments and move on. If you have given it sufficient thought and find you can't make a decision, flip a coin. Indecision is all about avoiding either the choice between two negative options or the choice between two fairly equal courses of action, so tossing a coin could makes sense.

People often say, "If I decide to be indecisive that's my decision." It is your decision. It's the decision to feel trapped and depressed.

Practice on the small decisions first so you force yourself to learn to make decisions. Determine not to get caught up in indecision and you will find you are much happier.

"The way to develop decisiveness is to start right where you are with the very next question you have to face" (Napoleon Hill).

Day 118

I took an IQ test and the results were negative.

Always reassure yourself that you are:

Okay
Worthy
Lovable
Attractive
Important
Intelligent
Good Enough

You are a good person, and you deserve to be happy, healthy, and successful!

It is vital to develop a good sense of self. Do not let the opinions of others make you feel insecure or lacking. Be the most you can be and appreciate yourself to the fullest.

A negative self-perception causes depression, indecision, procrastinating, isolating, overcompensating, rationalizing and projecting blame on others. By blaming others, you relieve yourself of the burden of doing something productive about your situation.

The strongest factor for success is self-esteem: believing you can do it, believing you deserve it, feeling you are as good as anyone else, worthy of respect from others as well as from yourself. The more you work at just being yourself the more likely you'll feel purposeful and significant in your life.

Albert Einstein said, "Everybody is a genius but if you judge a fish by its ability to climb a tree, it will live its entire life believing that it is stupid." Find your niche. Explore and pursue your personal abilities and talents. A strong positive self-image is the best possible preparation for success in life and, of course, nothing builds self-esteem and self-confidence like accomplishment.

Day 119

"I have not failed…I've just found 100,000 ways that won't work."—Thomas Edison

A prime reason for unhappiness is anxiety due to fear of failure. No one is immune to failure. The most successful people have failed in one area or another, or at one time or another. Developing a healthier approach to failure will help combat the anxiety.

Stanford University psychologist Carol Dweck suggests that our experiences of failure are influenced overwhelmingly by the beliefs we hold about the nature of talent and ability, and that we can train ourselves to improve that outlook. The "fixed theory" assumes that ability is innate and, therefore, people who hold this theory approach challenges as occasions on which they are called upon to prove this ability. They are, therefore, horrified of failure, which would show they tried to prove themselves but didn't measure up. In truth, this failure shows they may have the innate talent but didn't put in the effort to realize their potential. Unfortunately, when one thinks according to the fixed theory, failure causes them to give up, thinking they just didn't have the talent to succeed.

Those who believe in the "incremental theory" believe that ability emerges through tackling challenges and hard work. Failure for these people is evidence that they are stretching themselves to their current limits. It's analogous to weight training. Muscles grow by being pushed to their limit of current capacity.

If you are afraid of failure, set your mind to take on the incremental mindset. If you fail, realize it is because you are pushing at the limits of your present ability.

Take on an incremental outlook and in case of failure, feel I may not be where I want yet or achieved what I hope to yet, but I am now closer to getting there. This will replace the fear of failure with the hope for success.

"One of the marks of excellent people is that they never compare themselves with others. They only compare themselves with themselves and with their past accomplishments and future potential" (Brian Tracy).

Day 120

The pessimist may be right in the long run, but the optimist has a better time during the trip.

The esteemed, scholarly Dalai Lama said, "The very purpose of life is to be happy." He propounds a terrific set of "instructions for life" that he asserts will nurture a "good karma."

The following are a few of his ideas:

- Spend some time alone every day.
- Remember that not getting what you want is sometimes a wonderful stroke of luck.
- Don't let a little dispute injure a great relationship.
- Share your knowledge. It is a way to achieve immortality.
- Once a year, go someplace you've never been before.
- Take into account that great love and great achievements involve great risk.
- Follow the four Rs: Respect for self, Respect for others, Responsibility for all your actions, and Remember that silence is sometimes the best answer.
- Live a good, honorable life. Then, when you get older and think back, you'll be able to enjoy it a second time.
- Approach both love and cooking with reckless abandon.
- A loving atmosphere in your home is the treasured foundation for your life.

- Judge your success by what you had to give up in order to get it.
- Remember that the best relationship is one in which your love for each other exceeds your need for each other.

"One word frees us of all the weight and pain in life. That word is love." (Socrates)

Day 121

News: A tragic accident occurred in a sawmill today when a man lost his entire left side. He was immediately rushed to the hospital, and doctors report that he's all right now.

So you think you have something to be depressed about today? Read the following:

1. Fire authorities in California were assessing the damage done by a forest fire when they found a corpse in a burnt-out section of the forest. The deceased male was dressed in a full wet suit, complete with a dive tank, flippers and facemask. A postmortem examination revealed that the person died, not from burns, but from massive internal injuries. Dental records provided a positive identification. Investigators then set about determining how a fully clad diver ended up in the middle of a forest fire.

    It was revealed that on the day of the fire, the man went for a diving trip off the coast some twenty miles away from the forest. The firefighters, seeking to control the fire as quickly as possible, called in a fleet of helicopters with very large buckets. The buckets were dropped into the ocean for rapid filling, then flown to the forest fire and emptied.

    You guessed it. One minute our diver was making like Flipper in the Pacific, the next he was doing a breaststroke in a fire bucket three hundred feet in the air. Apparently, he extinguished exactly 5'10" of the fire.

Some days, it just doesn't pay to get out of bed. Put things in perspective. Do you still think you're having a bad day? Think again.

2. A man was working on his motorcycle on his patio, while his wife was in the kitchen of the house. Somehow, the motorcycle slipped into gear as the man was racing its engine. Still holding the handlebars, the man was dragged through a glass patio door and dumped onto the floor inside the house.

Hearing the crash, his wife ran into the dining room and found her husband lying on the floor, cut and bleeding, the motorcycle next to him and the patio door shattered. The wife ran to the phone and summoned an ambulance. Because they lived on a fairly large hill, the wife went down the several flights of long steps to the street to direct the paramedics to her husband.

After the ambulance took her husband to the hospital, the wife righted the motorcycle and pushed it outside. Because gas had spilled on the floor, she blotted up the gasoline with paper toweling, throwing the towels in the toilet.

The husband was treated at the hospital and released. Back home, he went into the bathroom, and while sitting on the toilet, smoked a cigarette that he then flipped it into the toilet bowl.

His wife, now in the kitchen, heard a loud explosion and her husband screaming. She ran into the bathroom and found her husband lying on the floor. His pants had been blown away, and he was suffering burns on his buttocks, the back of his legs and his groin.

Again, his wife ran to the phone and called for an ambulance. The same ambulance crew was dispatched, and his wife met them at the street again. The paramedics put the husband on the stretcher and carried him to the street. While they were going down the stairs to the street, one of the paramedics asked the wife how her husband had burned himself. She told them, and the paramedics started laughing so hard, one of them tipped the stretcher and dumped her husband out. He fell down the remaining steps and broke his arm.

When all is going well, take notice and appreciate it.

Day 122

If quitters never win and winners never quit, what idiot came up with "Quit while you're ahead?"

President Clinton's mother urged him "Never quit." No matter what one may think of Mr. Clinton, this sage message did serve to get him to the pinnacle, the most powerful, most sought-after position in the entire universe. And no matter what happened, he always bounced back.

Human beings are complex, flawed, difficult, and needy. Life is often demanding and daunting, At times we do unfortunate things that we regret. At times, we are met by unfortunate circumstances and setbacks or with individuals who stop or discourage us, but we must never quit.

President Bill Clinton told his daughter Chelsea's high school graduating class to "Dream big dreams and chase your dreams." He said, "My high school classmates who chased their dreams and failed are far less disappointed than those who left their dreams on the shelf for fear of failure."

Robert F. Kennedy said, "Some men see things as they are and say, 'Why?' I dream things that never were and say 'Why not?'" To paraphrase him: Don't just reconcile to what is, dream of what might be and then work tirelessly to bring that dream to a successful fruition. "Not all dreamers achieve, but all achievers dream." And action energizes the dream.

Believe in yourself. Don't give up on yourself, and by so doing, you can be, or make to be, almost anything you aspire to. Equally important and satisfying is that the ongoing process of working towards the fulfillment of some exciting, rewarding dream can be very gratifying along the way.

Decide your goal and pursue it. "Optimism is the one quality more associated with success and happiness than any other" (Brian Tracey), so never give up. It's difficult to wait, but it's worse to regret.

Day 123

The optimist fell out a window on the top floor of a skyscraper. As he passed the tenth floor, he was heard to say, "Well, so far, so good."

There is perhaps nothing, or anyone, more inspiring than Franklin Delano Roosevelt's defiance and refusal to surrender to the devastation of crippling polio. From his wheelchair, he was twice elected Governor of New York State, elected President of the United States four times during which tenure he gave hope to a Depression-stricken nation, and waged a winning global war. Roosevelt demonstrated and epitomized the ability to overcome and the absolute unimaginable power of positive thinking. He gave hope and courage to every American. It should show you and me the way. Franklin D. Roosevelt urged us to never get downhearted, for "the only thing we have to fear is fear itself"!

Cus D'Amato, probably the best boxing trainer of all time and the beloved mentor of the world heavyweight champion Mike Tyson, taught his fighters that "the will to win is more crucial than the skills to win," confirming the importance of mental attitude and positive thinking in determining the ultimate outcome in life's every endeavor.

The only self-limiting disability in life is a bad attitude. Use your power of positive thinking to overcome every shortcoming and every disability.

Day 124

"I was never an athletic kid. One year, I played Little League baseball, and my dad was the coach. Halfway through the season, he traded me to another family."
—David Corrado

The Minnesota Twins young superstar Justin Morneau, who in May 2005 had an unbelievably fantastic batting average of .400, was hit in the head by a fastball in the third game of the season. Previous head injuries had also landed him in the hospital.

As a thirteen-year-old hockey goalie, he was hit with a skate. Later, in a high school basketball game, he wound up having a head examination after he took a hard knee. And when he was playing baseball in 2000, his legs got tangled and he injured his head when he slammed into the ground.

After the aforementioned 2005 incident, Morneau was dizzy with headaches for a week, but eventually they went away. Morneau, who is 6'4" with big arms and curly blond hair, made his return in Detroit against Tiger's lefty Mike Maroth. He popped up in his first at-bat and hit a double in his second. In the ninth, he hit a game-tying home run against Troy Percival.

Morneau's dad says when Justin played hockey, "He got smoked with pucks, but he just got up and kept going. I didn't worry about him. I always told him to grin and bear it and don't be a wimp. Mope and it hurts more."

The temptation to give up is a common one and no one is exempt. Don't dwell on the misery, which with the right positive attitude, you will eventually overcome. "Never confuse a single defeat with a final defeat" (F.C Scott). As Newt Gingrich, former Speaker of the House, said, "Perseverance is the hard work you do after you get tired of doing the hard work you already did."

Day 125

I believe we should all pay our taxes with a smile, I tried—but they wanted cash.

"People wait all week for Friday, all year for summer, all life for happiness."

These are the 7 Rules of Life from *Whisper of the Heart*:

1. Make peace with your past so it won't disturb your present.
2. What others think of you is none of your business.
3. Time heals almost everything. Give it time.
4. Don't compare your life to others and don't judge them. You have no idea what they're journey is all about.
5. Stop thinking too much. It's all right not to know the answers. They will come to you when you least expect it.
6. No one is in charge of your happiness, except you.
7. Smile. You don't own all the problems in the world.

Day 126

Money can't buy happiness but it sure makes misery easier to live with.

"The conviction of the rich that the poor are happier is no more foolish than the conviction of the poor that the rich are" (Mark Twain).

Do you think you would be happier if you were financially better off? Economists have found that money makes truly poor people happier in that it relieves pressure from everyday life, such as getting food, a place to live and medical needs. But, it's been found that once people reach a little beyond the average middle-class income level, even large financial gains don't yield much, if any, increase in happiness. While it has been found that there is a correlation between happiness and income when basic needs are not yet met, people tend to overestimate the influence of wealth on happiness by 100 percent. Money does not cause happiness to the extent that people think.

A study showed that people who purchased tickets for a restaurant or theatre increased their well-being to a greater extent than someone with material possessions. The night out satisfied a higher order need, specifically for social connection and vitality, which gives one a sense of well-being.

Go out to a restaurant, a museum or theatre or anywhere you enjoy going. "Happiness resides not in possessions and not in gold, happiness dwells in the soul" (Democratis).

Day 127

All I've ever wanted was an honest week's pay for an honest day's work.

According to new research, relationships with co-workers are 23 percent more correlated to happiness at work than the same relationship with managers. The study stresses the importance of peer-to-peer support at work. Social support was found to be a key factor in creating well-being and reducing stress at work. Forging relationships is a proven way to increase happiness since people have a need for connection. Companies and their leaders, the study concludes, "must prioritize recruiting talent that is collaborative and team oriented."

Another important need, which when met, helps people feel happier, is connecting to their job. Research highlighted that many workers feel they are drifting aimlessly in their jobs. Only 42 percent of workers were able to pinpoint their company's vision mission and values. Senior managers were criticized for failing to communicate their goals to other members of their staff.

Try to find a job you enjoy which has co-workers you can relate to and leaders who are clear both on their goal and your responsibilities. Work is something most people do five days a week. If you can't find a job you like, tell yourself "It is only a job I am doing to earn a living." But, if you can find a job that makes you feel like you want to get up and go to work, it really has the power to increase your happiness.

Day 128

On a beautiful day like this, it's hard to believe anyone can be unhappy—but we'll work on it.

Wouldn't it sound foolish to ask who is happier, someone who won the New York lottery or someone who became a paraplegic? Believe it or not, data proves that a year after both these events, both these people are equally happy. This holds true for someone who won or lost an election, passed or failed an exam or got or lost a romantic partner.

Data further proves that in the case of a tragedy, with only a few exceptions, three months later, the tragedy has no effect on a person's happiness level.

Sir Thomas Browne said, "I am the happiest man alive. I have that in me that can convert poverty to riches, adversity to prosperity and I am more invulnerable than Achilles: fortune hath not one place to hit me."

Man has been blessed with a psychological immune system. This is an unconscious cognitive system which helps change a person's view of the world in which he is stuck.

Jim Wright, who due to a scandal was forced to resign in disgrace as chairman of the House of Representatives, later said, "I am so much better off physically, mentally, financially and in every other way."

A man who was falsely accused of a crime and spent thirty-seven years in prison, when he was released at age seventy-eight due to new

DNA tests, said, "It was a glorious experience. I do not have one moments regret."

Pete Best, the original drummer for the Beatles in 1994 said, "I am happier than I would've been with the Beatles."

These examples demonstrate that our minds are able to create synthetic happiness when we don't get what we want. We are able to rationalize our feelings. We control our minds.

Take control of your mind and train it to see the positive side. Don't spend so much time treading water and trying to keep your head above the waves that you forget how much you love to swim.

Day 129

"Trust your husband, adore your husband, and get as much as you can in your own name."—Joan Rivers

When our levels of trust, morality, and empathy increase, we feel happier. Findings show that as our levels of Oxytocin increase, so do our levels of trust, morality and empathy. A Clairmont Graduate University 2011 experiment showed that the simple act of eight hugs a day can increase internal oxytocin levels and result in a happier you.

Actions and the response to those actions, in this instance hugs and the feeling of connection and being cared about, cause reactions within our body, such as the production of oxytocin, which in turn, causes us to feel a certain way, in this case more trusting and more empathetic, characteristics which make us like ourselves and feel happier about ourselves.

Hug and be hugged at least eight times a day. Connect with other people. You will find yourself feeling much happier. "We are not here to see through each other. We are here to see each other through" (Anonymous).

Day 130

"Start every day off with a smile and get it over with."—
W.C. Fields

Experiments at Michigan State University (2011) found that people who smile as a result of cultivating positive thoughts can significantly and immediately improve their mood. By recalling pleasant memories and smiling because of it, people immediately became happier.

People who surrounded themselves by happy people were also shown to become happier in the future. This was shown in a study done in the University of California, San Diego 2008 study.

You have the ability to make yourself happy just by thinking happy thoughts, recalling happy memories and smiling, and by surrounding yourself with happy people. The effect is circular, your smile will make you a happy person who makes those around you happy and smiley and they in turn will keep you happy and smiling.

"Smile, it enhances your face value" (Dolly Parton).

Day 131

I'm writing a book on reverse psychology. Don't buy this book!

A psychology teacher handed out papers to her class, which to her students looked exactly the same, however, half the papers asked the student to recall the three worst things that happened to them that week, while the other half asked the student to recall the three best things that happened that week.

The teacher then asked each student to call out and rate his/her week on a 1-10 scale. Inevitably, the group that was asked to recall the worst things about their week scored their week around 4, 5 or 6. The group that was asked to recall the best points of their week scored the week at 8, 9 or 10.

By controlling our thoughts, by focusing on the positive, our entire perspective is altered and our mood is strongly influenced.

When you find yourself getting upset about little things in your life, things that just didn't go right, a game you lost, a conversation that went wrong, a job you messed up, consciously try to think of all the things that went right.

Make a list of everything that is going incredibly well in your life and you will find yourself in a better state of mind. Positive thinking is not about expecting the best to happen every time, but about accepting that whatever happens is for the best for this moment.

Day 132

Last night my girlfriend and I watched three DVDs back to back. Luckily, I was the one facing the TV.

Your outlook has the power to make or break you.

My friend, who lives in Cleveland, sent his 12-year-old son to a camp in the New York region, Catskill Mountains, whose bunks integrate regular and special-needs kids. There was a whole group of kids coming from Cleveland, so the parents arranged a minibus to transport the kids. Unfortunately, there was some sort of malfunction and the entire bus went up in flames. By the grace of G-d, nobody was hurt, though the kids lost all their stuff in the fire.

Upon hearing of this accident, my friend, who was on a business trip in Boston, rented a car and drove to the camp to check on his son and the other kids before returning to Cleveland.

While in the camp, he actually ran into my son who was on staff. He introduced himself and got a good laugh upon realizing that this staff member was my son. When my friend was checking on the other kids and in speaking to the camp director, he found out that one of the accident victims was still extremely shaken up. He was refusing to talk about it and was so traumatized that he was thinking of going home. The camp director was considering sending him home with my friend.

Later that day, the director informed my friend that everything had been resolved and the boy wanted to remain at camp. When my friend asked how the whole situation had been so positively resolved, the director responded, "We put one of our best guys on it, and he took care of it! Everything is fine now."

The director explained that my son had taken this young boy out to Walmart to get him away from camp a little. He was then able to get the boy to share what was troubling him. Apparently, this boy was the oldest on the bus, so he was tasked with saying the Traveller's Prayer. He, therefore, believed that the bus burning was his fault and that he had personally endangered the entire group! He must have thought he hadn't recited the prayer with the proper conviction and faith.

When he confessed this to my son, my son immediately explained to the boy that, in fact, the opposite was true: Not a single boy was hurt despite the entire bus burning down, and it was the boy's prayers that had protected all of them and allowed for such a miracle! This instantly changed the boy's entire perspective and uplifted his spirit. With the right view, my son was able to help this boy shed his guilt, boost his self-esteem and be happy.

To change ourselves effectively, we first have to change our perspective.

Day 133

**"I always take my wife morning tea in my pajamas, but is she grateful?
No, she says she'd rather have it in a cup."**—Eric Morecambe

Experiments have proven that one of the greatest contributing factors to overall happiness is how much gratitude we show. In a study at the University of Pennsylvania (2005), people who said "Thank you for…" as little as three times a day were found to be happier than the group that didn't.

An awareness and appreciation of what we do have takes the focus off the things we do not have and leaves us with a greater sense of well-being. Most people would be amazed if they started enumerating how very much they have to be thankful for from the ability to wake up, to dress themselves, to walk on their own, to see where they are going, to hear and to express themselves.

Try going through a day thinking how grateful you are for your life, for nature, for your job, your talents, your family, your friends, etc. You will find yourself whistling with appreciation and happy for your blessings. "Reflect upon your present blessings of which every man has plenty; not on your misfortunes of which all men have some" (Charles Dickens).

Day 134

If you ever find happiness by hunting for it, you will find it as the old woman did her lost spectacles, safe on her own nose all the time.

Learn to be your own best friend. A best friend doesn't allow you to focus on the disappointing, the depressing or the hurtful. S/he distracts you with enjoyable thoughts or experiences, seeks ways to lift you up, encourages you, inspires you and works on ways to make you feel happy.

That's the least you can do for yourself—be your own best friend. That is one of the most important secrets to success because nobody—not even the most devoted of friends—spends as much time with you, as you do with yourself. So, by all means think of what a best friend might do for you during whatever troubling experience you are living through and then do those things for yourself.

At first it may be difficult to do—to get out of the morass that can overwhelm you—but with concerted continuous effort and practice you will master that invaluable technique. Shopenhauer taught, "With will power you can do anything." If you want to make it happen, it will happen.

It can be one of the most fulfilling, self-gratifying actions you can ever take to lift your own spirits, to get your feet back on the ground, to be strong in the face of adversity.

Controlling your response to misfortune will give you a sense of self-worth and self-esteem.

Day 135

My horse was so slow he won the next race!

Ken McPeek's story is just the kind to provide hope and inspiration in the face of discouraging adversity. McPeek, a world-class horse trainer whose horse, Repent, was favored to win the Kentucky Derby in the winter of 2002, was sidelined by an ankle injury.

Then he became the trainer of Harlan's Holiday, which entered as the favorite to win the Kentucky Derby only to come in seventh in the Derby and fourth in the Preakness. Immediately, the disappointed owner of this favorite fired McPeek, who went from being the golden boy of the Kentucky Derby prep season to getting publicly embarrassed. But, if you can imagine, that was the least of his devastating experiences. Worst of all, his wife Sue learned that she had a rare form of cancer in 2000.

Amazingly, his wife recovered and his training career began to soar. His entry in the Belmont Stakes, Sevara, who based on his track record many wondered why McPeek even bothered to bring him to Belmont, miraculously went on to become the longest shot, at 70 to 1 odds, to win the Belmont Stakes.

As the sports writer for the *New York Times* described McPeek's saga, "When everything else failed, when the disappointed and disgruntled owner gave up on him, McPeek said there was nothing else to do but to take a step back and reload."

As he received his cherished trophy in the winner's circle, with all the sports world watching, McPeek said, "I had the belief that after terrible things happen to you, wonderful things are bound to follow."

HAPPINESS GUARANTEED OR YOUR MISERY BACK

He bounced back from seemingly hopeless adversity by holding out hope and pursuing the fulfillment of dreams that life can offer each of us. Adaptability and resilience are a necessary prerequisite to leading a life of fulfillment and happiness, even in the face of the inevitable, painful adversities that are part of every human being's existence on this earth.

Keep on fighting, keep reloading, keep pursuing, keep dreaming, keep believing that even the very worst shall pass and exciting, rewarding and truly wonderfully fulfilling experiences will be yours, when this present hurtful episode finally passes.

"The darkest night is often the bridge to the brightest tomorrow" (Jonathan Lockwood Huie).

Day 136

"My grandfather used to make home movies and edit out the joy."—Richard Lewis, comedian

"In the depth of winter I finally learned that there was in me an invincible summer" (Albert Camus).

It's imperative that we learn to close the chapter on any and all unfortunate events, adversities and tragedies. We must bring a sense of closure to these disasters or be weighed down by an overwhelming sense of misfortune. If we don't let go of our hurtful experiences, we remain oppressed and afflicted and cannot begin to thrive and launch ourselves into a renewed state of hopefulness and happiness. We dwell in the pain to our own detriment.

Every bad chapter has to be closed out. Conversely, every joyous chapter should be invited in, focused upon, highlighted, prized and relived over and over again.

In 2014, three precious boys were kidnapped and murdered in Israel, Eyal, Efrat and Naftali. Is there any more painful loss for a parent to endure than the futile loss of a young, innocent child? Rachel Frankel, Naftali's mother, heartbroken as she was, focused on the positive. She said that fortuitously, as a by product of the Israeli government's search for the boys, the secret underground tunnels from Gaza, which the Palestinians had planned to crawl through and cause massive, unimaginable damage on Israel were discovered. Rachel focused on how the unfortunate deaths of these three boys were responsible for saving the lives of countless Israelis. She put her focus on the national good that emerged from these tragic deaths and stressed the national benefit.

"Hardships often prepare ordinary people for an extraordinary destiny." All three sets of parents, some in a more private manner, some in a more outspoken manner, rather than expressing vengeful bitterness, stepped up as role models to inspire the world with their strength and unwavering faith.

Day 137

"We were dirt poor, living in a ramshackle tenement with no heat and no running water. There was never enough food on the table and our clothes were ragged hand me downs—and then came the Depression."—Red Buttons

Think about it for a moment. Would you trade places with any of the billions of people who are now dead, or who live with incurable, painful, devastating diseases and maladies such as tuberculosis, malaria, or AIDS, or with swollen stomachs, and who are completely devoid of any energy or hope, because of their calamitous impoverishment of food and medicine and their widespread homelessness and starvation?

Regardless of the disheartening experience you may be currently enduring, appreciate every relatively luxurious priceless minute of your existence. Each moment is a golden moment—a golden opportunity for you to work, to improve, to grow, to enjoy, and to make yourself more content and happier.

Use every moment to develop your attitude of recognizing and appreciating all you have been blessed with. If you have nothing to be grateful for, check your pulse! If you switch from expectation to appreciation, you change your world. "It is not happy people who are thankful. It is thankful people who are happy" (Anonymous).

"Legend has it that hummingbirds float free of time, carrying our hopes for love, joy and celebration. The hummingbird's delicate grace reminds us that life is rich, beauty is everywhere, every personal connection has meaning and that laughter is life's sweetest creation" (excerpted from Papyrus).

Day 138

"I don't want to make the wrong mistake."—Yogi Berra

In the game called life, you have to develop maturity and a sense of perspective in order to survive and thrive effectively.

In a crucial 1998 postseason playoff series game between the New York Yankees and the Cleveland Indians, Chuck Knoblauch, the Yankee star second baseman, made a major blunder by arguing with the umpire over a call while the winning run crossed the plate, allowing the Indians to win in extra innings.

Knoblauch, clearly hurt, embarrassed and devastated, said he hoped he would not be remembered for this egregious error before a national audience. Fortunately, he said, it would not be his last play and hopefully he would perform in such a manner as to minimize the impact to his reputation of that "bush league" mistake, leaving the world with the memory of his overall superior accomplishments.

He responded to the reporters by saying, "Life has its ups and downs and this was one of my downs."

Life has its terrible moments, disasters and indelible embarrassments even for the best of us! But life also has its ups, not just its downs.

Focus on the ups! It's not what you look at that matters, it's what you choose to see.

Day 139

The Big Bang Theory—G-d spoke and bang! It happened.

Short story: One evening, the prayers of a poor family were answered. There was a knock at the door, and tens of "people" stood outside. "Who are you?" asked the father. "I am 'happiness,' this is 'faith,' that there is 'joy,' this is 'health,' standing there is 'success' and the tough guy over there is 'power'… We are what you requested in your prayer," he said to the stunned family members. "But you are only allowed to choose one of us." The family members were perplexed as to what would be the best choice: success or health, happiness or power…? Eventually, the father went over and said, "We choose faith." As faith started to enter the house, she was followed by all of the other wishes. "What happened?" asked the astonished father. "You said that we could choose only one request." "That's right," explained happiness, "but where faith goes, we all follow."

Life is much more bearable when you believe G-d is running the world, so "if G-d is your co-pilot—swap seats!" Belief gives us what to hold on to, who to trust, who to turn to. "Faith is not knowing what the future holds but knowing who holds the future."

Day 140

The road to success runs uphill; so, don't expect to break any speed records.

Push off negative thoughts of any kind to the far off tomorrows that will, hopefully, never arrive. In the meantime, reflect upon and immerse yourself in thoughts that make you feel inspired, uplifted and gleeful.

Develop the attitude from *"Gone with the Wind"* where Scarlet deals with her disappointing loss at the end of the novel by telling herself, "I'll think about it tomorrow!" Meanwhile, have a happy, productive, self-fulfilling day, today and each and every day.

Don't hide from problems. Cope with them. Deal with them. This can be done more effectively and with much less wear and tear and personal self-destruction and bodily harm if you stay in a positive, constructive mood and a happy frame of mind. Use your anxiety (and everyone has anxiety) to energize yourself.

Recognize life isn't easy—it is a struggle. If you realize that and accept that reality then you approach life with a better perspective. You can better deal with the downs, the disappointment, the losses, the tragedies and face them as challenges to overcome.

"The difference between stumbling blocks and stepping-stones is how you use them" (Anonymous).

Day 141

Two weeks after John transferred into the promotion department, his boss got a call. "Didn't you tell me that while John was in your department he was very responsible?" "Yes, in the year he worked here the computers went down five times, the petty cash got misplaced six times and I developed an ulcer. And each time, John was responsible!"

Don't ever allow yourself to get into the cycle of evading responsibility by accepting or even thinking that your behavior won't make an enormous difference. Know for sure that it does. Realize that it's up to you to control how you want to feel, how you make yourself feel and thus how you will indeed feel.

Ultimately, others do not dictate your life. It is not whatever happens, happens. You are the all-powerful dictator of your mind and your life. You can let things happen, or you can make them happen. Do you want to tolerate, suffer and permit the uncontrollable vagaries of direction from the outside to influence you, or do you want to be in charge of the direction that your mind, your emotions and your life takes?

Choose to maximally direct your own attitude, your own path, your own thoughts, and your own existence. Always opt for a winning attitude, not that of a helpless victim tossed hither and thither by the ever-challenging winds of life. The most effective solution is to "FYOHO," Face Your Obstacles Head On. Stop being afraid of what could go wrong and focus on what could go right.

Day 142

And here are Adam and Eve living together in Paradise. You can tell it's Paradise. Not once does Eve ask Adam to take out the garbage.

It's so important to cultivate the appropriate frame of reference, one that generates a feeling of appreciation, good fortune and gratitude for the opportunities and the quality of life with which we are, comparatively, blessed.

Our ancestors would have thought our life is Heaven, the very Garden of Eden, Paradise. The standard of living we currently enjoy throughout these United States and much of the developed civilized world, the availability of fresh water, the endless variety of amazing foods and drinks, the quality of healthcare, the variety and abundance of entertainment, would stagger our ancestor's wildest imaginations. How fortunate we are!

As Oprah Winfrey said, "Be thankful for what you have: you'll end up having more. If you concentrate on what you don't have, you will never ever have enough."

Practice focusing on the good luck that has you alive, in this place, at this uniquely advantageous and this rewarding time, in the history of the universe. Learn to constantly feel gratified by that good fortune. By so doing, you can indeed feel that this is heaven and thereby infuse an emotional reaction that produces true happiness. "Look at everything as though you were seeing it for the first or last time. Then, your time on earth will be filled with glory" (Betty Smith).

Day 143

The man is such a worrier. When he greets you, he says, "Good morning—maybe."

After eighteen years of working his way up from in-house accountant to president, the head of Luby's Cafeterias couldn't face the embarrassment of reporting lower earnings in his first quarter. He left a suicide note for his wife and three kids and then rented a motel room where he stabbed himself through the neck. He was only forty-nine.

How does one deal with the panic and fear of overwhelming embarrassment? How does one conquer the fear that others, the whole world, will learn the secrets of how bad you really are, how ineffectual, how terrible, how deviant?

The first thing to recognize is that in almost every single case, your own negative evaluation of how bad you are or how shameful your actions are is immensely exaggerated in your own mind, both as to the level of evil that you imagine and in other people's level of concern or judgment. Do they really care as much as you fear? At that frightful moment, when you fear imminent discovery, it's imperative that you get hold of yourself and realize that it's only in your own oversensitive mind that this is such a big deal and then realize that "this too shall pass."

Don't allow embarrassment or shame to ever possess you for more than the briefest moment. Rather, turn your unpleasant experiences into constructive, corrective learning opportunities. Don't be debilitated by focusing on them, by allowing your mind to be end-

HAPPINESS GUARANTEED OR YOUR MISERY BACK

lessly filled or overwhelmed by these counterproductive, destructive, feelings. Learn to use every negative episode to generate some positive feeling or some productive resolution.

In his courses on "How to Stop Worrying and Start Living," Dale Carnegie teaches that when you are going through a difficult period, imagine the worst possible and frightening experience, actually feeling the horror. Then, congratulate yourself—how fortunate, how fantastic it is that you are not actually in that horrendously painful situation! Perhaps you are going through your own personal, hopefully temporary, torturous experience, but it's better than it might be.

Reassure yourself that there is hope. Visualize a more positive, hopeful future beyond the present agonizing trials and tribulations. "Don't worry about what's ahead. Just go as far as you can go—from there you can see further" (Bits 'n Pieces).

Day 144

A wife complained about her husband, "He's writing a novel. I don't know why. For three dollars, he can buy one!"

Colin Wilson, the British existentialist thinker and author of the best-selling book *The Outsider*, said that at an early age he was in such terrible despair that he wanted to kill himself. He was on the verge of swallowing a virulent poison when, almost miraculously, he says, "In a kind of magical epiphany, I glimpsed the marvelous immense richness of reality, extending to distant horizons."

Conscientiously achieving such moments of optimistic insight has been his goal ever since. He has discovered how to harness a human being's amazing power to wipe out gloom. He says, "The problem with human beings is that they are met with so many setbacks that they are quite easily defeated. Once you realize that you can conquer defeat, suddenly you begin to see the possibility of achieving a positive state of mind, a kind of steady focus, which means that you can and do see things as extremely good."

Through more than one hundred books, Mr. Wilson postulates that pessimism robs ordinary people of their powers, insisting, "Positive optimistic experiences can come only through effort, concentration or focus, and by refusing to lose one's vital natural energies through pessimism."

Another strong reason to "think positively" is a 2011 Michigan State University research study, which shows that if one adopts an uplifting "mindset," it produces a favorable difference in his or her

HAPPINESS GUARANTEED OR YOUR MISERY BACK

IQ. It actually measurably improves one's intelligence because the nature of someone's *attitude* determines whether they act productively or self-destructively in response to their various experiences and challenges.

Work at being optimistic to improve both your outlook and your brainpower.

Day 145

Life is an incurable condition: the only known treatment is to try to keep the patient comfortable.

Pesach Krohn relates a beautifully touching story of a woman dying of cancer. Her young teenage son asked her why this was happening to her and she gave him the most amazing heartfelt answer. She said, "When I was little and was a naturally good student and others were struggling with their work, I didn't ask 'why me?' When I was the first in my class to get married and some of my friends never found their life partners, I never questioned, 'why me?' When I got pregnant so easily and some of my friends have never been able to conceive, I didn't ask, 'why me?' So, what gives me the right to question G-d now? I just have to accept that all G-d does, although we don't understand His reasoning, is for the best."

It has been found that those who have faith find contentment, acceptance and happiness. "For those who question there are no answers. For those who believe there are no questions."

Day 146

"I like optimists. They show me how I'd feel if I weren't a pessimist."—Milton Berle

Stephen Holden, in a *New York Times* review of the renowned folk singer Judy Collins asserts that, "It would be easy for anyone who has not followed the details of Ms. Collins life to assume that she has led a charmed existence because she exudes a poised self-confidence that can easily be confused with serenity."

But he describes how in the past Judy Collins "struggled with alcoholism, bulimia, bouts of depression and panic attacks in which she feared losing her grip." He also describes how the toughest hurdle came with the suicide, at age thirty-three, of her son and only child, Clark Taylor, brought on by substance abuse and depression. She has since become a sought-after keynote speaker on suicide and suicide prevention.

It is apparent that Ms. Collins' serenity is hard won and maintained by rigorous self-discipline. She states, "Staying un-depressed is really the big one, isn't it? That's the key. The person I've been most influential in changing is myself. I practice optimism." Ms. Collins' profoundly adaptive behavioral response makes so much sense.

Train yourself to find a place inside where there is joy and then let the joy crush the pain, so you can go forward with optimism. "Don't look back, you're not going that way."

Day 147

When you're dissatisfied and would like to go back to youth, think of algebra.

If you are unhappy, fed up, frustrated, depressed, there is good news for you to be happy about. Studies show that even if you do nothing, just by growing older you will become happier.

A survey by the National Opinion Research Center, at the University of Chicago, found that almost 40 percent of Americans 65 or older rated themselves very happy as compared to 33 percent of those 35-49. These results were found in other countries as well. Happiness has been found to have a U-shaped curve, with people's happiness low point occurring at age 46 and 50. Jonathan Rauch wrote that "life satisfaction falls for the fist couple of decades of adulthood, hits bottom in the late forties or early fifties" and then until the very last years increases with age. Interestingly, the best years are the later ones.

It seems that the young idealize the future. They are full of hope and optimism but by middle age, late thirties, many feel disillusioned, even if they have done well. During these years, people are overwhelmed by their careers and family responsibilities. There is not enough time to accomplish what they have to, leaving them with a sense of losing control. In their late forties or early fifties, responsibilities diminish, careers peek, children leave home and ambition and youthful dreams decline. People accept their limits, the chance for failure lessons, the mismatch of expectation and experience narrows, people mellow and there is a reappraisal of life's purpose and meaning. The writer Donald Richie said, "Midlife crisis begins sometime in your forties, when you look at your life and think, 'Is this all?' And it ends ten years later, when you look at your life again and think, 'Actually, this is pretty good.'"

You can sit around and get older and you will eventually get happier or you can work at being happy now.

Day 148

A man goes into a Zen bookstore and hands the cashier $10 for a book that costs $9.95. He waits and finally says, "Where's my change?" The cashier says, "Change must come from within."

Samuel Johnson wrote, "He who has so little knowledge of human nature as to seek happiness by changing anything but his own disposition will waste his life in fruitless efforts."

The most helpful journey, the most effective, meaningful and advantageous quest that we need to pursue, is to change our selves. Anyone who thinks "I would really be happy if I could only change my spouse, my employee, my boss, or my fiancée" is bound to be disappointed.

Can you imagine the gross conceit that one indulges oneself in when he or she thinks that he can change someone other than himself over whom he surely has less influence than he has over himself? If we can change ourselves, and we surely can if we work at it, we can achieve unbelievably rewarding results. If our happiness depends on changing others, we are destined to experience frustration and disappointment. If we can develop a positive, optimistic approach to life, if we can inculcate the right winning attitude, despite what others may do or say and despite the unalterable circumstances, we can generate our own happiness.

Jim Loehr, author of *Stress for Success* and trainer of such outstanding world-class athletes as Pete Sampras and Andre Agassi, teaches people to be winners by using his "mental toughness" pro-

HAPPINESS GUARANTEED OR YOUR MISERY BACK

gram. He theorizes that positive thinking releases positive chemicals in the brain and makes you a winner, while negative thinking is damaging because it releases negative chemicals in your brain, making you a loser.

"When you see a dandelion*, you have a choice of seeing a weed or making a wish. Make a wish."

---

* a weed on which people blow and make a wish, as its flower easily disperses in the wind.

Day 149

An elderly gentleman was given a complete physical. Afterward, the doctor said, "You'll live to be ninety." The man said, "I am ninety." The doctor said, "See, what did I tell you?"

The prevailing wisdom is that "Politics is the art of the possible." That's surely accurate. It's equally valid to state, "Life is the art of the possible." Sometimes, perhaps too often, we expect too much of ourselves and then become disappointed and depressed at our perceived failure. It is essential that we not be so hard on ourselves. We must realize what is possible.

When you are going through a very difficult scary, threatening, period, do not allow thoughts of a frightening tomorrow dominate your thinking. Force yourself to get absorbed in some activity that focuses all your thought and energy on the activity you are participating in presently. Immerse yourself and even enjoy it, so that you are not overwhelmed by the probably largely exaggerated potential fear and aggravation. "Activity," as Plato famously said, "is what makes life worth living."

Your mind is on overload. It's just too much. You feel you can't take it anymore. It may not be possible to control a situation, but it is possible to control your mind. It is important to know what it is within your power to control and not demand more of yourself than you are capable. On the other hand, don't demand less of yourself either.

HAPPINESS GUARANTEED OR YOUR MISERY BACK

Do as much as you can. Be as productive as you can. Control what you do and how you perceive it. Perceive all you can in a positive light. It will lighten your burden and your life and help you to move on effectively and expeditiously to more uplifting, rewarding and happier experiences. Don't give in to despair or failure.

"The difference between winning and losing is most often… not quitting" (Walt Disney).

Day 150

There was once a wife so jealous that when her husband came home one night and she couldn't find hairs on his jacket, she yelled at him, "Great, so now you're cheating on me with a bald woman!"

There is a story of a king who had two sons. The younger son was ferociously jealous of his older brother. One day the king said to him, "Choose anything in the world that you want and I will give it to you. But, I will give your brother a double portion of that same thing." The younger son considered and then said, "Father, I want you to pluck out one of my eyes."

This boy had the opportunity for gold and silver, riches and love, but he was so blinded by jealousy that, rather than choosing what would make his life happier, he chose what would make his brother's life more miserable.

You work hard and are doing relatively well, but your neighbor is still more successful. Can you work harder or more hours or can you just alter your attitude? You have sufficient funds to have a good life but the envy is eating at you. Think logically. Is being jealous helping or hurting your quality of life? If your neighbor had less, would you have more? If your neighbor weren't as happy, would you yourself be in a better position? Learn to accept your circumstances, irrespective of what those around you do or don't have.

You can be the moon and still be jealous of the stars. Enjoy and appreciate what is given to you without comparing it with others who may have more than you.

HAPPINESS GUARANTEED OR YOUR MISERY BACK

Actively appreciate the blessings you posses. This awareness and enthusiasm of that which you do have will enrich you with a sense of gratification that will reward you with truly enviable, authentic happiness.

"The jealous are troublesome to others, but a torment to themselves" (William Penn).

Day 151

You can't have everything. Where would you put it?

"Happiness is not having what you want, but wanting what you have."

Think how lucky you are to be born in the best place in the world in the best time in history. You could have been born in places like Africa, South America, China or India, where millions of people are malnourished and diseased, living in starvation and filth without modern plumbing.

Before the twentieth century, a vast portion of the world's population suffered from epidemics and plagues that wiped out entire villages. The primitive state of medicine meant that one suffered tremendously in the process of dying or even during less critical illnesses. There were no modern-day painkillers. There were no anesthetics to put you to sleep during surgery or during the extraction of teeth. Life expectancy was a far too brief forty-two years or less. Almost every family lost members at a young age. Almost every mother lost one or more children at birth. If you got sick, you suffered and often died a slow, painful death.

With the lack of modern-day plumbing, medical treatment, transportation, air conditioning, heating, etc., life was often miserable to say the least. Now, how lucky are you? Smile. Be happy! Be elated! Count your lucky stars.

What about quality of life? What food or drink choices did you have then? What entertainment could you have enjoyed? By contrast, even a family on welfare and food stamps today enjoys a far more exciting variety of food and drink than any king who reigned 150 years ago. During most of our history, a king became excited at the arrival of a rare spice or tasty fruit from the Far East. Today, even a food stamps recipient can go to any local supermarket and bring home a countless variety of breads, cakes, meats, fruits, vegetables, cookies, crackers, ice creams, spices and sausages.

The same is true for transportation. Two centuries ago, the fastest, most efficient form of transportation was a horse. Today, we have automobiles, trains, buses and airplanes that exceed in speed and comfort anything available to the wealthiest king in the old world. Now, how lucky are you? Lean back in your La-Z-Boy and think how privileged you are.

What about entertainment? With radio, TV, movies and the Internet, you can access more variety and a superior quality of entertainment than any king in the entire history of man. A king and his court were excited if some theatrical troupe or circus passed through their town. No king ever had the comforts taken for granted by the average citizen in the Western world today.

We are living "the good life." Notice it. Be grateful for it. Appreciate it. Be happy because of your truly remarkable good luck.

Can't sleep? Count your blessings!

Day 152

An optimist is someone who always sees the bright side of your problem.

In the blink of an eye, someone on top of the world today can be on the bottom tomorrow. Someone wealthy can lose all his money as in the crash of 1929. Someone poor can make a fortune overnight. Someone who may be lonely now in one minute from now may meet his soul mate. Someone with a great family may lose a member. Someone barren may find she is pregnant. Your whole world can change for the better or worse in the next second.

"Hope is definitely not the same as optimism. It is not the conviction that some thing will go well, but the certainty that something makes sense, regardless of how it turns out" (Vaclav Harvel). "The essence of optimism is it takes no account of the recent, but it is a source of inspiration, of vitality and hope where others have resigned: it enables a man to hold his head high to claim the future for himself and not to abandon it to his enemy" (Dietrich Rushdie). The enemy is disheartenment and despair.

Don't be busy looking back or looking at what others have or worrying about the future. Appreciate this moment and go into the future with hope and optimism.

Day 153

A shoe salesman arrived in Africa and after observing the facts telegrammed his boss, "It's hopeless for me to spend any more time or effort here. Nobody wears shoes." Another shoe salesman arrived and e-mailed his boss, "My G-d it's terrific...nobody here owns any shoes—what a great opportunity!"

Always look for the really bright, most optimistic, side of a given situation. No matter what the situation, try to put the best possible face on it—see it in the most positive light. If it doesn't solve the problem, it can make you feel better about it. As it is said, "It may not help but it surely can't hurt." As Winston Churchill said, "For myself, I am an optimist. It does not seem to be much use to be anything else."

Roll with the punches, firstly because we really must, and second because it's the best possible adaptation. For example, if you're on a bouncing turbulent commercial airplane flight, you can, as some people do, go crazy, shake with fright, even cry and scream. Alternatively, you can simply recognize that you can't get off, that you must tolerate every scary bounce and make the best of it. Forget about it and concentrate on something else. Focus on the stewardess who does this every day and who knows that it's part of the reality of flying, and that it will ultimately experience, as it does in 99.9999 percent of the cases, a satisfactory ending—a safe landing!

For years, whenever I flew, I stayed nervous and on guard the entire flight. I stayed awake and alert to experience and suffer every shake and bump. Then, one day I adopted a new, more upbeat mindset. "This is out of my control. The pilot, with G-d's help is flying this plane. I can relax." When the fear assaults me, I repeat to myself, "It shakes but it lands. It shakes but it lands."

*Don't misunderstand, I still hate turbulence, but now I consider the time I fly surprisingly enjoyable.

Optimism is the stubbornness of maintaining that everything is best despite that everything is at its worst.

The lesson is this: to enjoy life, to get to your ultimate destination you have to ride out, often many, unpleasant, frightening bumps. Sooner or later, hopefully sooner, the bumps will stop and you will once again experience smooth and pleasant sailing. You'll always be far better off throughout the journey than the one who doesn't take that optimistic approach.

Don't worry. You will have a safe landing!

---

* Since laughter is the best medicine, I can't resist adding one of my favorite Rita Rudner jokes. **"My mother said, 'I shouldn't be afraid of my plane crashing.' She said, 'When it's your time to die, it's your time to die.' I said, 'I know, but what if it's the pilots time to die?'"**

Day 154

"So I was getting into my car, and this man says to me, 'Can you give me a lift?' I said, 'Sure, you look great, you can accomplish anything you set your mind to, go for it.'"

Thomas Edison handed a light bulb to his assistant who dropped it. It took Edison weeks to rebuild the bulb, but when it was ready, he handed it to the same assistant. A friend asked Edison, "What are you doing? He dropped it last time. He's unreliable!" Edison answered, "The last time, I was inventing a light bulb. This time, I'm inventing a person.

We each have the power to invent others, as well as ourselves. By the way, we think and act, we shape ourselves and affect others. We cause us to admire and respect ourselves by the way we treat people and handle circumstances. We shape our relationships by the way we behave and interact with others. By choosing to treat others with love, warmth, admiration, respect, care, friendship and trust, versus treating them with anger, hatred, disdain, distrust, control, indifference, aggression or belligerence, we create positive friendships and joyful exposures.

By reacting towards life in an upbeat, accepting, positive manner, rather than in a dowdy sad or angry stance, we are shaping the way we view our experiences, our life and those in it, as well as affecting the moods and outlooks of those around us.

As Winston Churchill said, "Attitude is a little thing that makes a big difference."

Day 155

If at first you don't succeed, don't try skydiving.

The truest route to success is doing everything you do in life with joy and in rejoicing in all your innumerable blessings, while being constantly cognizant and appreciative of them.

Even the best things in life can be a source of discomfort and frustration and pain if we do not approach them with a proper frame of mind. For example, there is no greater joy to parents than a newborn child, yet when that beautiful, priceless infant cries incessantly in the middle of the night, when you are exhausted and want desperately to cling to your bed and sleep, you can feel immensely disturbed and even angry so you can get up feeling tired and stiff, responding with anger to that mischievous infant, or you might remember how lucky you are to have this child and cuddle and comfort your precious gift. "Little children, little problems. Big children, big problems." It's part of life. Thank G-d for these children.

People often get frustrated that they have to take care of their elderly parents rather than being grateful that they still have parents to enjoy.

A big house to take care of, a new car to look after, a booming business to run, each can be viewed as a headaches or a blessing. Every positive has a negative and vice versa, choose to find and react to the positive.

Your attitude in any situation is always solely up to you. It can be constructive, heroic and ego enhancing, or it can be destructive, depressing and ego diminishing. Each one of us can create our own utopia or our own hell.

Day 156

A wife asked her husband, "What are you doing today?" "Nothing," he answered. "You did that yesterday," she angrily retorted. "Well," he shouted back at her, "I didn't finish."

In order to understand what it takes to achieve happiness, it helps a great deal to comprehend the cause of unhappiness, so that one can then adopt and pursue a counter positive, diametrically contrary behavior.

If you do nothing, if you are not productive or not working to achieve some goal, then that lethargic behavior produces a staleness, a boredom, a sense of guilt and inevitably an ensuing anxiety, malaise and depression. There is just no fun in that kind of inactive idleness. It instills sluggishness, bleakness and a gloominess of a futile blank future and generates a kind of emotional dullness, drowsiness and tedium. It makes one stultified and pep-less and, rather than helping one to become upbeat and excited, it provokes a sense of hopelessness and despair.

If being lethargic and lazy makes you more a somnolent vegetable than a lively human being with boundless potential, you should activate and arouse an action-packed, productive goal-oriented behavioral pattern and an arousing, vibrant lifestyle.

Tragedy should be used as a source of strength. No matter what sort of difficulties you might experience and despite how painful an experience is, if you lose your hope, that's a real disaster. You must stay optimistic, pull yourself up and Do! Do! Do! Be Busy! Work diligently toward achieving a dream. Yes, rest when it's appropriate and wise, but be restless to always be doing things which make you feel good about yourself, which make you feel you are making progress and growing, which make you feel both joyful and full of life, which doesn't allow you time to focus on what's not right or to sit around and mope about what might have been or what others may have.

"If lethargy is the mother of unhappiness, then activity gives birth to the happiness offspring."

Day 157

You only learn from your mistakes. That's why I make sure not to do anything right!

In the entire history of the human race there is no individual who didn't make some decision that caused him disappointment, loss, hurt and/or deep regret. It is human to err. We all make mistakes. There is not a one of us, be he scholar or saint, be he genius or king, who wouldn't wish, wouldn't give almost anything, to change some decision he made, cancel some action he took, or choose an alternative direction than one he pursued.

To second-guess oneself, to punish oneself for what one sees in retrospect as a clearly wrong, even a silly course of action, is counterproductive. It's the biggest waste of time and energy—a needlessly hopeless and demoralizing activity. Concentrate on where you are, not on past mistakes, misfortunes, disillusionments and hurts.

As Winston Churchill, one of the greatest government leaders and statesman of all time, so brilliantly surmised, when he urged Parliament not to look back at the mistakes they made when they ignored the dangers of Hitler and Nazism, "Of this I am certain, that if we open a quarrel between the past and the present, we shall find that we shall have lost the future."

Regret is nonproductive. It only brings you down. You can always think of another "If only…then I would be happy. If only I had done. If only I had been. If only I had…" So many of us live under the illusion that if we only had achieved a certain outcome, then we would be really happy.

The actual reality is that it's not some specific or imagined new outcome that delivers lifelong durable happiness. Happiness is acquiring the ability to either find pleasure in what you have done, what is or what you hope will be.

Forgive yourself for your mistakes and learn from them. "Don't regret what you've done because at one time it was exactly what you wanted" (Anonymous). Don't dwell on what went wrong—find what to do next.

Day 158

I'm not an optimist but hopefully some day I will be one.

The productive thing to derive from our missteps and mistakes is to learn from them in order to avoid similar acts in the future. We can, and, of course, to some extent, we do suffer and pay the price for unwise or even unlucky decisions. But, it serves little purpose other than to further aggravate us and consequently cause us to experience even greater damage than necessary.

Don't delude yourself. We often rationalize and defend our faults rather than realizing we have done something wrong. When we overcome denial, the correct perception of reality allows us to function better and achieve greater happiness.

It helps to understand that we are human and that we all do, and will, make many mistakes, some of which are avoidable since they are due to our own actions, but many are beyond our control due to unforeseen, unexpected occurrences.

What we can do is to convert these negative, disappointing experiences into inspiring lessons is to make wiser decisions in the future and to use the lesson to stimulate our minds and our personal growth.

Some problems are for solving—others are for living with. Since we can't change what we already did, what has already occurred, it's foolish, futile, and self-destructive to engage in second-guessing oneself. No matter how terrible, in retrospect, your course of action was, no matter how terrible the consequence, there is only one sensible course of action to take now—move on!

Learning from the past, rather than being captured by it, is the constructive way to deal with the setbacks, reversals and mishaps of life. The future is changeable and that's what your mind should be focusing on. "If you can change your mind, you can change your life" (William James).

Day 159

My luck! I'll have nothing all my life and then they'll discover oil while they're digging my grave.

Jim Clark, a co-founder of Netscape and a billionaire several times over, told the *New York Times* how, at age thirty-eight, he fell into a rut of self-pity. He had run through two marriages and several college teaching jobs. He remembered sitting at home and saying to himself, "You can dig this hole as deep as you want to dig it." He had achieved nothing, in his estimate. But then, he said, "I developed this maniacal passion for wanting to achieve something." This reinvented him and launched him to unimaginable wealth and success in life.

However, even after Clark became a multimillionaire, he was still miserable, finding himself as ill-designed for life in a big corporation as he was for life inside a big university. He sank into another dangerous depression, and sowed strife and discontent in his own enterprise, endlessly distraught about the future. He was increasingly alienated from the company that his genius and vision had created. He said what pushed him on was that "I assumed that the best motive for wanting to change the way things are is that you're unhappy with the way things are."

It sounds so obvious but it is really a brilliant insight, the kind of inspirational perception that can drive you and me to make fundamental changes. If you are unhappy, do something about it! Change things. Reinvent yourself. Know that optimism yields positive results. Think futuristically. Think positively. Get passionate about something and act to work toward fulfilling an aspiration, a dream.

Move on. Don't give in to the seductive pull of self-pity. Acting like a victim threatens your future. Propel yourself forward to do things, which bring you happiness. "Respect yourself enough to walk away from anything that no longer serves you, grows you or makes you happy."

Day 160

Laziness is nothing more than the habit of resting before you get tired.

Stephen Covey, the author of the best-selling motivational book *The Seven Habits of Highly Effective People* advocates the following seven ideas to use in your daily life until they become automatic and habitual:

1. Be proactive
2. Begin with the end in mind (visualize your goal)
3. Put first things first
4. Think win-win!
5. Seek first to understand, then to be understood
6. Synergize (cooperate, use teamwork)
7. Sharpen the saw (The *New York Times* writer Paul Brown translates this to mean engage in personal renewal)

Following the aforementioned concise, but brilliant advice, has helped many people become more targeted, more effective and significantly more productive. In the process, it has helped them to be more inspired and more fulfilled and considerably happier with their careers and their lives.

Plan to incorporate these habits into your life. "If You Fail to Plan, You Plan to Fail."

Day 161

When happiness shows up, give it a comfortable seat.

People who understand the nature of human life do not look on ill fortune as ill fortune. They see the glass half full. They accept that there is no rainbow without first enduring the rain.

Live this life! It's not a dress rehearsal so enjoy it, don't suffer it. Don't allow anything to drag you down and destroy the limited valuable time you have. It's the only life you have so make the very best of it.

You aren't anything until you have it really bad and overcome. Until you have it really bad, you don't appreciate how good you have it. When things are not so bad, think how well off you are. In the midst of strife, there is hope. In the midst of darkness, there is light.

Bring about your own solutions by being the sole determiner of what you think. Let go! Get beyond any situation, relationship or adverse event that disturbs you, overwhelms you and eats you up. Many of us cling to the very thing that bothers us most. We focus on it. We dwell on it. It's as if we refuse to get beyond it or end it. In so doing, we actually behave as our own worst enemy.

Try saying to yourself, "I don't care. I just don't care." If you take that attitude, even if you have reason to worry, you will be more relaxed. It's no use grumbling and complaining. It's just as easy to rejoice.

Don't look back unless it's joyful. Only look forward with a sense of exciting expectation—then make it come about. If you dream it, it is.

"Happiness, like unhappiness, is a proactive choice" (Stephen Covey).

Day 162

"Happiness is the quiet lull between problems."—Paul Reiser

At one time or another, we all go through times that are disillusioning, discouraging and even disastrous. As a consequence, not unnaturally, we become cynical, angry and severely pessimistic. If we stay with that condition, we become the cause of our own continuing and growing despondency. We, in effect, nurture our own despair, wretchedness and misery.

Instead of remaining mired in a rut of despair, we must become "born-again optimists." We must as rapidly and effectively as we can limit, soften and subdue the hurt and the pain that emanates from such reversals, from such terrible calamities and with a religious fervor raise ourselves, our spirits, from the ruinous damage that such pessimism and negativism can perpetrate on our physical being and on the quality of our life. If a problem can be solved, there is nothing to worry about and if it can't be solved worrying won't do you any good.

Pack up your troubles, and throw them to the wind. Induce hope when hope is gone. Revitalize! Start a new life. It's rewarding and ego enhancing to lift yourself up by becoming a dedicated, committed "born-again optimist."

Accept, as Steve Jobs said, "You cannot connect the dots looking forward: You can only connect them looking backwards, so you have to trust that the dots will somehow connect in your future." Believe everything happens for a good reason. Learning from a challenged past helps create a brighter future.

There is nothing more positive than being positive.

Day 163

When your ship comes in, be sure you are not at the airport.

Don't fight reality. Sometimes, things do go against you, but into each life—yours and mine, there arise unique opportunities to exploit your potential for achievement, success and very "special situations" for happiness.

We all have "one beautiful pitch." When it comes, it's up to us to recognize it and pounce on it so that we can do like Ted Williams' spectacular feat and bat what would be the equivalent of batting 400. When we get up each morning, we get up to the plate in the batter's box that is life. We have to keep our eyes open and alert for that "one beautiful pitch" that will turn our own days and our own lives into a happiness-winning lifetime existence.

If it's important to win the MVP (most valuable player) award in baseball when that's your career, how much more so is it important to win the MVP award for yourself in the career of life? When life serves you a lemon, make lemonade but when life serves you lemonade, drink and enjoy it.

Take advantage of, recognize and maximize the numerous opportunities for joy and blessedness, for doing something you are proud of, for helping someone in need of your help, for achieving your particular home run.

Day 164

"If you don't think every day is a good day, just try missing one."—Cavett Robert

To fully enjoy the benefit, the bounty, the lavish rewards that life in this world has the potential to afford us, we must first realize and accept the reality that nothing is perfect, not this world, not human beings, and not life.

Why must we accept something that seems so discouraging and depressing? Because, if we don't accept reality, we will be devastated by it. When the inevitable disappointments and demoralizing events do occur, we won't recognize that these experiences are intrinsic to human existence and part of the very fabric of life. Instead of confronting adversity and working to overcome it and move on whatever it is and whatever it takes, we will be far more devastated, for far longer periods of time, with far more hurt and pain, suffering, anger, resentment and an unmerited sense of personal misfortune than we need necessarily allow ourselves to tolerate.

To increase the sum total of the happiness in contrast to the quantity of unhappiness, we must, of necessity, be prepared for adversity. We must overcome it as effectively and as quickly as humanly possible so as to experience all of the exciting, fulfilling and uplifting adventures of life. In large measure happiness is a direct result, a by-product, of immersing yourself in life, and particularly in the "feel-good" experiences of life. In the final analysis, it is about how you deal with all your life experiences, good and bad, and feeling good about how you travel through the challenging intriguing adventure which we call life.

Each of us ought to consider our lives a rich pioneering adventure that is so special and beautiful because it belongs so completely to each of us.

The Greeks say, "We suffer our way to wisdom." Each adversity that we suffer can be exploited to teach us lessons that will make us wiser and more capable of dealing with the future so as to make it more fulfilling.

Learn to use every experience as a stepping-stone to a more exciting, adventurous and happier future.

Day 165

No matter how great your triumphs or how tragic you defeats—approximately one billion Chinese couldn't care less.

"Oh, my friend, it's not what they take away from you that counts; it's what you do with what you have left" (Hubert Humphrey).

All glory is fleeting. One year Newt Gingrich is elected Speaker of the House and is designated *Time* magazine's "Man of the Year." Shortly thereafter, he is savaged, vilified, embarrassed and forced to step down as Speaker of the House, resigning from Congress as well.

"Newtie, you have to get on with life," said Mrs. Gingrich when Newt asked his mother how she maintained a positive attitude after the recent loss of her husband and the health problems that forced her to give up her home.

"Many are the thoughts in man's heart, but it is G-d's will that will prevail" (Psalms).

When you come to a dead end in the road, find another path. Life has many disappointments. You must be able to adapt. If your dreams get shattered, dream new dreams.

Day 166

"Son, I'm worried about you being at the bottom of the class."
"Don't worry, Pop. They teach the same things at both ends."

The best way to stay young and excited about life is to keep constantly learning. As you learn new things, you continually renew and grow and open up whole new worlds. You never really get old if you learn new things. It's like pursuing and experiencing an entire undiscovered adventure. You become an adventurous pioneer, discovering new vistas that open up your eyes and your mind. You afford yourself the opportunity that generally is the exclusive domain of the very young, who are always thrilled to experience the excitement of learning anything new and feeling the special joy of such growth.

Watch the happiness of a young child when s/he achieves some new milestone, learning to do something s/he has never done before. Through adopting that behavior, you can replicate that same feeling of youthfulness and growth and adventure throughout all the days of your life regardless of age. In that sense, you become ageless and ever young.

If you think you are complete, that you have little to learn and no new goals to reach, then you exclude and destroy your capacity for growth, new adventures, and the unparalleled joy of learning.

Open yourself up to new experiences and new knowledge. Learning is exhilarating.

Day 167

The experienced sea captain was putting a young naval officer through his paces. "What would you do if a storm sprang up on the starboard?" asked the captain. Said the sailor, "Throw out an anchor, sir." "What would you do if another storm sprang up aft?" "Throw out another anchor, sir." "And if another terrific storm sprang up forward, what would you do?" "Throw out another anchor." "Wait a minute," said the captain. "Where are you getting all your anchors from?" Replied the sailor, "From the same place you are getting all your storms, sir."

Life may be full of storms. When things are terrible and you think you can't take anymore, make up your mind to take a single course of action and retrench, rebuild, renew. Don't react by moaning and sulking which just further adds to your debilitating condition. Make up your mind which single action you can start with right now, today, and what sequence of actions you might take to change what "is" and that will make for a better less tormenting, more stimulating and invigorating future.

Don't ever succumb to passivity, indifference, paralysis, or defeat. Make up your mind to fight your way back—to lift yourself out of the ashes of disappointment. When you feel down or inept or unworthy or just lousy, taking action is the cure. It immediately begins to make you feel better.

Every day, experience the excitement of being born anew, of resurrection and new creativity and adventure. If you dedicate yourself to pursue that attitude, not only will you relieve yourself from the morass that inevitably confronts us all in life at one time or another, but you will be more productive, more successful and achieve an inspiring spirituality that will reward you in degrees of happiness beyond your most ambitious dreams all the days of your life.

"Learning is a gift, even when pain is your teacher" (Maya Watson).

Day 168

Q: Did you hear about the blonde who shot an arrow into the air?
A: She missed.

You have to be adaptive to be successful and to create for yourself a sense of happiness. Albert Einstein said, "We cannot solve problems with the same thinking we used when we created them." No matter how far the course of your life deviates from your hopes or expectations, you have to adjust and make what comes along into the very best for you.

If your life doesn't exactly hit the target you planned for it, adjust it so that you can revise the bull's-eye accordingly and thereby enjoy the adjusted target. You can rearrange your own bull's-eye. There is more than one way to lead a happy life. The opportunities, the adventures, the challenges, the joys are limitless.

When challenges arise, don't give up on your goal, either find a new path to reach that goal or a new goal which will be as fulfilling. "Surrender to what is. Let go of what was. Have faith in what will be" (Sonia Riccoti). Retain your confidence, your enthusiasm and your drive. "You can't live a positive life with a negative mind."

Day 169

We are born naked, wet and hungry. Then, things get worse.

"If happiness is activity in accordance with excellence, it is reasonable that it should be in accordance with the highest excellence" (Aristotle).

I can tell you innumerable stories of individuals who lived through the most challenging, horrendous experience, and as a consequence of their practicing the kind of behavior I am urging you to adopt, have not only survived but actually managed to convert their terribly torturous situation into a positive, inspiring, uplifting opportunity that ultimately served to develop and enhance their character and personal growth.

An outstanding example of responding constructively to anger and resentment in the face of exorbitantly unfair treatment is that of Nelson Mandela, who spent twenty-seven years as a prisoner for his leadership against apartheid in South Africa. Upon his release, he was asked if he carried a grudge, hated, or felt angry and embittered toward his jailers. He responded that, if at the moment of achieving his undreamed of freedom and the sense of gratification that that miraculous milestone brought, he clung to bitterness and anger he would still continue to be a prisoner.

As a consequence of this constructive attitude, he became the first president of post-apartheid South Africa and, in fact, as a result was able to bring together the divisive factions that had divided his nation. He never, as so many others of us surely would have, pursued

HAPPINESS GUARANTEED OR YOUR MISERY BACK

a vendetta of wrath, vindictiveness and revenge in retaliation for the years of depravation of freedom, abuse and suffering.

In behaving in such a magnificent, indeed saintly, manner, he earned the respect and admiration of all of the world leaders. Best of all, and most meaningfully for him personally, was that he was able to avoid the pain one inflicts on oneself as a result of anger and bitterness. He was able to enjoy, with an ever-present smile on his face, a truly productive, constructive, immensely admired, wonderful long life.

Nelson Mandela's behavior, can serve as an invaluable lesson, a guide, to all of us of the enormous rewards that can come from a positive, never resentful, always cheerful attitude in life, even in the face of unfairness, hopeless obstacles and tortuous punishment.

Train your mind to release the anger. As Ralph Waldo Emerson said, "For every minute you remain angry, you give up sixty seconds of peace of mind."

Day 170

She decided to bury the hatchet—between his shoulder blades

Two children will fight and say, "I hate you. I never want to play with you again." For two or three minutes, they play separately, and then they begin playing with each other again. How can children be so angry one moment and play together the next? It's easy. They choose happiness over righteousness.

How does a married couple get past their disagreements? They agree to disagree and choose a good marriage over winning each battle. The same holds true for partners who put their successful partnership before their egos.

Arguing with people not only angers the other person, it frustrates you. A disagreement with someone that is not that important to you, like someone who cuts in front of your car or someone who rudely bumps into you while you are walking down the street, is something you should calmly take in your stride. Save your effort for resolving conflicts with people you value. Even if you're right about something, don't stubbornly demand recognition of it. Sacrifice the victory for the sake of happiness.

Healthy disagreement, which leads to understanding and compromise, is fine and admirable. Of course, sometimes despite how difficult and frightening it may be, in order to feel fulfilled you may have to follow your moral compass and/or your heart and stick to and stand up for what you believe.

HAPPINESS GUARANTEED OR YOUR MISERY BACK

When it comes to a disagreement, judge the situation. Know in which instances, under what circumstances and with whom it is appropriate to settle or to stick to your guns. Recognizing this difference and doing what is right will keep you happy.

"Relationships include fights, jealousy, disagreements, faith, tears, disagreement. But, a real relationship fights through all that with love."

Day 171

How do you relate to the Soviet government? Like a wife: part habit, part fear and I wish to G-d I had a different one.

Natan Sharansky, perhaps the most renowned dissident of the tyrannical Soviet Union, was arrested and imprisoned for publicly promulgating political views that challenged the embedded, arbitrarily cruel, dictatorial Soviet government. He was jailed on all kinds of trumped-up, outrageous charges, locked up repeatedly and endlessly deprived of any semblance of freedom or self-esteem.

He maintains that even at the time of his most unjustified and extreme punishment and, what was seemingly total deprivation of any human rights, he trained his mind to inculcate a mental attitude that produced a positive state of mind, which remarkably gave him far more freedom than that of his prison guards. The prison guards were so regulated, controlled and disciplined that they felt a greater sense of enslavement than he did and, thus, caused them to become so depressed and joyless that during the duration of his imprisonment several of the guards were actually driven to commit suicide.

Sharansky read, wrote, told jokes and enjoyed a sense of psychological freedom. This, he says, helped him not only to experience an enriching survival but helped him to become a world-class political leader and statesman, as well as a successful role-model freedom fighter who, as a consequence, helped inspire the Soviet Union to ultimately become a Democratic nation. He became an outstandingly magnificent spokesman for freedom and liberty throughout the world.

HAPPINESS GUARANTEED OR YOUR MISERY BACK

Hold Sharansky's experience, his ability to control his thinking process, his mental attitude under the most dire circumstances, as your incontrovertible proof and reminder to you that one can manage and effectively manipulate one's own state of mind to induce the most rewarding results despite any challenge one may confront. Remember, when life's path is steep, keep your mind steady and don't allow yourself to be pulled down.

Day 172

Two pals, one an optimist the other a pessimist, were involved in an accident. While waiting for the ambulance, the pessimist said, "I think all my bones are broken." The optimist answered, "You're lucky you're not a herring."

When Tony Snow, former press secretary to the President of the United States, was asked how he was coping with colon cancer, he responded, "I don't cope. I live each day fully with excitement and with the knowledge that many people with this condition survive and go on to live quite a long time after treatment. I retain the faith and belief that I will be one of them. I live each day with a sense of hope and optimism. We all die at some point. The important thing is for me to live and appreciate and, in so far as possible, to enjoy and be productive and do good things for my family, for myself and for others."

From this remarkably adaptive and constructive approach to what is clearly one of the most discouraging and distressing experiences one could ever be confronted with, we can derive a most useful, happiness facilitating and emboldening example as to the most effective and rewarding way to live life—even in the face of the most challenging and disheartening frustrations and setbacks.

As motivational writer Zig Zigler says, "A lost battle is a battle one thinks he has lost." Don't just cope. Fight to make each day hopeful.

HAPPINESS GUARANTEED OR YOUR MISERY BACK

Live each day! Enjoy each day! Appreciate each day! Do this and you will thereby enrich your everyday life and be rewarded with an enviable, amplified quality of happiness throughout your life. "Life is not about waiting for the storm to pass…it's about learning to dance in the rain."

Day 173

First senior citizen: "Hello, Rose. How are you?"
Second senior citizen: "Fine, fine, but I'll be all right."

"Every day may not be good, but there's something good in every day." There are always innumerable daily and even hourly experiences and involvements that can irritate you, frustrate you and cause at least momentary aggravation and anxiety. These include issues with spouses, children, bosses, co-workers, traffic jams, rude drivers, bad news, declining stocks, planes delayed, personal illnesses, or accidents.

So how should you manage in the face of so much that can and does consistently and recurrently go wrong and which tends to generate and incite despair, disillusion and unhappiness?

The only wise and healthy response is to figure out how to minimize the annoyance and pain that emanates from these untoward, hurtful experiences by, in so far as possible, rolling with the punches. "Don't miss the sun today worrying about the rain coming tomorrow." Try to recognize and know that with time and, in most cases, with the appropriate effort on your part, these distressing episodes will pass. Believe that at a time in the near future, good and even wonderful new experiences and blessings will be forthcoming in your life. This will not only help you feel better, it will effectively help you survive the difficult times and even help those better times manifest themselves more rapidly.

Try to remember what you were worried or upset about at this time last year. Chances are you can't.

Day 174

"I had a tough childhood. I could tell that my parents hated me. My bath toys were a radio and a toaster."— Rodney Dangerfield

In the course of my life, there have been ups and downs and lots of adversity. How I dealt with and overcame was very important to my survival. I learned, through trial and error, that you could be effective no matter what happens. It's about being in control of your life rather than letting external events control your life. That's the real secret of happiness. We all have adversity. We all have letdowns. We all have losses. We all have disappointments. We all have frustrations. None of us will ever achieve everything that we hope to in life.

I had a tough childhood. Life has never been easy, from school to work. I have enjoyed meaningful highs but also experienced great disappointments. At every point where I thought, "I have arrived" or "I have achieved success," I was always let down somehow. People disappoint you and events disappoint you, so it is important that no matter what happens, you have internal control.

Focus on the people and the things that didn't disappoint you but rather bring joy and meaning to your life. You will be surprised how much you have to be grateful for if you let the good images dominate your thoughts.

I focus on my wife, my children and my grandchildren and the pride, joy and laughter they add to my life.

Focus on the surprises, the unexpectedly wonderful events, the blessings G-d showered you with that you didn't necessarily deserve, the good times and the good people that are part of the fabric of your life. You are the accountant determining the positive value of your life.

Always be aware that happiness is an inside job.

Day 175

A basketball coach bumped into an old lady while leaving the game. He looked at her and said, "No offense." The old lady snapped, "You can say that again! And no defense either."

On June 5, 2006, The *New York Times* sports section ran an article entitled "Embarrassing Defeat Fueled Ride to Finals." That piece described how a thirty-six point loss, 112 to 76, by the Miami Heat to the Dallas Mavericks in a nationally televised game acted as their wake up call, inspiring them to win the next ten games in a row and ultimately the 2006 NBA Championship.

The article tells how Pat Riley, the Miami coach, thinks of that ignominious night and smiles, asserting, "From that day on we got better." The humiliation woke the team, changing them into a cohesive group that could win the national championship.

This particular episode can serve as a very powerful lesson. Too often, we fall apart when we suffer a reversal or an adversity, which, as a consequence, inhibits our ability to succeed. Teams often start off behind and then proceed to bounce back and in the end excel and achieve a championship!

It's not those individuals who avoid failures that come out on top in life. Rather, it is those who constantly deal with, confront and overcome the worst experiences and then rise up and achieve the greatest degree of happiness.

Often when people feel helpless in one area of their life, they not only give up in that area, they give up in all areas. A setback at work often causes a failed relationship. An argument with one friend may cause you to lose trust in others. Our helplessness spirals out of control, often impeding our success in all walks of life.

We must try to see why we failed and how we can do better next time, all the while keeping our attitude positive. Challenges must energize us. Failures must motivate us. Many company managers became frozen and ineffective during the economic crisis, but some kept their company's spirits high, re-evaluated the companies goals and redirected them into new projects. It is not the adversity itself but what we do with it that determines our fate. You must gather your wits, capitalize on your strengths, try thinking out of the box, and forge ahead.

Take your failures and learn from them. Successful people are the ones who demonstrate resiliency—the ability to bounce back from reversals, disappointments, failures, and even from seemingly devastating tragedies. Those who are flexible don't get bent out of shape.

Day 176

He can't pitch, catch or field. So, they put him in a league of his own.

Frank Robinson, one of the great ballplayers of all time and the last player to win the triple crown (consisting of the highest batting average, the most home runs and the most runs batted in), one of the most difficult accomplishments in all of sports, could not attend the celebration of that momentous victory because the establishment where the celebration was being held did not serve Blacks. Although the proprietors let Robinson in when they recognized him, he walked right out, angry and humiliated.

The memory of that treatment, Robinson says, helped make him a tenacious competitor and instilled in him an unwavering sense of purpose. He used it to inspire himself to become a Hall of Fame baseball player, team leader and major league manager.

He not only overcame the blatant discrimination and racial abuse, which African-American players experienced in those years, staying in segregated hotels and drinking from "colored only" fountains, but he channeled and mobilized that anger and humiliation to elevate his professional career to unbelievable superstardom. Instead of quitting, as others had done, or being defeated and destroyed by this totally unjust, abusive treatment, he converted this injustice into a passionate inspiration that produced an almost matchless greatness. In 1961, when the Cincinnati Reds won the pennant, Frank Robinson won the national leagues MVP award.

Utilize adversity, so that it energizes you and inspires you to convert that negative experience into a positive elevating condition. All growth emanates from initial hardships. As you can readily learn from any farmer, sweat, tiredness, pain, constant worry about the weather, plowing, and planting ultimately produce a sweet, rich, lavish growth.

It's up to each of us, in fact, it is incumbent on us, to translate and transform adversity into creative new personal growth and ever new heights of inspiration, accomplishment and success—a well-earned gratifying success—that can make us feel triumphant, proud and immensely happier.

"A certain darkness is needed to see the stars. Even if things are not going well, remember that something nice is happening around you. If you look for it, you will find it even in the darkness" (Helen Keller).

Day 177

A man stood before G-d, his heart breaking from the pain and injustice in the world. "Dear G-d," he cried out, "look at all the suffering, the anguish and distress in the world. Why don't you send help?" G-d responded, "I did send help. I sent you."

Times try our souls and through the pain, we grow stronger.

An outstanding scholarly teacher of mine expostulates that "stress is about bringing me to a sufficient frustration level, or more, a sufficient level of suffering which will motivate me to feel that I absolutely must change."

Some things are in our power to control. Some, such as terrible accidents, arbitrary fatal diseases or other fateful events that during a lifetime inevitably befall each of us, are not.

As Dr. Rabbi Abraham Twerski says, "We may be angry at G-d when we are in distress, but we turn to Him for security and pray for the serenity to accept the stresses in life."

When challenges occur, we can choose the light or the darkness. Always choose light. Always make up your mind to be positive in your attitude and in your actions. Mobilize all your resources, become energized and then, as a consequence, you can and will make good things happen to your mind and body as well as for all those around you and even, in many instances, unto the entire world.

Witness the legacy of so many people faced with major adversity or irreversible tragedy that launch meaningful, successful research efforts to deal with the very challenges and tragedies they themselves have been confronted with.

There is a Nietzchian dictum that goes, "That which does not kill me, makes me stronger." It is true that if you successfully overcome adversity and the challenges that confront you, you will feel stronger and develop a certain pride in yourself that can help you feel happier.

A crisis is a terrible thing to waste. It can be the catalyst that jumpstarts one to a new appreciation, a new attitude, a new better way of life. For example, mothers who lost children to drunk drivers established MADD (Mothers Against Drunk Driving) to prevent such tragedies from occurring to other innocent children.

People who suffered from cancer have raised funds and established foundations to do cancer research. Nancy Brinker set up a wonderful and effective breast cancer research foundation in response to this terrible malady.

Kris Carr, a thirty-two-year-old New Yorker diagnosed with a rare and incurable Stage IV cancer called Epithelioid Hemangioendothelioma in her lungs and liver, challenged her disease by adopting a new nutritional lifestyle and published a series of successful self-health books, documentaries, and a wellness website that has 40,000 followers. She has become one of the most prominent health experts on healthy living and has celebrated a decade of thriving with cancer.

When President Ronald Reagan was shot by the mentally deranged John Hinkley, his Press Secretary Jim Brady was permanently brain damaged. Brady's wife, Sarah, launched a successful campaign leading to beneficial gun control legislation against the instant availability of guns to any purchaser without a background check or a minimum waiting period.

Clearly, one can even deal constructively with the most terrible tragedies. Helen Keller, blind, deaf and mute, led a life of real achievement. She became a magnificent role model for every human being, whether disabled or healthy.

Direct your energies in a healthy productive manner, turning sorrow into accomplishment, turning disabilities into successes. It

HAPPINESS GUARANTEED OR YOUR MISERY BACK

will bring fulfillment and help cure the pain with which we are each often challenged.

"It is better to light a candle than to curse the darkness" (Chinese proverb).

Day 178

A student told her mother, "I'm not bright or intelligent enough to write my term paper." "What is it about?" asked her mother. The student replied, "Self-esteem."

You need to like yourself in order to feel happy. Do something that makes you feel good and proud of yourself.

If you like yourself, you feel good. If you depend on others to like you, you will never achieve a significant sense of self-worth. If everyone loves you but you don't like yourself, you are destined to be perpetually unhappy.

You will like yourself when you help someone, give unselfish love, tutor a child, comfort a friend, work for a worthy charity. Start slowly. Visit one sick person a month. Call one friend who is feeling down. Say one kind thing to your spouse. Boost one person's ego. Recognize one nice thing your child has done, even if it's just a pretty scribbling on the floor. Control your temper during one argument. Finish one thing on your to-do list. Help someone carry her groceries. Hold a door open for an elderly person.

Do something for yourself, take a course that enhances your potential, build something, paint a picture, read a book, play ball, cook a meal or bake a cake.

Indulge in these and similar activities to raise your self-esteem, making you proud and pleased with what you do. The best way to feel good is to do good.

There are two types of rings, a marriage "ring" and "suffering." The first is clearly a much-desired choice; the second intrudes upon us without invitation. But, the "rings" that can help significantly in vanquishing adversities in our lives are "caring" and "sharing" smiles and love. It costs so little and means so much and yields its givers the most genuine and worthy joy.

It is indeed better to give than to receive, for in giving, you are the ultimate recipient and true beneficiary. The very act of giving, whether it is love, advice, gifts, or charity, rewards you immediately with an inner, lasting joy.

You don't have to wait for the appreciation or the plaudits of others, which are difficult to attain and are often superficial or phony. They do not make you feel as good as the appreciation and sense of worthiness and greatness that come when you derive the authentic pleasure from the feeling that you have done something good. "To be doing good deeds is man's most glorious task"(Sophocles).

By appreciating the value in yourself, of being "a giver," you will find self-admiration and self-inspiration. As Albert Einstein said, "The value of a man resides in what he gives and not in what he is capable of receiving."

Day 179

Just be yourself, everyone else is already taken.

I like myself because I try to be, and believe that I am, a good person. I try to do what's right. I try to be a good and giving spouse, parent, grandparent, child, relative, friend, and community participant.

I try to give of myself, of my time, of my money, of my energy and of my care. I try to recognize the kindnesses that others have done for me, the joy others have brought to me and the care and concern others have shown me.

I try to be the type of friend I would want to have, the type of person I would like as a role model, the type of child I would like my children to be, the type of spouse I would want my spouse to be.

I try to forgive others, understand others, accept others and love others unconditionally.

I try to be sad for each person's pain and happy for each person's joy.

I try to be the best I can and accomplish the most I can. I try to treat all people with respect, honesty and sensitivity. I try to always put myself in the other person's position and try to comprehend their situation and feelings. I try to give every person the benefit of the doubt. I work on watching what I say and in correctly interpreting and filtering what I hear. I try to lend a listening ear and be of assistance when I can. I do this for others and I do this for myself for when I like who I am, I am happier for it.

HAPPINESS GUARANTEED OR YOUR MISERY BACK

I've learned to appreciate the difference between wanting and needing. I've learned that doing for others or problem solving for others is great but often a person only wants a listening ear, sympathy, encouragement or validation. I've learned to try to empower others but that people, in truth, must empower themselves.

I try to give to those both less and more fortunate than me. I've learned that it's more fulfilling to give than to take and that it's important to give a pauper a piece of fish but so much more amazing to teach him how to fish.

I've learned that it's important to give your child a warm, loving home and permission to leave it (though I pray, they will hopefully come back to visit often).

I've learned that in order to feel good we must stretch in our thinking, in our accepting, in our belief, in our giving, in our learning and in our character growth.

"You are not a good person because you like doing what is right. You are a good person because you do what is right even when you don't like it."

I've learned that the best connection one can make is his connection to G-d, which gives one security, stability, and a vital lifeline.

I've learned that we allow negative events to color our lives rather than focusing on the whole beautiful picture.

I've learned that if I indulge in things that are bad for me, I am happy for the moment and sad in the long run. If I indulge in self-pity, I endure the moment but I am wasting precious G-d given time.

I've learned that every second holds new potential for good or for bad. The moment must be cherished, noticed, appreciated. I've learned to choose to see the positive side in people and situations in life.

I've learned that it's often a struggle to be happy, especially when you are only as happy as your least happy child, parent, relative, and even friend, but that when we don't see the good in this moment, often things get worse and we pray that we could only recapture this moment when things weren't quite as challenging.

I've learned that having people to love and having people to love you back is the greatest gift one has to enjoy, bask in, notice, and thank G-d for.

I've learned that setting a goal, no matter how small, and achieving that goal is extremely satisfying and rewarding.

I've learned that it's important to be honest with yourself and others, like yourself for what you are rather than being disappointed with yourself for what you are not. If you choose to be more, you can be more. I've learned that if you set and meet even the smallest goal, life feels fulfilling.

I've learned that a hug can wipe away a tear and that sometime we have to turn off our thinking brain, throw the problems up to G-d and just force ourselves to think happy and smile.

Day 180

For Sale: Parachute. Only used once, never opened, small stain.

Some people I interviewed as I wrote this book found it amazingly effective to pour their emotions into newly directed endeavors, such as expressing themselves by painting on a canvass, putting into writing their innermost thoughts which became their short stories or novelettes, composing their own unique poetry, or shaping and molding clay into creative sculptures (or even not so "creative" sculptures). All of these activities they found exhilarated them constructively chased away and released them from what was their oppressively heavy-hearted, somber depression and generated for them a healthy transformation. It helped to unburden them and, in fact, it served to invigorate and revitalize them, so as to once again help them feel hopeful, exuberant and zestful.

New, intriguing, activities can likewise prove tremendously enticing and enthralling and generate in you an enchanting, uplifting salvation thereby producing a winning and fascinating new lease on life. You may find that for you too this can be the kind of strategic tactic that will yield astonishingly gratifying results. At the very least, it's potentially one more possible road map to consider and to follow whenever you are hit with the overwhelming feeling that life has saddled you with calamitous adversity, dejection and grouchiness. It can help navigate you to a renewed sense of the excitement that life can offer and thereby instill a passionate new lust for life which will, in turn, invigorate and elevate your spirits and inspire a hopeful, radiant mood and a propitious state of mind. It can and will engender that very sense of happiness that is our ongoing ultimate quest.

Choose a new activity—try skydiving. I am told it gives you new perspective and a new appreciation of life.

Day 181

The psychiatrist said to his new patient, "I'm not aware of your problem so perhaps you could start at the very beginning." "Of course," replied the patient. "In the beginning, I created the heavens and the earth…"

Get involved. Be involved. Control your inner self. We must see ourselves as captains of our lot in life—the vessel we command. We travel the sea of trials and tribulations. The voyage is as long as the days of our lives. Since, as "captains," we are responsible for the welfare of all that surrounds us, the most banal deeds become imbued with meaning. Every turn in life carries tremendous possibilities.

We all have our problems. Decide that you can meet and defeat even the most horrible thing that can possibly happen to you and then you will be able to put your fears and worries to rest.

In life, there are only two things to worry about: those things that you can control and those that you can't. When we live like "captains," responsible for our lives and the lives of those around us, we feel empowered to deal with life's challenges and we too will come into contact with our essence, causing our lives to be imbued with tremendous purpose and meaning.

Create your own heaven on earth and steer your ship through the storm, over the waves, towards happiness.

Day 182

"I couldn't wait for success, so I went on without it!"
—Jonathan Winters

None of us ever achieves total, absolute success. It just doesn't exist. Not in this world anyway. That's not stated to discourage you, only to ensure against your being disappointed by harboring or pursuing unrealistic, unachievable expectations. We will never achieve total knowledge but that should not deter us from learning as much as we can. It's the striving to ever improve and better ourselves that distinguishes us from all other living things. It's the chase, the quest itself, the pursuit of happiness as one moves up the ladder towards the eventual goal that is gratifying and fulfilling.

Even though striving for the ideal of absolute happiness is not possible, working towards, reaching for that exalted goal, will dramatically and meaningfully enhance your life and your capacity to achieve substantially greater happiness.

As Zelig Pliskin relates in the preface of his excellent book, *Gateway to Happiness*, a teacher of his encouraged, "You might not catch any stars as you try reaching for them, but at least you won't get your hands stuck in the mud."

Go for it. Even if you could, it's not important to catch a star. You still will be a real winner in the happiness race and achieve the most important thing—enviable "stardom," in that most critical of all contests—the competition, the goal of being a champion in your own life's pursuit of happiness. That's the ultimate goal for all of us.

HAPPINESS GUARANTEED OR YOUR MISERY BACK

Your life is your personal Olympics. Achieving satisfaction and happiness is life's ultimate prize! Work at it like you're going for the highest *gold* medal. It's every bit as important and far longer lasting and worthwhile.

In the process of pursuing your goals, you improve, become a better person, become more mature, and become more knowledgeable. You attain a greater self-respect and self-admiration and that will make you feel proud and produce a sense of genuine joy and happiness.

We absolutely have a right, and obligation, to strive for the best, to work at it, to make it happen, and to have the highest goals and the most exciting and enticing dreams. However, we must keep our expectations at least realistic, if not deliberately low. That way, if we don't expect too much—for example, actually finding a knight in shining armor or the perfect mate—and if we understand and fully realize that human beings are imperfect at best, we'll never feel let down.

Peter M. Senge writes in *The Fifth Discipline* that a problem is "the creative tension between the way it is and the way you want it to be." Life is always the creative tension between these two. It is important to strive for the most, but to want only what we need and, most importantly, to appreciate everything we've got.

Day 183

This is what he knows about art: if it hangs on a wall, it's a painting, and if he has to walk around it, it's sculpture.

Tsereteli, the Russian artist/sculptor, who has created some of the largest memorials, was given a hard time when he created a memorial for New Jerseyans who lost their lives at the World Trade Center on 9/11. The sculpture was rejected by Jersey City because it was thought to be "too big and ostentatious." Tsereteli did not give up and eventually his "tear drop" sculpture was enthusiastically accepted by Mayor Joseph Diora of Bayonne and placed on its shoreline. There, like the Statue of Liberty, it is visible to ships passing into New York Harbor.

Mr. Tsereteli said he was far happier with this site than the original one that had been selected in Jersey City. And regarding the controversy, he said, "I always look forward; I never look back. To appreciate art takes time. People thought da Vinci was nuts. What famous artist is not controversial?"

Indeed, for many years, critics argued about the site of the Statue of Liberty and the Eiffel Tower, yet, as the *New York Times* pointed out, "Without those renowned symbols, these places would be unimaginable."

Never get discouraged; keep working at overcoming and succeeding. "By persistence, the snail reached the ark."

Day 184

When we are flat on our backs, there is no way to look but up!

Dr. Seuss, the beloved author of more than forty-six children's books, was originally considered too outlandish. His first book, *And to Think That I Saw it on Mulberry Street,* (1937), was rejected by twenty-eight publishers before it finally found a home at Random House. It was one of the company's most prescient decisions.

Former Random House President Bennett Cerf once remarked, "I've published any number of great writers, from William Faulkner to John O'Hara, but there's only one genius on my author's list. His name is Ted Geisel." Before Cerf discovered this, Geisel had to put up with frustration and disheartening disappointments.

Stephen King, after having his first novel rejected thirty times, threw it in the garbage. His wife retrieved it and encouraged him to finish it. Today, King has sold over 350 million copies of his books, besides his many movies.

Steven Spielberg, one of the most prolific filmmakers of all times, who created *Schindler's List, Jurassic Park, E.T.* and *Jaws*, was rejected from USC, the film school of his choice. Later on, USC gave him an honorary degree and made him a trustee of the university.

Steve Smith, a successful astronaut, was rejected five times before he was finally accepted. He never gave up; because he continued to believe in himself, he did achieve his dreams.

In *Inspirational Stories* or *Why You Shouldn't Listen to Anyone Who Says 'You Can't,'* Catherine Pratt writes that Walt Disney was turned down by over one hundred banks when he tried to get funding to develop Disneyland. In fact, he also suffered several bankruptcies before developing it. Furthermore, he was fired from his job at a newspaper for "not having good ideas and lacking imagination."

These, and countless others, persevered despite obstacles and were able to turn their dreams into a reality. They did not give up. Don't you!

My grandfather, in his ever brilliant wisdom and ability to pass on sage advice, in order to encourage me to never despair, would tell a story of a soldier whose sword broke, so that faced by devastation and fear, gave up and fled the battlefield. A second soldier quickly grabbed that sword, pursued and killed the king and won the war.

"When the world says, 'Give up,' hope whispers, 'Try it one more time'" (Anonymous).

Day 185

It took Brahms five years to compose his memorable lullaby. He kept falling asleep at the piano.

Try singing a song you love. It can serve to release your frustration. Military experts from all over Europe gathered together after Napoleon's defeat, wishing to uncover the secret of his many victories in battle. After extensive research, they attributed much of Napoleon's success to the musicians he hired to play throughout the soldier's camps. With the happy melodies and rousing marches they were commissioned to play, the musicians kept the troops in good spirits, vanquishing despair and filling the men with hope and courage.

Singing can change your mood from down to up and from sad to happy. It's definitely a technique worth trying. In the course of my research, I found that many individuals attest to the fact that this exercise really works for them.

In the midst of the most sustained, demoralizing and destructive bombing of Great Britain during World War II, British citizens sang the hopeful, positive, forward looking, uplifting song "There'll be blue birds over the white cliffs of Dover, tomorrow, just you wait and see."

Remember, and even repeat loudly, the words from the Broadway play *Annie*, in which Annie, at her saddest moment, starts to sing, "The sun will come out tomorrow."

One of the best pieces of advice on how to achieve happiness is provided in the lyrics in the song "Look for the Silver Lining." As a matter of fact, in its opening verse it conveys, "Here is the happy secret of it all." This really is the best secret to learn and to constantly practice. Sing upbeat, inspiring lyrics that envision a hopeful, better future, beyond the immediate tribulations currently agonizing you.

When things are at their worst, try singing. It surely can't hurt and it may very well make you feel good.

Day 186

Don't give up; Moses was once a basket case.

F. Scott Fitzgerald wrote, "One should be able to see things as hopeless and yet be determined to make them otherwise." The fact is that we have little control over life's circumstances. We are confronted with what happens and with what is. Ten percent of life is what happens to you, and 90 percent is how you deal with it! What we can and must do is to make the best of whatever situation we are dealt. The most effective first step is to take control of your mind and your thought processes, so that you approach even the grim parts of life with a positive, hopeful attitude. This can help you achieve the maximum happiness.

Take charge; decide you are the boss. Get active! If you can do something to solve the problem, do so. Then, you're not just a victim letting it happen to you, but a dynamic entity, a factor in bringing about a change for the better.

If it is a situation that is completely beyond solving, then find an activity that will help you to feel that despite the mishap, the misfortune, even the tragedy; there is still much that exists in this world which can bring you satisfaction and self-gratification and fulfillment.

Consciously initiate an action that will serve to help you quickly break out of that rut and cheer you up. Willfully, do whatever you can to distract yourself from your hurt, that can excite, inspire and uplift you and help you break out of the counterproductive, dysfunctional "rut" that can only unnerve, agitate and demoralize you.

Indulge yourself in some mouthwatering, chocolate ice cream read a great novel, go out and hit some tennis balls, fantasize, buy something, till your garden, go to a zoo, lay on a warm beach, get absorbed in a challenging game of chess, help a sick child or console a mother who lost her baby. Take a warm bubble bath and a luxurious massage. See a show, go to the opera, visit with friends or just sit and talk to a best friend, your spouse or anyone who makes you feel good when you talk to them. Play with your children or grandchildren, travel, even start a new adventure you always thought about or a new relationship that can bring you new pleasure and love.

Focus your mind on wonderfully constructive things and do activities that will distract and cheer you and you will find that despite your troubles, you will feel better.

A study showed that people who just thought about watching their favorite movie actually raised their endorphin levels by 27 percent. (Endorphins inhibit the transmission of pain signals and may also produce a feeling of euphoria very similar to that produced by other opioids).

"Pain is temporary. Quitting lasts forever." The trick, and the challenge, is to enjoy life. Don't wait for life to get better, make it better.

As Hans Christian Anderson so aptly wrote, "Enjoy life. There's plenty of time to be dead."

Day 187

I try not to worry about the future, so I take each day one anxiety attack at a time.

During the 9/11 memorial in 2004 at the site of the World Trade Center where the most horrendous, terrorist mass killing of innocent men and women had occurred, a TV interviewer asked a man from North Carolina why he had come. The man explained that coming back every year gives him perspective, reminding him not to get aggravated over the innumerable hardships, reversals, irritations and difficulties of everyday life.

A middle-aged man, interviewed while reassembling his house which was devastated by Hurricane Charlie even as it was being threatened again by Hurricane Ivan, showed remarkable upbeat resiliency, "We just have to get on with our lives." Even in the face of the most distressing and agonizing events, it's most useful and constructive to move to the future with hope and optimism.

Senator Joseph Biden of Delaware lost his wife and two children in a car accident. When asked by David Letterman how he had endured and functioned in light of this terrible tragedy, he said his father had always told him, "Get up." With two small children to raise, he had to "get up."

When life is not going as you'd hoped, put things in perspective, get up and get on with your life. "Three grand essentials to happiness in this life are something to do, something to love and something to hope for."

Day 188

Swallow a frog in the morning and nothing worse will happen to you or the frog for the rest of the day.

"The game of life is not so much in holding a good hand as playing a poor hand well" (H.T. Leslie Don).

Don Hewitt, the genius producer of the perennially top-rated TV show *60 Minutes*, was honored at the Museum of TV and Radio celebrating his 50th anniversary at CBS. There he said he couldn't explain why he was so lucky and so blessed to have been involved with this exciting original magazine news show and all its wonderful people: Mike Wallace, Ed Bradley, Morley Safer, Leslie Stahl, Dan Rather, Andy Rooney, and on and on. He said he learned so much by being exposed to these individuals and the vast knowledge they offered. He loved the thrilling opportunity to do enlightening, stimulating stories, especially ones that made him think, "I didn't know that!" For example, he said, "Until *60 Minutes* did a piece on smoking, I never realized that it caused impotency in men and women, with devastating effects on their sex lives."

When asked how he started *60 Minutes*, Hewitt told about a former boss at a TV station who said to him, "Don, you're too big for this job." The comment made him feel good until one of his associates exclaimed, "Don, don't you understand? You've been fired."

He was devastated, depressed, and even suicidal at the ignominy and the hurt of being fired. For several months, he was miserable and felt hopelessly defeated. Then, he talked with Mike Wallace about producing TV news stories similar to print magazines. The format evolved into the most successful show of its kind in the history of television.

As a result of apparent adversity, Hewitt reached a happiness he otherwise may never have known.

After he was fired by Maryland Public TV in 2002 at age sixty-nine, following years as the host of a popular financial talk show, Louis Rukeyse wisely observed, "Pessimism is a losing strategy." He went on to do a new and better show. His upbeat philosophy largely accounted for his success on the TV show and in his entire life.

We all need inspiration during trying, painful times. Believe that you can overcome, and indeed convert, what seemingly are life-destroying misfortunes. The vision of a hopefully brighter future to come is one of the most useful and effective means of achieving a sense of happiness. We must learn from people like Don Hewitt and Louis Rukeyser, each of whom built a fantastic castle on the ashes of destruction.

"Success is the ability to go from one failure to another with no loss of enthusiasm. Hope is being able to see that there is light despite all of the darkness" (Desmond Tutu).

Day 189

The skies opened and the rain poured down. Noah looked up at his son and said, "I knew I shouldn't have washed the ark this morning."

Don't look back! Whatever happened, happened. Move on and spur yourself forward by optimistically thinking that lots of good things are ahead for you. If you think that way, it will actually help make it become a "self-fulfilling" reality.

Oprah Winfrey was sexually abused from ages ten through fourteen and felt ashamed, guilty and terribly fearful that her secret would come out. When her secret became public, she was worried that people would consider her "wicked" and would reject her for what she had done, and particularly for being pregnant at age fourteen.

But, she asserts, it helped her immensely that her father advised her, "What you have done is in the past and you alone get to determine what your future will be." Clearly, that counseling was effective. What an amazing future she determined and created for herself despite her painful past.

"Today is the tomorrow you worried about yesterday" (Dale Carnegie). The secret is to look beyond today.

Day 190

"In the book of life, the answers aren't in the book."—Charlie Brown

A very brilliant, learned and scholarly woman, whom I greatly admire, told me that when she was eight years old, a couple vacationing in a nearby summer bungalow was killed. Her father, a renowned scholar and spiritual leader, saw how this tragedy overwhelmed her; he told her to think of her heart as having many pockets. She should place this terribly hurtful thought in one of those pockets and draw positive, happy thoughts from the other pockets to the forefront of her mind.

Later in life, when this woman lost her twenty-one-year-old daughter, her father's earlier advice and guidance helped her contend with this devastating loss. By putting the painful thought in one of the pockets of her heart, she was able to go on living.

In the course of our lives, each one of us will inevitably be subjected to painfully depressing tragic experiences from which, if we can't adapt and somehow effectively move on, can paralyze us or even threaten our sanity. It may help you to deal with these untoward, potentially permanently devastating experiences by inculcating this unique wisdom and placing, indeed forcing, such of these into one of the pockets in your heart, letting it out only occasionally, reluctantly and briefly while drawing out of one of the other pockets positive, uplifting and inspiring experiences and memories that will induce a happier frame of mind and constructively liberating and rehabilitating emotions.

None of us can totally avoid adverse, even wretched experiences. What we can and must learn is how to most effectively initiate, implement and accomplish those adjustments to help us best live through, "weather the storm" and to overcome, and then to revitalize, reenergize and triumphantly achieve a successful adaptation. We can then effectively move on to a not only more bearable and contented future but also indeed to a resiliently exuberant and heartwarming one.

The leading character in the movie *Mrs. Doubtfire* articulates incisively and consequently promulgates what is clearly a wonderful approach: "The bad things fade away and I only adhere to the fond memories."

Day 191

"Every day begins with an act of courage and hope: getting out of bed."—Mason Cooley

"We must free ourselves of the hope that the sea will ever rest. We must learn to sail in high winds" (Aristotle Onassis). Life will always have its ups and downs and we must learn to survive the rough times.

Happiness is not euphoria, a perennial high, endless instant gratification, or the absence of all problems. That can never be. Happiness is making life work for you through a constant commitment to control your life and your thinking by your not being overwhelmed by what happens to you, but rather by what you do about what happens to you. To achieve this, you must view the problem as merely a bump in the road of life (maybe a major, intimidating, life-threatening bump, but still only a bump to get over, around, through or to somehow completely disregard) and to avoid its implications, so that you can avert it as a factor in your life.

Your aim is not to deny reality. Problems for all of us are real. There is no evading that fact. Only, perhaps, in death are we free of problems and that's not a viable or worthwhile option. Living—the very word and condition—is inevitably almost synonymous with problems. That being the case, we must see that as our challenge. It's our mountain to climb. It's our race to win. It's our puzzle to solve and resolve. It's our story to write. It's our channel to swim, to overcome the cold, the tiredness, the sharks, the fear, the improbability. It's our life to live. And, the way to live it is with optimism, seeing reality and then seeing it with a sense of optimism beyond any prevailing wretched reality. It's in that way that your mind, how you think, not what is actually happening, but how you let your mind perceive it that is the ultimate determinant of the quality of your life and the degree of happiness, or for that matter unhappiness, that you will experience and achieve.

Don't let external events run you or define you. You are separate from these external events. They will pass. Believe they will pass. Don't mope. Don't even expect them to suddenly get resolved or disappear, but develop the capacity to appreciate any little improvement. Appreciate the process towards the solution and you will begin to feel better, more optimistic and hopeful. In the last analysis, we are creatures who live on hope. That is perhaps our single greatest blessing. Hopeful thinking can get you out of the fear realm into the appreciation realm. "Remember: you are the only person who thinks in your mind! You are the power and authority in your world."

Day 192

If chocolate is the answer, the question is irrelevant.

Think big thoughts and relish small pleasures.

    I WISH FOR YOU

I wish for you…
Comfort in difficult days
Rainbows to follow the clouds
Laughter upon your lips
Sunsets to warm your heart
Gentle hugs when spirits sag
Friendships to brighten your being
Beauty for your eyes to see
Confidence for when you doubt
Faith so that you can believe
Courage to know yourself
Patience to accept the truth
And love to complete your life.

And if you can't have all that…
Then I wish you enough chocolate to make it through the tough times. (Anonymous)
    "Do what makes you happy. Be with those who make you smile and laugh as much as you breathe" (Rachel Ann Nunes).

Day 193

Gravity always lets you down.

"Experience is not what happens to a man. It's what a man does with what happens to him"(Aldous Huxley).

How can you be happier in your marriage? How can you make more sales this month? How can you be a better parent? How can you achieve higher grades? How can you improve your tennis game? How can you help someone in pain? How can you make your mark on this world? Do what you love, and love what you do. Deliver more than you promise and get ahead.

Have something special you are living for, a goal or dream, something you would love to see come about, something you can bring to realization.

When you have an idea, a dream that consumes you and for which you become a crusader, enormous power will come from your intense dedication to a cause you believe in and work to achieve. It makes your life meaningful and worthwhile. Your self-respect, self-image and ego will grow enormously. You will feel positively wonderful about yourself. That's real happiness!

Don't be afraid to work hard. As Theodore Roosevelt so wisely said, "Nothing in the world is worth having or worth doing unless it takes effort, pain, difficulty… I have never in my life envied a human being who led an easy life. I have envied a great many people who led difficult lives and led them well."

Think like a doer and you will be viewed and indeed feel like a winner. Successful people work for their success. As Albert Einstein said, "It's not that I'm so smart, it's just that I stay with problems longer."

Day 194

"By trying, we can easily learn to endure adversity. Another man's, I mean."—Mark Twain

Make the necessary personal investment in self-education and training. Pain serves a purpose. Athletes say, "No pain, no gain." In one's body, pain is a signal that something is wrong and we need to take action to correct it. If we did not possess that mechanism, we would be robbed of the warning system that helps us survive. G-d forbid one loses that capacity, what a calamitous and dangerous existence, and probably a very short one, that would be.

Pain, though we hate it, is useful. You might even call it a gift. Yes, the instant we have it, we must do everything we can to minimize the period that we must tolerate the pain. We obviously want to increase the pain-free moments of our lives, the pleasant, pleasurable moments.

Pain warns a mother of a child's discomfort, or his possible needs, as he cries out. Without pain, few of us would have survived long. Appreciate the gains that come from frustration and pain.

Physical and mental pain or anguish is an inescapable part of life. Comfort yourself, as Mayor Ed Koch did when he lost his re-election attempt. He counseled himself saying, "There is a good reason for everything." He told me, he now lives a far better, more diverse, exciting and financially rewarding life than he ever dreamed of. He became a popular radio talk-show host, wrote a stimulating column for the *New York Post*, became a TV media star as a courtroom judge, and launched a very successful new career as a partner with a major law firm.

There is life after pain and loss. The important thing is to know that and to move on.

Day 195

A few days ago, while working on the roof, I fell off. Torn and bloody, I managed to make it back into the house. My son asked, "What did you bring me?"

So many parents think that breaking their necks and working endless hours so they can attain success and buy all the things they want for their children is the important objective. That's a gross misconception. Ask any grown child, even from the richest, most successful family, what they value most as they look back. The material things, the money, the objects all take a backseat to the time they spent with Mom and Dad, the lessons they taught, the stories they told, the adventures they shared, the warm conversations they had and the moments of warm affection.

I doubt that many parents regret that they didn't work hard enough to give their kids more material wealth or regret that they didn't spend more time at work, but almost every parent, particularly fathers, regret that they didn't spend more time with their kids.

A house is just a house, no matter how big, how expensive, how luxurious. It only becomes a home when companionship, love and warmth are introduced and made part of it, and it is only then that it becomes a place of excitement, serenity and happiness. The most modest house can become the happiest place. The most expensive estate can be a place of depression and misery.

Bring happiness into your heart and home. It's what you make of what you have that makes a world of difference.

Day 196

Sometimes, I wake up grumpy. Sometimes, I let him sleep...

One of the greatest gifts a parent can give his child is security, confidence in his parent's unconditional love and confidence in his own ability to succeed.

The same holds true for a spouse. The most precious thing you can give the one you love or that the person you love can give to you is the security that you love him and are loved by him unwaveringly, that you are not continuously judging and questioning or being judged, studied, or doubted, despite any reasonable differences and disagreements.

This rule holds true in all circumstances and with every person you encounter. Everyone wants to be accepted, understood and even forgiven. You appreciate a boss who, despite setbacks, stays firm in his belief in your ability. You value a friend, a neighbor, a teacher, anyone who believes in you, whether its in your ability to succeed, or your willingness to just try, or someone who retains faith in your potential or in your goals, or even just in your gumption and willingness to face and fight to overcome challenges. Everyone values someone who doesn't give up on them, even when, they themselves have given up on themselves.

True happiness comes from being surrounded by these types of people and inculcating their view of you within yourself. Just as you should be there for others, your circle of friends can and should encourage you to be all you can be. By believing we can be and convincing ourselves to reach a bit higher, we are all capable of being more than we are.

All too often, life's challenges, wounds and even shatters our very fragile self-esteem. It is up to each of us to incorporate the belief in ourselves, to ceaselessly strengthen our inner confidence and the self-worth of our children, our spouses and all those we come in contact with.

It is each of our thought processes, hopefully teamed with the help of our past ingrained learning, our positive experiences and our amazing support system, when coupled by extreme effort, which give each of us the tools and the self-confidence to rebuild our hopes and dreams and the happiness we crave.

Day 197

I have what no millionaire has—no money!

    Material wealth does not produce the feeling of emotional contentment and happiness that we all hope to achieve. It's not one's net worth but one's self-worth that engenders the psychological enchantment, gratification and truly fulfilling pride that constitutes a sense of inner satisfaction and happiness.

    A businessman who sold his business for over $500 million was emotionally miserable. He worked one hundred hours a week to provide the financial security and lifestyle he assumed his family wanted, which he himself did not enjoy growing up. His daughter, resentful that he did not give her any of his time and love, became involved with an unaccomplished older, married man and had his child, while his son, for whom he had such great hopes, feeling the same deprivation of his father's time and love, became a conspicuous and flagrant drug addict.

    Many people in our materialistic society believe that by getting rich they will achieve happiness. Accordingly, they spend their lives pursuing financial success, only to find that, even after acquiring great wealth, they are deeply disappointed. Materialism does not mean happiness if at the same time you haven't learned to inculcate a positive mindset and an invigorating sense of uplifting self-worth.

    Always be cognizant that the things that money can't buy are more valuable than the things that money can buy.

Day 198

"Its money. I remember it from when I was single."
—Billy Crystal

 Money can be and often is lost, or even if it isn't, most of us who acquire great wealth learn that it is an illusion that having money leads to happiness. In fact, it often leads to unhappiness. What you thought would be the answer—cash—just doesn't do it. It is deeply disappointing. Unless you find a more genuinely worthy goal, you'll be let down and left unfulfilled.
 I have had friends that had more money and more priceless possessions than almost anyone can ever hope to have and, in addition, were considered to be major successes in their careers, but nevertheless, they suffered heartbreaking depression and in two cases were even driven to committing suicide despite their enormous riches.
 I have had other friends that literally worked full time just to get by, but had a positive, always hopeful attitude, did things which they enjoyed and who had developed a sense of prideful "self-worth," that have lived happy, fulfilling and genuinely successful (in the gratification they experienced) lives.
 Remember, no one ever dies wishing he had spent more time at his business. But, most of us wish we had spent more time and invested more of our efforts with our loved ones, especially our children, who can give us such really unimaginably worthwhile dividends and rewards.
 Re-examine your lifestyle. Prioritize. Put your "real" wealth before your material wealth.

Day 199

"I feel bad that I don't have children. I'm afraid that if I don't have kids, my grandchildren will not have parents."—Paula Poundstone

Figure out how rich you are. Count your assets. Do you have a child whom you love and who brings you joy and pride (even if not all the time)?

Would you take one billion dollars in exchange for your child? No way! Not even five billion dollars! There is no amount of money that would make you give up your child, so you are worth at least one billion dollars.

Even if you are losing money in the stock market, or your business is terrible, even bankrupt, or you are broke, you must still recognize your luck. Be aware and appreciate this fact that on your balance sheet you have an asset that's worth at least one billion dollars. This is clearly so since you won't agree to accept one billion dollars in exchange for that child.

So, even if you have little else in the way of assets or even if you have liabilities in the form of debt that you may feel is a gnawing burden, on balance, against that one billion dollar priceless asset you have, you are still immensely blessed and truly rich.

Suppose you don't have that asset of immeasurable worth—a child. Do you have your health, or at least relatively good health? Almost none of us are without some deficiency, pain or malady at one time or another or for many of us even constantly, but assuming you are relatively healthy, ask yourself would you give up your health

HAPPINESS GUARANTEED OR YOUR MISERY BACK

and accept a crippling, debilitating, constricting, constantly painful condition for one million, ten million or even one billion dollars? Hardly! Nobody in his or her right mind would do that.

Do you have your eyesight? What would you do if you were blind? How much would you pay to see? Certainly, you'd pay every last cent you had and then some. You can see. You're clearly rich.

What if you had no arms or legs, no hearing, no speech? What would you pay to obtain them? Anything? Everything? Of course! You're clearly rich in the most vital measures of what you need in life.

Recognize how rich you are. You have priceless assets on your balance sheet, your health, your family, your friends, your abilities, and your faith. Value that immeasurable wealth. Don't take your wealth for granted just because you don't deposit it in a vault. Appreciate the truly priceless G-d-given assets that you possess every waking moment of every day. It's only if we stop to appreciate that which we have, that it provides happiness.

Day 200

There is a light at the end of every tunnel. Just pray it's not a train.

Too many of us are led to believe from a very early age that if we can only be successful and become wealthy, we will be everlastingly, enormously happy. Yet, Howard Hughes, one of the wealthiest men in the world with $2.2 billion at that time and an envied tycoon who lived in the most sensational penthouse in Las Vegas for his last twenty-two years, complained that he never had one day of happiness.

So, what does make one happy? You make yourself happy by developing a positive optimistic attitude, teaching yourself how to appreciate what you possess, counting your blessings, and visualizing your future as holding interesting, exciting adventures and inspiring promise. Happiness is within your very own power and not through such shallow externals as popularity, fame, material possessions or wealth.

It's the remarkable (G-d-given) ability, which fortunately you do possess, to control your own state of mind that ultimately will determine the degree and nature of your happiness. It is the ability to look at yourself, at your life and at the world around you, and to decide, despite all the negatives, life is good.

The truth comes to be that which we convince our minds it is. Men who have become billionaires can be miserable, yet survivors of the Holocaust who experienced the most horrific of nightmares, somehow, miraculously, survive and build happy lives. They do this by controlling their thoughts and managing to focus on the hopeful

HAPPINESS GUARANTEED OR YOUR MISERY BACK

positives of the future rather than surrendering to the hopelessness of the unchangeable past. Nothing is forever. Even the horrendous Holocaust came to an end and the optimistic survivors live on. Shalom Aleichim wrote, "You've got to survive, even if it kills you!"

You have a voice in what you are and what you stand for and how you interpret unfolding events. If you take the wrong approach or the wrong attitude, if you give up control, you become ineffectual and devastated. On the other hand, if you choose to follow the upbeat path, life will become an ongoing, exciting adventure and you will be the master of your own fate.

Each morning, when you open your eyes, say to yourself, I, not events, have the power to make me happy or unhappy today. I can choose which it shall be. Yesterday is finished, tomorrow hasn't arrived yet, I have just one day, today, and I am going to make it a happy one.

Day 201

Hard work never killed anybody. But then, relaxing is responsible for very few casualties.

Paul Guenther was the chairman of the New York Philharmonic, a securities analyst, a banker, the head of a brokerage firm, on the board of a number of nonprofits, and a Catskills farmer, all of which he did with admirable success. He attributed his successes to his father who told him, "Do what you want to do—but do it well."

He professes, "I've had the chance of doing what I loved in the world's greatest and most generous city." He very clearly seems to be a very successful and immensely satisfied man.

The profound formula, which his father gave him, is one of the special secret axioms—a straightforward golden rule, which will go a really long way toward fulfilling our mission to bring you success and happiness. As Winston Churchill said, "Real success is finding your life work in the work that you love." Mark Twain declared, "If you love what you do, you never work a day in your life."

Michael Bloomberg asserts that he found the greatest high is staying busy, that working hard at something you can be excited by is more than satisfying—it's fun, it's even thrilling and perhaps is the most important contributor to a person's happiness.

In strategizing life's plan, amongst the highest priorities should be determining what you most enjoy doing and then see if you can design your education, so that it will help you attain a career or a private business endeavor that will entail that activity.

HAPPINESS GUARANTEED OR YOUR MISERY BACK

Do and pursue what you love. If you are smart enough, or perhaps lucky enough, you can end up experiencing what legendary hard-striving Thomas Edison described when he proclaimed, "I think work is the world's greatest fun."

Day 202

Bankruptcy is when you plan for early retirement and your company beats you to it.

David Hayden, was a dot-com entrepreneur, who at one time was worth over two hundred million dollars, owning a 7,000-square-foot mansion in one of San Francisco's wealthiest neighborhoods, other property in Sun Valley, Idaho, and a luxurious Gulfstream jet. Now, he finds himself essentially broke. He is being sued for thirty-eight million dollars, and is selling his furniture and paintings to pay his bills. It could force him to file for personal bankruptcy.

Nevertheless, despite the terrible situation, which he attributes to the bad advice and mismanagement of his finances by the very same financial institution that is now suing him for the thirty-eight million, the *New York Times* reports, "He appears to harbor surprisingly little bitterness."

"It's better in the end," Mr. Hayden asserts. "Otherwise, you focus on stuff that doesn't matter. It's just stuff and it's important not to let stuff get in the way of what's important—people, happiness, health, children and putting money in the right places."

At this very time, when he is going through these exceedingly troubling and hurtful events, he is appropriately and wisely, resiliently launching a new entrepreneurial venture called Jeteye. Forever fighting back and moving forward with hope and working to realize new dreams in the future is the ideal way to confront and overcome adversity and still retain a sense of optimism and happiness.

"A challenge only becomes an obstacle when you bow to it" (Ray A. Davis).

Day 203

**Pupil: I don't think I deserved a zero on this test.
Teacher: I agree, but that's the lowest mark I could give you!**

Life is a test…if it were the real thing, we would have been told where to go and what to do.

When you are faced with a challenge, take the attitude "This is my test. G-d has given me this test for my benefit and I am going to pass it. I am going to grow stronger because of it."

The more we handle, the more capable we become. The more we are aware of our own ability to surmount life's obstacles, the more confident we become in ourselves and the more able we are to deal with the next challenge which comes our way.

You can't enjoy your challenges but you can recognize their benefit. Don't be daunted by your challenges; rather, be spurred on by the knowledge that this is your opportunity for growth and expansion. Each test you pass moves you further along.

When a couple passes a test together, it becomes a building block in strengthening their relationship.

Remain happy and upbeat even in the face of challenge. As Albert Einstein so brilliantly put it, "In the middle of every difficulty lies opportunity."

Playing in the penultimate game of any football career, the Indianapolis Colts linebacker Gary Brackett was accurately described in an article by Mark Cannizzaro of the *New York Post* as someone who "faced more land mines" than most human beings. Within the span of sixteen months, he lost his father to a heart condition at age fifty-seven, his mother to complications from a routine hysterectomy at age fifty-one, and his brother to cancer after he had given him his own bone marrow in an effort to save him.

Brackett summarized, so incisively, his ability to withstand this disastrous series of overwhelmingly painful tragedies by assuring himself that everything happens for a reason and "I guess the reason was to make me stronger. Now, I feel I can accomplish anything I put my mind to."

It's this kind of positive thinking that moved him, despite the crushing adversities, to reach the very epitome of his profession and to be part of a "super" bowl. By facing life's challenges with this kind of constructive mental attitude, you can achieve genuinely contented and noble happiness.

"I am not a product of my circumstances, I am a product of my decisions" (Stephen Covey).

Day 204

Well, today was a total waste of makeup.

Heidi Klum, one of the most beautiful models in the world, was asked, "Were you ever turned down by a man you liked?" She answered, "Yes, of course, even more than once."

No matter how great you are, how special you may be, how apparently gifted or fortunate you seem to be, at some point of your life, you are bound to experience disapproval, even disappointment, and will countenance disillusionment and frustration.

Sometimes, far too often, you look around and see someone who is apparently very successful and very blessed and you may feel jealous and envious, or at least wish you could be so lucky as to be in that persons place, only to learn later how unhappy and depressed that person is because of something he has sought and failed to control or accomplish. No one always gets everything he or she wants. Even people, who seem to have everything they want, just don't.

Growing up, every time I went to the beauty parlor I would see this tall beautiful, meticulously made-up woman, who had just come from playing tennis to have her hair done. She wore lots of expensive jewelry and she looked like she had it "all." One day, sitting next to my sister, she burst out crying and told my sister that it was the anniversary of the death of one of her twin sons. She said that when she lost this child, she was beyond devastated and a therapist advised her that in order to be able to go on with her life, she had to create a routine. From then on, every single day she forces herself to get up, get dressed, play tennis and go to the beauty parlor. Suddenly, I came to understand that what looked to outsiders like the dream life was in reality a torturous attempt to survive and thrive. No one can know or understand what anyone else is going through and what challenges the next one is facing. We each must accept and appreciate our own circumstances and predicaments.

Happiness is a product of feeling blessed and deriving joy from what you do have. It's all attitudinal. "It isn't our position but our disposition that makes us happy."

Day 205

An oil company's public relations man said, "Of course, we spilled eight hundred thousand gallons of oil in the ocean, but after all, who wants a squeaky ocean?"

Philip F. Anschultz, a multi-billionaire, at the very inception of his entrepreneurial business career received a call from one of his supervisors with the bad news that the oil well he was drilling was on fire. If the fire kept burning, it would bankrupt him. But, he saw the bright side. He surmised that the fire meant that he had struck oil, so he quickly went out and contracted to buy up all the land around the area of that burning well.

Not only that, but he invited a Hollywood studio to shoot an episode of a John Wayne thriller showing the legendary oil field firefighter, Red Adair, putting out the blaze.

Mr. Anschultz proclaimed, "There's always a point if you go forward you win." As an outgrowth of that positive, constructive, courageous and emboldened attitude, he is a business tycoon, who controls railroads, real estate, movie theaters, newspapers, telecommunications entities, soccer teams and on and on.

Failure is often a prelude, sometimes even a launching pad toward eventual success. We must not only derive a useful lesson for the future from each failure we experience but we may actually find, as in the case of this billionaire, that it points to the direction and presents the opportunity to the implementation and realization of eventual success.

Don't just get depressed. Get inspired! As Florence Nightingale said, "I attribute my success to this: I never gave or took any excuse."

Day 206

Two golfers were strolling toward the green when they happened to see two women come up behind them. One said, "Here comes my wife with some old witch she must have found in the clubhouse."
The other golfer said, "Mine too!"

Embarrassment is the dismay brought on by public humiliation and is often the stimulus for major depression. The fear that members of one's family or one's community will know something shameful about you often leads to psychological devastation, and in extreme cases, even suicide.

Eugene Black worked himself up from the lowest levels of the economic ladder to become President and CEO and the major shareholder of United Fruit, a Fortune 100 company. It was the largest banana company in the world and important enough for the US Government to send battleships to Central American countries when a United Fruit farm was threatened. This action came to be known in our history books as "gunboat diplomacy."

This rags-to-riches, Horatio Alger storybook tycoon, fearful that his corporation would be embarrassed since it had paid commissions to intermediaries that would be viewed under newly passed legislation as bribes, jumped out of the forty-second-floor window of the Pan Am building in New York, carrying his attaché case along with him.

In the ensuing time period, it was discovered that many major corporations were guilty of similar violations and none was ever

HAPPINESS GUARANTEED OR YOUR MISERY BACK

criminally indicted. Had Eugene Black hung around a little longer, he would have learned and realized that he would not be viewed as the terrible person he obviously perceived he was, which caused his violent self-destruction.

Moreover, if he stayed around, he would have enjoyed seeing his son, Leon Black, become one of the most successful bankers on Wall Street and a billionaire as well as experience the joy of his beautiful grandchildren. What an unnecessary, unfortunate irreversible decision. The trouble is, once you jump you can't make a U-turn.

No one ever needs to take that horribly final escape route. One needs only to control one's thought processes to avoid such self-destructive depression.

Look beyond the immediate seemingly insurmountable, devastatingly embarrassing situation. Survive and be around to live a better day.

Day 207

I've never had money problems. Lack of money problems, yes!

Rabbi Noah Weinberg of Jerusalem, a revered clergyman and religious leader, asked hundreds of people of all ages and of diverse backgrounds, "Would you rather be rich or happy?" The universal answer was, "I'd rather be happy than rich." Rabbi Weinberg continued, "Why don't you stay with me for three months, only ninety days, and we'll teach you to be happy." He was referring to a happiness based on learning to trust that whatever G-d does is for the best, learning to appreciate all we are blessed with, learning to appreciate family, education, talent, the G-d-given things over material wealth and learning to value our spiritual needs.

The almost unanimous response was "I'd love to, but I can't stay."

Rabbi: "Why can't you?"

Respondent: "Because my airline ticket back home is booked for next Tuesday. It's impossible!"

Rabbi: "But who made the reservation?"

Respondent: "I did."

Rabbi: "So you can change it or cancel it?"

Respondent: "Yes, but I really need to get back. I have things to do."

Rabbi: "But wouldn't you like to learn how to be happy?"

Respondent: "Of course I would, but I can't."

Rabbi: "But why can't you?"

Respondent: "It's just impossible. I can't. I really would like to, but I can't."

Rabbi: "If I promise you four hundred thousand dollars would you stay for ninety days?"

Respondent: "Well, yes, for four hundred thousand dollars, I'd arrange to stay."

Rabbi: "But didn't you just say you can't?"

Respondent: "For four hundred thousand dollars I'd arrange to stay."

Rabbi "Well, four hundred thousand dollars is a lot of money, but it won't allow you to retire or to live the life of the rich. And yet, for only a relatively modest fraction of riches, people will do what they claim is, otherwise, utterly impossible."

We all value happiness, but we won't pay its price. We won't even make the investment in time and effort. Instead, we literally kill ourselves making money, trying to get rich, so that we can become happy. No effort, no amount of dedication, no personal sacrifice is too great when we're earning a buck. Yet, there are countless people with limited material assets, some, indeed, just simply poor who are genuinely happy and many really wealthy, even immensely wealthy people, who are unhappy and often depressingly miserable.

Wealth does not make one happy! Of course, I do not discourage hard work for financial success, but the real riches of a great life are internal, not external. It's not the pile of paper currency or extensive possessions, but the essential, fundamental self-development that you inculcate in your nature that will result in your being happy.

If we would put in the same effort to find fulfillment as we devote to getting rich, we would be the beneficiaries of true magnificent success and happiness.

"Don't let making a living prevent you from making a life" (John Wooden).

Day 208

Mere wealth can't bring us happiness,
Mere wealth can't make us glad,
But we'll always take a shot
At being rich and sad!

    A front-page *Newsday* story entitled "He's Long Island's Richest Man" says that James Simons, an outstanding math professor who became a hedge fund manager is now worth two billion dollars. That is really phenomenal wealth and also a really enviable achievement.

    The article goes on to say that "counterbalancing" his business success, are personal tragedies. He and his wife had five children. However, sadly, their thirty-four-year-old son Paul was killed in 1996 riding a bicycle, their 23 twenty-three-year-old son Nick drowned in 2003 while on a trip to Bali in Indonesia, and their daughter Audrey suffers from autism, a terrible medical condition.

    While Mr. Simons and his wife certainly deserve immense respect and admiration for the really wonderful and effective charitable and philanthropic foundations and research efforts they have founded and supported in the names of these children, there are those who are envious of them. But, would anyone really want their total package?

    A family had just lost their home and everything in it because they had to evacuate it within a forty-five-minute evacuation warning. They had to leave just about everything they owned and loved to the uncontrollable Los Alamos fire that wiped out over two hundred homes. The fire completely burned everything to ashes. The mother

HAPPINESS GUARANTEED OR YOUR MISERY BACK

seeing a flat, burned-out piece of land on a television monitor where their lifelong irreplaceable possessions and home had been still courageously smiled. When asked why, she wisely responded, "Though we lost all our material possessions and so much of what we loved and can never replace, we are grateful because we could have perished."

Consider these people, their hardships, their attitude, and your attitude. Appreciate the good fortune of the totality of your package. Do count and carefully enumerate your blessings. You're much better off and richer than you think.

"There are people who have money and people who are rich" (Coco Chanel).

Day 209

"**Money is better than poverty, if only for financial reasons.**"—Woody Allen

In our own lives, we can't avoid being swept along by the imperatives of contemporary society. We need larger houses, faster cars, the latest technology, and more complex and lucrative investments because we are convinced these things will deliver perfect bliss. And so, we pursue the shimmering mirages of material success with all the energy and single-mindedness that the frenetic pace of today's world demands.

You will never be happy running after money. There is always somebody richer. Even if you are the richest man, you will find out that it doesn't produce happiness. I know millionaires, even billionaires, who are the unhappiest people because they are so driven. They are never satisfied because somebody always has more than they do or somebody is more successful. Human beings are insatiable.

The best things in life are free. Being with friends you love, enjoying the warm, bright sun, the shining moon at night, the lively breaking waves in the ocean, the playful, pleasurable sands on the beaches—these things are there for every one of us.

G-d's incomparable paintings are around us every moment: the ever-changing rainbow colors in the sky above, the greens and browns and reds of the trees and plants and flowers, the calm of the stream and the rushing white waves of the ocean, the special quality of every living creature and of every amazingly unique human face, the beauty of a woman, the strength of a man and the lovely shining image of a child.

HAPPINESS GUARANTEED OR YOUR MISERY BACK

Rich people don't have more real friends than poor people. In fact, it may even be quite the contrary; poor people spend more time visiting and talking to each other because they don't have all the luxury play things that a rich person has.

People forget what life's real riches are. If you want to know how rich you really are, think about what you would have left if tomorrow you should lose every material thing you own.

Husbands and wives and children too often become like ships passing in the night, with little more than a friendly wave to sustain their relationships. We're searching for happiness in all the wrong places. If we would only invest a fraction of all of our effort into appreciating our families and friends, we would find boundless spiritual rewards already at hand and draw much closer to the ever-elusive goal of perfect bliss.

Remember, "The best things in life are not things."

Day 210

What's the use of happiness? It can't buy you money.

Maintain a frame of reference. One afternoon, I was feeling really beat up and aggravated. I had just lost a great deal of money when shares of a drug company in which I had a very large position dropped dramatically after the FDA rejected a very promising drug the company had developed. I was thoroughly devastated until a close friend called me about a project we were working on together. He sounded depressed, so I asked him what was wrong. He explained that his son who was studying at Harvard had just been diagnosed with a malignant liver cancer. He was starting chemo and had to obtain a liver from an organ donor.

I suddenly realized how foolish I was to be so agitated and depressed about losing money. Sad as it was, money can always be made back, but something like a child's health cannot. The unfolding tragedy of seeing one's beloved child subjected to that kind of life-threatening malady and all the pain and suffering that he would be subjected to (even if he were lucky enough to ever overcome that frightening outcome), made me appreciate how fortunate I was.

As Lee Strasberg, the great acting coach said, "Good health is the most important thing. More than success. More than money. More than power." But, "the love of family and the admiration of friends is much more important than wealth and privilege" (Charles Kurait, CBS Journalist).

Why must we wait for the storm to appreciate the calm? Constantly be cognizant of how fortunate you are!

Day 211

"Worry kills more people than work does because more people worry than work."—Robert Frost

In his first-ever commencement address, Governor George E. Pataki urged graduates of Siena College and Colgate University not to let fear of failure hold them back. "Those who walk slowly and timidly through life, for fear of taking the wrong step, might very well achieve their goal of not taking the wrong step," Mr. Pataki said. "But, what will they ever accomplish?"

The governor cited himself as an example of someone who took risks even when the odds were overwhelmingly against him. He also quoted Theodore Roosevelt, Charles Dickens and Motown Records mogul Berry Gordy, urging students to seek success in fields that were important to them.

"I always did something I was a little not ready to do. I think that's how you grow. When there's that moment of 'Wow, I'm not really sure I can do this,' and you push through those moments, that's when you have a breakthrough" (Marissa Mayer). "Take risks; if you succeed you will be happy. If you fail, you will be wiser."

Happiness is achieved by pursuing one's goal.

Day 212

"You might want to consider a career change when you hope for a natural disaster as an excuse to go home for the day."—Jason Love

Elycia Rubin, an author who holds a full-time job at Twentieth Century Fox, contends, "Almost nothing compares to enjoying what you do—be it a job, work at home or whatever." When Elyse Glickman, a writer for *Lifestyles*, asked her, "When do you find the time to have fun?" Elycia answered, "Doing all of this is fun! I write at night and on weekends and I spend however long it takes. I make the time to write because I don't see it as a chore and when I complete something, it feels very fulfilling. When you pursue things you're passionate about, you're in the right place at the right time."

A study at the University and Manchester Business School in England said even a modest drop in job satisfaction can lead to burnout of "considerable clinical importance." It also found that depression and anxiety are the most common reasons for people claiming long-term sick benefits, surpassing ailments such as back pain.

If you belong to this group, make a move, change jobs, change careers, do whatever it takes. Find something that gives you job satisfaction, a sense of accomplishment, and, if possible, even excitement.

For most of us, the work we do, our job, takes up most of our waking hours. It is absolutely imperative to pursue an activity, a job, and an assignment, which contributes to your feeling good and satisfied and which makes you a more upbeat and happier person, even if it is monetarily a poorer choice.

HAPPINESS GUARANTEED OR YOUR MISERY BACK

Don't be passive. Don't settle. Don't just accept what life throws your way. Find a job that will make your life more pleasant and gratifying. "Pleasure in the job makes perfection in the work" (Aristotle).

Day 213

**"Why are you quitting? The wages are good."
"I know, but I'm keeping a horse out of a job!"**

Work hard. Visualize human beings as a motor with eight cylinders. Fortunately, for those of us who are willing to work hard to beat out the others and rise to the top, most humans operate on only about two cylinders. Therefore, if we extend ourselves even a little, since it is likely that no one ever operates up to his full potential, if we operate on even five of our eight cylinders, we will exceed our fellow man and excel at whatever we choose to work.

The reason that there is always the most room at the top is because people don't want to put in the energy to get there. You can't just dream about success, you have to work at it. Success is the sum of all the effort you invest. As Collin Powell said, "A dream doesn't become reality through magic, it takes sweat, determination and hard work."

Success is usually accompanied by a rewarding feeling. Make up your mind to work for success and you will succeed and feel good about yourself.

"Successful people are not gifted; they just work hard, then succeed on purpose" (G.K. Nelson).

Day 214

My brother has a great way of saving money. He uses mine!

"Neither a borrower nor a lender be." I had never quite understood the meaning or value of this seemingly esoteric advice. I thought that lending money to a friend or business acquaintance or someone in dire need would be a good deed and make him a better friend. In several cases, this was indeed the case. However, unexpectedly, disappointingly, in more instances than I care to admit or recall, when it came time for the promised repayment of the loan, which I had so generously extended and eventually requested repayment, suddenly they wouldn't take my calls. Moreover, if I pursued repayment, they often complained that I was annoying them and badgering them. In the end, instead of winning or cementing a friendship, I earned animosity and sadly, hurtfully, not only didn't I get my money back, but they even viewed me as an enemy. I lost a number of friends, whom I really liked, even several I had treasured, by being a lender.

As to the first part of that superb advice, about not being a borrower, I have learned over the course of my career and my long life how appropriate and how exceptionally smart that advice and guidance is. At times, when I had borrowed money, simply because I had easy access to a credit card, I almost unconsciously spent much more than I could reasonably pay for and was hit with enormous penalties and egregiously high interest charges much to my painful chagrin. And later when I borrowed and bought shares of stock on "margin"—because of my desire to own more shares than I could actually pay all cash for, so I could, perhaps greedily, make more profits on the larger number of shares I would own as a result of those borrowings—when the shares declined in price, I lost money faster (on the shares I had paid my own cash for and on shares which I had borrowed funds to buy).

Even worse, on several occasions I could not put up more money to meet the "margin calls" by the broker who had lent me the money to buy those extra shares. I lost my entire investment. In retrospect, if I had paid all cash and not borrowed, even if the shares declined, I could have retained some value and in most cases would have been able to hold onto the shares and survive what eventually proved to be only a temporary, although very sharp, decline. In the end, I would have ultimately experienced a good profit when the share price subsequently rebounded and rose to a higher price than I had initially paid.

As you see, I learned the hard way that it's unwise and sometimes very costly and exceedingly painful to be a borrower.

In fact, if you do even a minimal amount of research, you will quickly find that many good and honest, hardworking people have lost their homes or businesses as a consequence of being unable to repay the lenders from whom they borrowed.

You can clearly see borrowing can lead to instability, aggravation and disaster. You will indeed lead a more serene, happier life if, when possible, you avoid borrowing! "Before borrowing money from a friend, decide which you need more, the friend or the money."

Day 215

It seems ironic that all the people who hate the rich are the ones in line buying lottery tickets.

One of the great puzzles of human nature is why humans strive for more material things—money, jobs, homes, cars, flat-screen televisions—when they do not seem to make them any happier in the long run. Not only does greater wealth not guarantee happiness—even when you get what you want—research indicates that you will not find it as satisfying as you had hoped, and you will want something else.

This cycle of desire and dissatisfaction tends to keep people on an endless treadmill. This may sound self-defeating, but that is the point. Why not get off the treadmill and pursue a life with fewer material ambitions? You will be happier.

Claudia Senik, professor of economics at the Sorbonne, believes that the struggle for achievement offers a peculiar reward all its own. It's not so much having the stuff that people really enjoy, but the struggle to obtain it. The anticipation, independent of the outcome, seems to bestow happiness in the present.

There is pleasure in progress. We are proud to aim at something—to earn a degree, get a promotion or buy a house. When you work to reach a higher position or earn a higher income, you are already happy today, but it doesn't matter because you've already spent the last few days looking forward to it. Dr. Senik's research suggests that it's fine to crave the condo and the car as long as you realize there may be more pleasure in striving for those goals than in actually achieving them. Get off the materialistic treadmills. They are exhausting. Enjoy the pursuit but don't allow the need for success to consume you.

Day 216

An elementary school girl from an exclusive neighborhood was asked to write about a poor family. She wrote, "Once upon a time, there was a poor family. The father was poor; the mother was poor; the sisters and brothers were poor; the butler was poor; the chauffeur was poor; they were all poor."

Food for Thought:
In 1923, nine of the world's most successful financiers attended a very important meeting at the Edgewater Beach Hotel in Chicago. Those present included:

The president of the largest independent steel company
The president of the largest utility company
The president of the largest gas company
The greatest wheat speculator
The president of the New York Stock Exchange
A member of the President's cabinet
The greatest "bear" on Wall Street
The head of the world's greatest monopoly
The president of the Bank of International Settlements

Certainly, we must admit that here gathered a group of the world's most successful men. At least, men who had found the secret of "making money." Twenty-five years later let's see where these men are:

The president of the largest independent steel company—Charles Schwab—died bankrupt and lived on borrowed money for five years before his death.

The president of the greatest utility company—Samuel Insull—died a fugitive from justice and penniless in a foreign land.

The president of the largest gas company—Howard Hopson—is now insane.

The greatest wheat speculator—Arthur Cutten—died abroad insolvent.

The president of the New York Stock Exchange—Richard Whitney—was recently released from Sing Sing Penitentiary.

The member of the President's cabinet—Albert Fall—was pardoned from prison so he could die at home.

The greatest "bear" on Wall Street—Jesse Livermore—died a suicide.

The head of the greatest monopoly—Ivar Krueger—died a suicide.

The president of the Bank of International Settlement—Leon Fraser—died a suicide.

All of these men learned the art of making money, but not one of them learned how to live. Don't live just to earn a living; earn a living so you can live.

Day 217

You can stop trying to keep up with the Joneses. They've died of exhaustion.

If you have billions and you're not satisfied, you will feel frustrated and miserable. If you make much of even the little you may have, you will feel becharmed, lucky and psychologically fulfilled.

Go for more, but learn to be satisfied with the less that you already have. The children in the story *Mama's Bank Account* grew up happy despite living with very little because their mother provided them with security of savings in her fictitious bank account.

We may have "life" and "liberty" but "the pursuit of happiness" isn't going so well. As a country, we are richer than ever. Yet, surveys show that Americans are no happier than they were thirty years ago because we aren't good at figuring out what will make us happy. We constantly hanker after fancier cars and fatter paychecks that initially boost our happiness. But, the glow of satisfaction quickly fades and soon we're yearning for something else.

According to the American Psychology Association, money is our number one stress factor. When we were living in caves, we fought for physical survival, and now we all fight for financial security. The statistics tell us that most Americans are in financial trouble. On the whole, we are spending more than we're making. Seventy percent of us report living paycheck to paycheck. Everyone has a need to impress the next one.

Neither money nor financial riches is the answer to happiness. "Success is getting what you want, and happiness is wanting what you get." Let us remember what is written in *Ethics of our Fathers*: "Who is happy? He who is satisfied with his lot!"

Day 218

An elderly man is hit by a car. A woman runs over to him and asks, "Oy Mister, are you comfortable?" He answers, "I make a living."

Donald Trump, who is clearly one of the most dynamic, creative and successful entrepreneurial business leaders and one of the richest men in the whole world, proclaims that the most critical and useful advice he himself follows, which he advises us to follow as well, is to "never, ever, give up!" He says that this fighting attitude has proven to be so constructive for him in his own career that it has, in a number of significant cases, turned what seemed to be hopeless losers into major winners.

These "pearls of wisdom" that Donald Trump offers need to be employed by all of us in every aspect of our lives and particularly in our pursuit of success and happiness. When things look worse and we get so depressed we want to throw in the towel and just give up, we should firm up our backbone, our mental attitude and enlist this superb Trump injunction to "never, ever, give up." Then we must energize our fighting spirit to induce renewed good fortune.

It's not just by accident that Donald Trump is so successful, rather, precisely because he practices this imperative that he strongly believes in that accounts in no small way for his fantastic achievements and resiliency. Likewise, if you follow this effective and salient precept, your achievement of success and happiness won't depend on fortuitous accident or luck but will be a result of your behavior and winning attitude.

Trump your goal of achieving exalted, ongoing success and happiness by imitating Donald Trumps constructive, success producing attitude and behavior. "Success is not final, failure is not fatal; it is the courage to continue that counts" (Winston Churchill).

Day 219

A man carrying a cigar box ran into a friend. The friend said, "Look at this. Times are tough, and you're walking around with a box of fancy cigars." The other man said, "I'm moving. This is my luggage!"

My wife Rozi has a distant relative, a much older charming aunt named Sally Avery. Sally was married to a struggling artist, Milton Avery, who has now become a renowned, world-class artist, whose paintings, today sell for millions of dollars each and are part of the invaluable collections of the most important museums.

But Sally remembers the days when she and her husband didn't have enough money to pay for paints or canvasses. They desperately sought to sell paintings for one hundred dollars each. She painted too but her husband Milton is the one whose paintings have won universal acceptance, fame and enormous value. She says that of course it makes her feel good when one of Milton's paintings sells for over a million, or even many millions. But, she says it in no way compares with the phenomenal joy and gratitude which she and Milton felt when in those old days when they really needed the money and they sold a painting for the petty sum of only one hundred dollars so they could buy the paint and canvass that allowed them to do the activity they so enjoyed and loved.

The "less" of those sales was so much more fulfilling, satisfying and rewarding than the multimillion dollar sales, the "more" she now experiences.

The lesson is that we need to feel a sense of happiness, not by the size or amount of the given asset or experience, but from immersing ourselves in the appreciation and gratitude that even the smallest blessing can provide us.

"Be thankful for your allotment in an imperfect world. Though better circumstances can be imagined, far worse are nearer misses than you probably realize" (Richelle E. Goodrich, *Smile Anyway*).

Day 220

A man went to a library and asked for a book on how to commit suicide. The librarian said, "Forget it, you won't bring it back."

Become a "possibilitarian." No matter how dark things seem to be or actually are, raise your sights and see possibilities—always see them, for they're always there (Norman Vincent Peale).

Martin Gray, author of *For Those I Love* and twelve other books to date, lost his entire family—his father, mother, two sisters and a brother—in the German concentration camp, Auschwitz, in Poland during the Nazi-perpetrated Holocaust. He managed to evade Nazi captivity and helped feed starving people in the Warsaw Ghetto. He then spent years in a Polish forest in the underground as a freedom fighter. When the Russians recaptured Poland, he joined the Russian Army. Disillusioned by the barbaric, inhuman behavior of this army, he ran away, eventually ending up in the United States.

In New York, he did well financially, in business. But, since he was determined to be a writer, he immigrated to a more sedentary and accommodating creative-writer and literary-productive environment in France where he rebuilt his life. But, once again, misfortune followed him and he lost his wife and four children in a terrible forest fire.

He was totally devastated and wished to die but then determined that he must do something meaningful and memorable in order to honor the life of his wife and kids. So, he embarked on a dedicated campaign with the enthusiastic cooperation of the French government to save other people's lives by helping to prevent forest fires.

He later related that while making loads of money in New York was kind of exciting for him, he felt that helping to feed people in the Warsaw Ghetto was the most satisfying activity he had experienced in his far too adventurous life. He felt it was a truly noble task—"as if he were reaching the sky."

Even at his advanced age, Martin Gray is touring the world promoting his newly reissued, updated book, *For Those I Love*. His books and courageously resilient life serve as an inspiration to millions of people who, during their own trials and tribulations, take heart and derive hope and the expectation of a better, more rewarding and enriching future in their own lives.

If you spend your time thinking predominantly about your problems and misfortunes, you will impel your mind to become dispirited and dejected, which in turn, will induce sadness and cause emotional depression. If, instead, you think of all the possibilities, joyful happenings, inspiring adventures and exciting prospects that lie ahead once this situation or problem is overcome and behind you, you will almost instantly be emotionally uplifted and exhilarated and you will begin to feel better and happier.

No matter how distressing and painful your situation may currently be, adopt a positive, optimistic belief and attitude and go on to find courage, happiness and a rewarding life. Make it to the moon even if you have to crawl.

Day 221

"If you try to fail, and succeed, what have you done?"—
George Carlin

Don't ever become depressed by failure. Certainly, don't beat yourself up or think of yourself "a loser" because of any specific failure. We're all human and we all fail. Failure is an inevitable step in the process of any success. Think of each failure as an opportunity to progress. It's part of the learning curve. Even in those cases where the government spends billion of dollars, it often initially experiences a series of discouraging disappointments, until it finally achieves success. When we worked desperately, and invested enormously, to beat the Soviet Union to land a man on the moon, we tried solid fuel, then liquid fuel and finally gaseous fuel; each time, we failed, we learned something vitally important which ultimately helped us win the battle and achieve that urgent goal of being first to land a man on the moon.

You need to recognize that it's fundamentally a very basic human nature to fail, often innumerable times, before we can effectively succeed. Watch a young baby as it tries to get up and walk. It falls, thus fails, not one time or ten times but maybe one thousand times or more. And each time it falls, it hurts itself and even cries, but each time it gets up and tries again until one day, amazingly, it succeeds. And, of course, it benefits from this determined valiant effort all the rest of its life.

As the proverb goes, "If at first you don't succeed, try, try again." Don't get disillusioned and depressed. Understand and grasp the critical insight that with each failure, you are learning, progressing and moving ever closer to achieving the goal you are striving to accomplish. Once you understand that, instead of becoming depressed, you can become inspired, motivated and move productively forward—smiling and even feeling encouraged. You will view each failure as actually moving you a step closer to arriving at that ultimate, exhilarating, desired success.

Researchers found that women diagnosed with breast cancer experienced growth, such as increases in spirituality, compassion for others, openness and eventually an increased appreciation of life. After trauma, people with optimistic, positive, attitudes, who are willing to face their situation and are determined to deal with it, who decide that they will make the best of their condition, often as a result of the trauma, report enhanced personal strength, increased self-confidence, and improved social relationships.

"There is no telling how far you will have to run while chasing a dream" (Anonymous), but persistence turns failure into extraordinary success.

Day 222

Reality is the leading cause of stress among those in touch with it.

When asked to define his idea of success, Tom Perkins, a mega-millionaire, a partner in the most successful venture capital firm, Kleiner Perkins, and the author of the novel *Sex and the Single Zillionaire*, said, "stress successfully overcome is triumph." With all the enormous success he has achieved—his venture capital firm was an original investor in Google, Yahoo, America Online and many other astronomically successful companies on which it earned billions of dollars—it's astounding that that simple statement is his best summary of his idea of success.

It is absolutely profound that if you can handle and overcome stress, you become stronger, more effective and ever more able and likely to lead a rewarding, successful and certainly hope-fulfilling and happier life. Just as stress debilitates, distracts and destroys one's effectiveness, overcoming stress strengthens, invigorates and empowers one to achieve an unbeatable, robust success.

At one time or another, we are all faced with stress. The three most important words to learn in order to succeed are, "Yes, I can." I can be understanding, forgiving, patient, flexible, accommodating, gracious, accepting. Yes, I can handle it. I can manage it. I can overcome. I can survive. I can choose to ignore it or deal with it. I can laugh through it or smile at it. I can recharge. I can cope. I can choose to believe or grow from it or learn from it or just move on. I can fight it or challenge it. Yes, I can work toward my goals. Yes, I can control my thoughts, my outlook, my attitudes, my perceptions, my judgments, and my responses. I can think uplifting, inspiring, encouraging, positive thoughts. Yes, I can choose to be happy.

Yes, I can let the stress get me down but I won't. I can sing or dance or write to keep my mind off it. I can go for a walk or a ride or visit and talk to a friend. I can breathe through it or go to bed for a while or take a relaxing bath. Yes, I can reminisce on the good things or count my blessings or think about all I have to look forward to or just stuff myself with a chocolate ice cream sundae. Yes, I can focus on what I can do rather than what is out of my control or I can pray to the one who does have control. I can ask for a hug or spend time with family and feel surrounded by love. I can go out and do a good deed or give someone a warm smile. I can look for the opportunities in the challenge. Yes, I can be strong. Yes, I can be a success. I can choose not to regret but rather to realize that if it should've been, it would've been. Yes, I can realize that while there is life there is hope and opportunity.

"A diamond is just a piece of coal that handled stress very well" (Anonymous).

Day 223

"People don't realize that the 'future' is just now, but later."—Jim Norton

Being nervous, anxious and tense, overwhelmed and trying to meet deadlines, is frustrating and depressing. Your professor needs your research paper first thing in the morning. Your boss needs your brief by tomorrow. Your wife wants you to be home by six for a dinner engagement. Your son wants you to be at his Little-League game. The bank needs you to pay your mortgage by the end of the week. So many commitments, so many obligations, so many responsibilities and so many people who count on you or to whom your actions matter.

You might think you would be happy if you had no schoolwork to feel pressured by, no job to report to, no boss, spouse or children to consider and no commitments to think about. If you so desired, you could sleep late, perhaps till 10 a.m. or till 12 or 4 or 8. Perhaps you don't have to get up at all. You might be happy and relaxed for a day or two, but how would you feel after that? Your time is your own. You are in control of your life—or are you? Being bored, directionless, unnecessary, having no goal, no reason to get up in the morning is beyond maddening. Life feels purposeless. Feeling good comes from feeling accomplished, feeling needed, feeling challenged and motivated.

The key to happiness is finding a balance and managing your life with optimism. Willingly taking on more responsibility or obligations than you can handle is irresponsible. Doing less than you are capable of doing is wasteful.

Too often, we get frustrated or discouraged and allow setbacks and disappointments to stifle and break us. The wonderful thing about being alive is while we have life we have hope, we have the ability to turn our lives around, to build a future despite a tragic past or an unbearable present. Challenges aren't easy, but succumbing to them, giving up on yourself, on God, and on hope, is painfully intolerable.

Sometimes when you have nothing else, hope is all you have, but if you have hope, you have everything. Get moving. Build up your self-esteem by taking small steps toward your goal. Use your potential and continually recognize and appreciate your progress. Take on challenges that you can handle but which still stretch your brain, and challenge your efforts and your growth potential. Only you can turn your hopes into your reality.

Day 224

Happiness: the agreeable sensation felt while contemplating the misery of others.

"To be upset over what you don't have is to waste what you do have" (Ken S. Keyes).

The heart requires very little—quiet, joy, peace, and dreams. But, we drive ourselves crazy by intensely desiring and pursuing so much of what we don't need—what is in fact often harmful to us and contra-indicated to the achievement of contentment and happiness. Don't let these illusionary values and aspirations ruin your life.

Unfortunately, we live in an advertising-driven age that molds our values and our needs, that paints the trivial as attractive and the unnecessary as seemingly urgent. We just "must have and can't do without." In the process, we lose track of what is really important, worthwhile and fulfilling. Remember, "things" just don't mean happiness.

We continually want more. We even lose our perspective on appreciating things that do have value. Years ago, my little son fell and tore his eyelid. Originally, I begged G-d not to let him lose his eyesight. When I was finally told that his vision would be fine, I begged G-d not to let him look deformed. Emergency surgery was quickly performed and thankfully, the doctor was able to do trauma surgery and restore his eyelid. I was then informed that one stitch was missing and there would remain a tiny slit in his lid. I ran to the top plastic surgeons in an effort to replace the single missing stitch, so that there wouldn't even remain a tiny trace of the horrible accident my son had so miraculously survived. I realized the outrageous progression of thought I had experienced, first only wanting sight now wanting perfection. In the end, I was advised not to push my luck and to leave the tiny, barely noticeable slit, which my son exhibits with pride, remembering how grateful he is to G-d.

It's reminiscent of the Jewish prayer Dayeinu that we recite on Passover, which states that if G-d had only taken us out of Egypt, it would have been enough. If G-d had just given us the Torah, it would have been enough and if G-d had just given us the land of Israel, it would've been enough. But thankfully, he gave us so much more.

All we have is all we need. All we need is the awareness of how blessed we really are.

Day 225

"I hated my last job. My boss asked, 'Why are you two hours late?' I said, 'I fell down the stairs.' He said, 'That doesn't take two hours.'"—Johnny Carson

If and when things are not going so well or when you just experienced what you feel to be a major disappointment, tell yourself: "Better things will happen to me in the future!"

Repeat it over and over again: "Better things will happen to me!" Just repeating and believing it will immediately help you feel better and it will become a self-fulfilling prophecy. Pessimism leads to weakness while optimism empowers you.

A friend of mine lost his job as a television announcer and was devastated. His very wise and caring wife encouragingly lifted his spirits by saying, "There must be a reason for this untoward happening and that it will lead to some better, more rewarding career opportunity and gratification." She repeatedly reassured him that there was a good reason why this "temporary" reversal occurred. Just hearing this made him feel better, more upbeat and more inspired and capable to pursue a new opportunity, which he did. He ultimately went on to enjoy a rewarding career as an impressive TV sports announcer, a career he never would have pursued had he not lost the earlier position.

In the face of disappointment or any adversity, encourage yourself that "things will be better in the future." Optimism is essential to achievement because it allows you to build up courage, and courage leads to progress. As Franklin Delano Roosevelt said, "The only limit to our realization of tomorrow will be our doubts of today."

Day 226

There's a simple secret to long life. Get to be a hundred and then be careful!

Your most cherished fantasies can come true. But first, you must believe it. Move forward in life with the confidence that it will happen for you—that if you "will it," it will be. Believe that G-d will be on your side (maybe after testing you first) before it finally actualizes.

Don't let anybody or anything inject heartache. Reject heartache! Drive it out as instantly as possible, as if it is a menace, which it surely is, to your health and to your future.

Life gets better—there are new inventions, new cures, and new happenings every day. My father-in-law always inspired me by pointing out "The sun is always there, you just need to brush away the clouds."

Keep family values. Develop a close relationship with your spouse. Stay involved in each other's lives. Grow together. Talk together. Share good times. Share your thoughts, your goals, your dreams, your youth, and your old age.

Stay involved in your children's lives. Care, share and be there for them. Be aware if they are going through difficult times, as most children do. Help them make it through those difficulties.

Don't complicate your life. Don't hurt the people you love. Remember family values.

Keep life simple. Keep your life uncomplicated. Break up problems into segments, dealing with each part separately. As you solve each segment of your problem, you begin to feel better. Simplify!

HAPPINESS GUARANTEED OR YOUR MISERY BACK

Avoid and get out of any situations that will lead to frustrating complications, inevitable aggravation and uncontrollable headaches. If someone, for example, tells you something great about someone with whom you plan to do business or with whom you might enter into a serious personal relationship, listen, digest it, but be skeptical of what they say. Check it out. They may be right, but they also may have a personal interest in misadvising you. If someone warns you off and tells you not to trust a certain person, or that he is dangerous for whatever combination of reasons or behavior patterns, run away and don't get involved. Life is far too short to risk getting mixed up with such potentially trouble-generating associations. Yes, you may miss an opportunity, a relationship or whatever—but in all likelihood, what you will miss is a serious misadventure. You'll miss inviting a lot of punishing entanglements and endless headaches. Weigh the cost-benefit relationship of any action you contemplate pursuing.

We all know, for example, some women who have been warned to stay away from a certain man because he is an alcoholic, a womanizer, or an abuser. Yet, despite such warnings, they continue pursuing the relationship. Likewise, I have known businessmen, and I must confess that on at least two separate occasions I have been guilty of such behavior myself, who went into partnerships with or employed key personnel or invested with someone whom they were strongly advised against. We indulge in the same rationalization that "Under my guidance and influence he will be different," only to experience painful losses and even major catastrophes.

Protect yourself. Lower your pain threshold. Don't allow yourself to suffer. Don't allow yourself to be vulnerable, fooled, mislead or cheated.

If sorrow befalls you, raise your spirits. Open your eyes to the positives. Let love pervade your life.

When you fall down, get up. When you first learn to walk and fall down you tend to lie there and cry, but as you get a little older when you fall down you quickly get up and move on.

Let the past remain in the past. It's counterproductive and self-destructive to dig into a hurtful past. You will find that it is necessary to let things go simply because they are too heavy...heavy on your heart, heavy on your soul. You can't reach for anything new if your hands are filled with yesterday's junk. Remember and celebrate the good times and those that were a major part of it. Appreciate all that you have, all you have been blessed with and all that you have to look forward to in the future.

Day 227

Life is like Facebook. People will "like" your problems and comment, but no one will solve them because everyone is too busy updating theirs.

A study by Anxiety UK showed that nearly 50 percent of people are worried or uncomfortable being away from their e-mail or Facebook accounts. These studies show that we need to re-establish control over the technology we use.

Studies show that heavy cell phone use has been shown to increase sleep disorders in men and increase depression in both men and women. People who are constantly available by cell phone are most likely to report mental health problems. Men who use computers intensively are more likely to develop sleep problems. Men and women who stay up late using computers develop sleep disorders, stress and depression. Those who are heavy users of both cell phones and computers exhibit even stronger stress issues. The light from TV and computer screens affects melatonin production and throws off our circadian rhythm preventing deep, restorative sleep and causing increased stress and depression.

Decide to control your use and dependence on technology rather than allowing technology to control you. Talk to your family, friends, even business associates rather than only sitting in front of the TV or computer, texting and e-mailing.

Real communication allows for developing deep, intense friendships, which are a major ingredient for happiness.

Day 228

So, what if a guy breaks up with you. You can still enjoy your lunch.

Infatuation is instant desire, one set of glands calling to another. Love is friendship that has caught fire. It takes root and grows one day at a time. Decide that you want real love.

A feeling of insecurity marks infatuation. You are excited and eager but not genuinely happy. There are nagging doubts, unanswered questions, little bits and pieces about your beloved that you would just as soon not examine too closely because it might spoil the dream.

Love is quiet understanding and the mature acceptance of imperfection. It is real. It gives you strength and grows beyond you to bolster your beloved. You are warmed by his/her presence, even when he is away. Miles do not separate you. Though you want him nearer, you can wait because you know he is yours.

Infatuation says, "We must get married right away. I can't risk losing him." Love says, "Be patient. Don't panic. Plan your future with confidence."

Infatuation has an element of sexual excitement. If you are honest, you will admit it is difficult to be in one another's company unless you are sure it will end in intimacy. Love is the maturation of friendship. You must be friends before you can be lovers.

Infatuation lacks confidence. When he's away, you wonder if he's cheating. Sometimes, you check.

HAPPINESS GUARANTEED OR YOUR MISERY BACK

Love means trust. You are calm, secure and unthreatened. He feels that trust, and it makes him even more trustworthy. Infatuation might lead you to do things you'll later regret, but love never will.

Love is an upper. It makes you look up. It makes you think up. It makes you a better person than you were before.

Don't settle for infatuation. Love is worth searching for because true love brings true happiness.

(From an Aish HaTorah fax and an Ann Landers column)

Day 229

Never laugh at your girlfriend's choices…you're one of them.

True intimacy is contingent on positive self-esteem. If we don't value our selves and respect what we are, we may avoid real closeness with other people for fear they will discover our flaws. We must perceive ourselves realistically. Each of us may not be perfect but we each have value. To be happy we must decide to appreciate ourselves.

Too many people are driven to unhappiness because of unrequited love. When someone you believe you love rejects you, you may be feeling the pain of rejection rather than real loss. You try to hold on because you can't tolerate the rejection. Do not be fooled into thinking you love the other person so intensely that you cannot live without him or her. True love is reciprocated. If it is not true love, why try to preserve the relationship?

As long as you look for someone else to validate who you are, by seeking their approval, you are setting yourself up for disaster. You have to be whole and complete in yourself. Say to yourself, "I am special. I am worth loving and the right person will appreciate me and value what I am and the love I have to offer."

As Mark Twain said, "The worst loneliness is to not be comfortable with yourself. You need not be perfect. We all have flaws." Elizabeth Taylor said, "I don't approve of some of the things I have done, or am, or have been. But, I'm me. G-d knows I'm me."

HAPPINESS GUARANTEED OR YOUR MISERY BACK

As Brigham Young asked, "Why should we worry about what others think of us? Do we have more confidence in their opinion than we do in our own?"

You must have a humble, but reasonable, confidence in your own powers in order to be happy and successful. As soon as your brain tells you that you are not good enough, not capable or smart enough—that you can't do whatever you set out to do—tell yourself, "I can do it. I can make it happen. I can make my dreams a reality."

Day 230

I have lots of friends in high places. I hope the police can talk them down.

Make sure you choose the right friends!
A friend doubles the joys and halves the grief.
A friend is someone we turn to when our spirits need a lift.
A friend is someone we treasure, for our friendship is a gift.
A friend is someone who fills our lives with beauty, joy and grace
And makes the world we live in a better and happier place.

The A-Z of Friendship
A Friend...
(A)ccepts you as you are
(B)elieves in "you"
(C)alls you just to say "Hi"
(D)oesn't give up on you
(E)nvisions the whole of you
(F)orgives your mistakes
(G)ives unconditionally
(H)elps you
(I)nvites you over
(J)ust to "be" with you
(K)eeps you close at heart
(L)oves you for who you are
(M)akes a difference in your life
(N)ever judges

HAPPINESS GUARANTEED OR YOUR MISERY BACK

(O)ffers support
(P)icks you up
(Q)uiets your fears
(R)aises your spirits
(S)ays nice things about you
(T)ells you the truth when you need to hear it
(U)nderstands you
(V)alues you
(W)alks beside you
(X)plains things you don't understand
(Y)ells when you won't listen and
(Z)aps you back to reality

As Elton John's beautiful song goes, "In good times and bad times, I'll be on your side for ever more…That's what friends are for." Surround yourself with good friends. They make your life happier.

Day 231

This year, our basketball team plans to run and shoot. Next year, son, we hope to run and score.

Robert Horry is an NBA basketball clutch player who has been on more playoff-winning teams than any other professional athlete in history. During the 2005 finals, he was a member of the San Antonio Spurs. Detroit, who had won the National Championship the prior year, was their opponent. San Antonio, playing at home, won the first two games handily and it looked as if they were going to win the series easily. However, Detroit returning home for the next three games in this best of seven series won the next two games just as easily with similar large margins.

With the series tied at two each, the fifth game was crucial—especially for the Detroit Piston team since the next two games were to be played back in San Antonio's home court. In the final few seconds, Detroit was leading when Robert Horry made several long three-point shots and two clutch foul shots to tie the game and send it into overtime. In overtime, Detroit had the lead with 5.8 seconds left, when Robert Horry perfected a three-point shot to give San Antonio a one-point lead, which turned into a San Antonio win when Detroit missed its final shot.

What's the point of this long "megilah"? Simply this: When the TV interviewer asked Horry how he managed to stay calm and effective under such pressure, he astutely responded, "I know that even if I miss, my family loves me and tomorrow is another day." That kind of positive attitude makes one effective, successful, happy and able to risk failure without fear, dramatically increasing one's functionality and success, and maximizes results. Surely, it serves to maximize happiness.

It helps to always remember two vital facts: First, the people that really matter love you, and second, tomorrow is another day. This second idea may be even more important than the first because tomorrow brings the opportunity, the adventure and the excitement for new experiences and the chance to win (if you don't already have it) the love of people—family, friends, colleagues, etc.—that really count and who can contribute enormously to your ongoing and future happiness quotient.

The best thing in life is to be surrounded by people who love you unconditionally. These are the people that make you want to live another day.

Day 232

"They say such nice things about people at their funerals that it makes me sad to think I'm going to miss mine by only a day."—Garrison Keillor

"There must be one day above all others in each life that is the happiest. What if you've already had it?" (Lucy Van Pelt).

"If you don't like something change it; if you can't change it, change the way you think about it" (M. Mary Engelbreit).

Senator John Kerry's wife, Mrs. Heinz Kerry, who lost her first husband, Senator Heinz, in a plane crash and who, as the daughter of a physician, is very involved in medicine and healing, advises dealing with loss by "embracing the tiger." In other words, the best way to deal with grief is to confront it and accept it. She quotes a monk who was a meditation student she met at a spa who urged her, "Cry, shiver, hold it, and then let it go."

Clearly, one can't change or deny a disastrous loss or episode once it occurs. Therefore, the most constructive and effective way to deal with such an experience is not to deny it or repress it—which can only prolong the psychological suffering—but to confront it, deal with it directly and then to finally accept it and let it go.

Move on, as Mrs. Kerry did after losing the husband whom she loved and to whom she was married for twenty-five years. She then went on to launch a new exciting life with a new marital partner.

Facebook CEO Cheryl Sandberg wrote an amazing article in the *New York Post* when she finished her thirty-day religious mourning period, Shloshim, for her husband, Silicon Valley executive, Dave

HAPPINESS GUARANTEED OR YOUR MISERY BACK

Goldberg. She said a rabbi quoted to her a powerful one-line prayer, "Let me not die while I am still alive." Cheryl wrote that when tragedy occurs, it presents a choice. You can give in to the void, the emptiness that fills your heart, your lungs, constricts your ability to think or even breathe or you can try to find meaning. She says she has spent the past thirty days lost in a void and is certain that she will experience many future moments consumed by the vast emptiness, but she chooses life and meaning. She said she learned so much from those who shared their experiences with her in order to help her pull through. Her goal is to share her new realizations in order to help others. She says she has gotten a more profound understanding of what it means to be a mother, both through the depths of the agony she feels when her children scream and cry and appreciating her own mother for the support she is giving her while connecting to her pain.

Cheryl says she has learned that she never really knew what to say to others in need. A friend diagnosed with late-stage cancer taught her the worst thing to say to her is "It's going to be okay." Real empathy is sometimes not insisting that it will be okay but acknowledging that it is not. Cheryl says, when people tell her, "You and your children will find happiness again," her heart tells her, "Yes, I believe that, but I know I will never feel real joy again." She appreciates those who are tuned in enough to say, "You will find a new normal, but it will never be as good." Even a simple, "How are you?" asked with the best intentions makes her uncomfortable. She would rather people ask, "How are you today?" recognizing that each day is a struggle and that she is doing the best she can right now to get through each day.

Cheryl also claims to have learned gratitude for the things she, and all of us, take for granted. She appreciates life. She now looks at her children and rejoices that they are alive. She says, "I appreciate every smile, every hug. I no longer take every day for granted."

She appreciates her friends who stand by her. She tells of how she was talking to one of these friends about a father-child activity that Dave won't be there to do. They came up with a plan to fill in for Dave but she burst out crying that she wants Dave. She wants option A. The friend said, "Option A is not available. So, let's just kick the hell out of option B," to which she agreed, although she knows she will always mourn for option A. Cheryl ends by writing, "there is no end to grief…and no end to love."

Cheryl, in her deep grief, has decided to choose life, has chosen to give to her children and has chosen to give her new, hard-learned wisdom to benefit the world.

"Death leaves heartache no one can heal. Love leaves a memory no one can steal" (Anonymous).

Day 233

Some people don't know what they are more scared of death or taxes.

"Don't focus on the darkness; always focus on the glimmer of light." What most of us probably consider the worse of all tragedies—the death of a loved one—as much as we would hope that such an eventuality would never happen, it is really critical and may even be helpful to realize that death is a natural, in fact inevitable, reality of our very existence on this earth.

We are repeatedly told: "One can't avoid death or taxes." Actually, it is possible to go through life without paying taxes. But, if one lives long enough, one is bound to experience the loss of someone he loves and cherishes. That being the case, we must deal with that reality in the most functionally adaptive way possible—in a way that does the least psychologically hurtful damage. Since we are blessed with feelings, it's impossible not to grieve and one needs to go through a period of recovery and rehabilitation. It takes time to recover from a significantly meaningful loss and the resultant saddening emptiness. However, in a sense, it's just like any major wound, although the scar may remain forever, with the passage of time the wound does heal and generally is no longer a factor in your ongoing life, as you tend to adjust and move on.

Just as you can reduce the pain and suffering and accelerate the healing process of a wound or a surgical procedure by practicing appropriate rehabilitating behavior, so too you can reduce the magnitude and length of time you experience the hurt, anger, disappointment and suffering inflicted by the loss of a loved one.

You can do that in numerous ways. For one, many religious people often soothe themselves by believing that the beloved individual has passed on to a better place. Others move healthily and constructively forward by doing positive things that pay tribute to the one lost in a way that will not only honor that person, but whose exalting activity will revitalize your spirits, by serving to make this world a better place. For example, setting up a cancer research initiative in that person's name will surely immortalize that cherished person. Always remember:

"Those we love don't go away
They walk beside us every day.
Unseen, unheard, but always near.
Still loved, still missed and very dear" (Anonymous)

Of course, it is easier said than done but it is vital to do things, to be active, to renew your life without that person as rapidly as possible through new relationships and productive philanthropic, physical and psychologically uplifting activities. The person you lost would want you to move on and be happy.

Day 234

A little girl cried to her mother upon the death of her cat. The mother comfortingly answered that the cat was now with G-d. "What," said the little girl, "does G-d want with a dead cat?"

There is a beautifully touching true story of a rabbi whose two sons passed away on the Sabbath. Because she was aware of the dictum, "Thou shalt make the Sabbath day not only restful, but happy in every way possible," she prepared the most scrumptious meals, kept on a cheerful face and sang heart-warming songs that she knew would please her revered husband. Right after the Sabbath ended, she said, "My husband, can I ask you a question? If someone loans you a precious jewel and allows you to enjoy it and get unlimited pleasure from it, when this person decides to take back this gift, does one have the right not to show appreciation and give it back acceptingly?" "Of course not," said the Rabbi. "If someone gives you anything, even for a very brief period, my cherished wife, you're suppose to be grateful and appreciative." At which point his wife said, "G-d gave us two invaluable gifts, two jewels, and allowed us to enjoy them for many years, but G-d gives and G-d takes and now he has decided it was time to take back the loan of these gifts and we must respectfully accept that." Only then did she tell him of their great loss.

A wealthy man lost all his money. When the rabbi went to break the news to him, he too used this same reasoning, asking the rich man if a lender has the right to take back his loan. "G-d gives and G-d takes." We never question why he gives us good fortune, what right do we have to question why he withdraws it. An amazing explanation I was told is that G-d gives individuals wealth to see how they will use that wealth. When they pass that test, G-d sometimes withdraws that wealth to see how they will handle the test of being poor. Being rich or poor are both challenges. Having and losing children are both challenges. Everything we are blessed with gives us an opportunity for responsibility, recognition, appreciation and the ability to use that possession wisely. Everything we lose or are never given gives us an opportunity to develop character, acceptance, understanding, and drive. Both, having and not having, give one the chance for growth.

Day 235

"If love is the answer, could you rephrase the question?"—Lily Tomlin

A woman gave her boss a card that read, "You make a difference! The world is a better place because of you!" and told him that she appreciated his concern for his employees. Then, she asked him to pass the card on to another deserving individual within twenty-four hours.

That night the boss came home late. As he was walking down the hall, he noticed his teenaged son's light shining from under the door. He knocked and asked if he could come in to the room. "Son," said the man, "I know that I haven't been a very good father. I work late and don't spend much time with you. However, I want you to know that I love you and that you make a big difference in my life. I received this card today and I want you to have it." They hugged, they kissed, they cried.

As the father was about to leave the room, the son said, "Dad, there is something that I want to give you that I won't be needing." He pulled a loaded revolver from under his mattress. "I was going to use this tonight because I didn't think you loved me. Now, I don't need it."

Tell someone you love him. It will make a difference in his life—and in yours.

Day 236

A few of us wake up and find ourselves famous. Most of us wake up and find we're a half hour late.

I, like so many of us, grew up believing that fame and popularity constitute happiness. Despite this almost universal perception, this is the furthest thing from the truth. Perhaps nothing demonstrates this more than the life story of Marilyn Monroe. Many historians consider Marilyn Monroe the most popular, beautiful, famous and perhaps most admired and beloved woman (or even person) of all time. She was the movie "star of stars." She was married to Joe DiMaggio, one of the greatest baseball stars of all time, and to Arthur Miller, an outstanding playwright. If being famous, popular and overwhelmingly beloved and admired could make one happy, then no one should have been happier than Marilyn Monroe.

But despite her beauty and talent, in her mind, she was unattractive and unsuccessful. She was so unhappy that, at the very height of her popularity, she committed suicide.

The outstanding actress Judy Garland also committed suicide despite her apparent success, due to her poor self-image and disillusionment with life.

Elvis Presley is another world-famous superstar who couldn't attain personal contentment or happiness. To overcome his ever-present depression, this legendary superstar had to resort to alcohol and drugs, which ultimately destroyed him and brought his life to a premature end.

HAPPINESS GUARANTEED OR YOUR MISERY BACK

Tatum O'Neal was the youngest person ever to win an Oscar, which she received at the age of ten for Best Supporting Actress, playing Addie in 1973's *Paper Moon*, which co-starred her renowned father Ryan O'Neal. She had money and fame—supposedly, what we all dream of and what we all believe will make us happy.

In 2008, *New York Post* columnist Andrea Peyser wrote, "I talked with a woman who had hit rock bottom. This lady had just spent a night on a greasy mattress in a fetid Manhattan holding cell, lying next to ladies you would not touch without the protection of a hazmat suit. She was destroyed. Desperate. She was Tatum O'Neal.

"Tatum spent years hooked on heroin, sobered up, and then, one day decided to score crack and cocaine from a drug panhandler on a downtown street. She acted like a common junkie. And she was busted." This "lucky" woman was once so addicted she lost custody of her three kids to John McEnroe following eight years of marriage.

The reason Ms. Peyser was writing this tragic history was because Tatum's oldest son, Kevin, whom she had with former tennis superstar John McEnroe, was busted as he tried to score drugs—allegedly buying six bags of cocaine, twenty oxycodone tablets and/or morphine pills from a drug dealer.

Ms. Peyser interestingly asks, "Why did this young man and his now fifty-year-old mother—people with money and famous names allegedly attempt to score garbage? Was it a quest for cheap thrills? A walk on the wild side?"

How many great Hollywood personalities have turned to drugs or have taken their own lives? Clearly, "luster" simply isn't what it's cracked up to be. Don't strive for stardom and glory in your pursuit of happiness. Each of us can consider ourselves truly "lucky" if we are just wise enough to count and appreciate our own blessings, to feel like a star in our own minds and life, to enjoy family, friends, relationships, personal growth, helping others, loving and being loved.

Day 237

Life is full of misery, loneliness and suffering...and it's all over much too soon.

"Don't give until it hurts. Give until it feels good!" We are shaped by our deeds. Good deeds will change your life and make you feel better. An esteemed rabbi urged his daughter to smile even when it seemed as if there was nothing to smile about. He told her, "If you smile, G-d will give you something to smile about." Try it. It works.

Walking around with a sour face turns you into a thief. You rob other people of their own good feelings and smiles. Make a difference in someone else's life! A smile is the universal language of kindness. It's the one thing you can give to someone else and still retain. Not only that, but when you give it to someone, they usually give you one back and both of you wind up feeling happier.

In 2015, a terrorist attack in Israel caused the death of a young girl's father and brother just a few days before her wedding. She and her remaining family were doubtlessly in unfathomable, horrific pain. Yet, to combat the horror and to show that life and the people of Israel have and continue to survive, to smile and to retain hope and faith, they sent out a general invitation to all the world inviting everyone to come join in their wedding celebration. Thousands upon thousands of people attended this ceremony, "smiling at one another through our tears," singing and dancing and connecting.

HAPPINESS GUARANTEED OR YOUR MISERY BACK

This family, as do many families suffering tragedies, sacrificed their privacy to help give hope and cheer to others. People turned out by the droves to give a supportive smile and a warm, appreciative thank you to the family.

"A smile is a curve that sets everything straight."

Day 238

Single people die earlier. Marriage is healthier. If you're looking for a long life and a slow death, get married!

A king commissioned the leading artist in his realm to create a painting of perfect bliss. He gave no other instructions, so the artist set out to discover what people considered perfect bliss.

"A victory parade with thousands of cheering people," said a general. "Finding the solution to a very perplexing problem," said a scholar. "Making lots and lots of money," said a merchant. "Spending lots and lots of money," said a young bon vivant.

Ultimately, the artist used his own judgment. When the king unveiled the painting, he saw an elderly couple sitting on a park bench in the dappled sunlight, smiling devotedly at one another. The king stroked his chin thoughtfully and then nodded his assent. "Well done," he said. "Yes, perfect bliss."

Sharing your life and growing old with someone you love is perfect bliss.

Day 239

"You've got friends, and then you've got your best friends. Big difference. To me, a friend is a guy who will help you move. A best friend is a guy who will help you move a body."—Dave Attell

Cultivating good friends and spending time with them, enjoying shared experiences, confiding your intimate secrets, concerns and exciting plans and projects can add enormously to the quotient of happiness you will savor in your life.

A needlepoint pillow, which my wife bought me, wisely summarizes this truism proclaiming, "In the cookies of life, friends are the chips."

Find good friends. Be a good friend. Develop strong friendships. Enjoy the chips. They make life fun. "A single rose can be my garden…a single friend, my world" (Leo Buscaglia). Having a solid, reliable, caring, giving friend to share life with makes your world feel happy and secure. A good friend helps you retain your smile, your sense of humor, your self-esteem, your confidence, your equilibrium, your hope, and your courage. He keeps you from feeling lonely or alone. "Good friends are like stars. You don't always see them but you know they're always there."

There is nothing that will make you happier than a friend, unless it is a friend with chocolate.

Day 240

A man called up the law firm and asked, "Can I please talk to Mr. Finkelstein?" The receptionist responded, "Mr. Finkelstein passed away." The man called again the next day and asked, "Can I speak to Mr. Finkelstein?" The receptionist responded again, "Mr. Finkelstein passed away." The third day the man called again, "Can I please speak to Mr. Finkelstein?" This time the receptionist answered, "I told you! Mr. Finkelstein passed away." On the fourth day, the man called still again, "Can I please speak to Mr. Finkelstein?" This time she angrily said, "I told you Mr. Finkelstein passed away. Why do you keep calling?" Whereupon the caller answered, "Because it makes me so happy to hear that."

Don't get me wrong. I don't hate all lawyers. In fact, two of my daughters, one of my sons-in-law and three of my grandsons are lawyers and I love them a bunch. But, if you ever get involved in a lawsuit in the American court system, and despite the fact that it's probably the best in the world, you'll find to your chagrin that it's one of the least satisfying, most frustrating experiences a person encounters.

Whether you're a plaintiff or a defendant, it takes forever just to get to trial. You'll find reality in the saying, "Justice delayed is justice denied." Your adversaries use many delaying tactics and the lawyers wind up with nearly all the money.

No matter how valid and justified your position in the case is, when you finally get to trial, you hear the other side recite insulting distortions and lies. And in the end, it's not necessarily the "just" or the "right" that prevails but often the one represented by the most effective lawyer, or the one who is the best "liar." One of the top lawyers in the US once said, "This is the legal system. If it is justice you are looking for, you are in the wrong system."

If you and the witnesses on your side aren't as adept or impressive in their presentation as those of your adversary, then you may lose, even if you are totally in the right. Witness the outcome in the O.J. Simpson trial, where the alleged perpetrator of this horrendous act was found innocent and let off scot-free. And there are cases, on the other hand, where innocent people are found guilty and serve jail sentences because of wrong verdicts.

In some cases, government prosecutors enlist criminals who become witnesses for the prosecution in return for the promise of lighter sentences. They say whatever they need to say in order to win lighter sentences, and in the process, they may help imprison innocent victims. Prosecutors also coerce testimony out of witnesses by threatening those very witnesses with prosecution.

And does a jury of your peers truly try you? Biases are often rampant in the judicial system. Jealousy is uncontrollable. Does a poor jury member forgive a wealthy defendant? Can a layman understand a complicated business case? Can a businessman relate to a homeless man's perspective? Does a person of one race side with his own people or envy and look to harm another? Sadly, prejudice and anti-Semitism are rampant.

If a prosecutor wants to achieve a major win, does he care that it is at the expense of your loss? If a judge is awaiting an appointment to the Supreme Court and must get noticed by bringing in a major guilty verdict, are you the sacrificial lamb?

Does the government threat against you, if you fight and lose, carry such ridiculously harsh consequences that despite your innocence, you are forced to plea bargain and admit guilt?

How much, inventing, distorting and withholding of evidence is involved? How many people are misjudged due to tainted evidence or inadmissible evidence?

Most painful is when people have no boundaries as to how low they are willing to sink in their effort to hurt or frame you—can a person of value, fight that?

Whether you win or lose, fighting against the unlimited resources of the government or of major corporations can destroy you financially, so even when you win, you lose. And, even if you win, the accusation that was so outrageously and boldly emboldened in the front-page headline is inconspicuously withdrawn in a tiny article on page 65. Many, who have unfortunately been victims to this injustice, have been known to ask, "Now, where do I go to get my reputation back?"

My advice to you is "If you can possibly avoid it, don't litigate." Stay out of court. It's difficult to beat an unjust system. Don't get involved with lawyers or the court system. Life is too short and the aggravation too great and too extended to get involved (unless, of course, you're the lawyer earning the ever-ballooning fee as the clock keeps running).

This essential advice is not meant to serve to directly increase your happiness but rather to avoid the tremendous irritation and unhappiness as a consequence of the discouraging, humiliating, costly aggravation and frustration (and often financial devastation) that emanates from this generally unrewarding, time-consuming litigious activity.

"No truth, no equality. No equality, no justice. No justice, no peace. No peace, no love. No love, only darkness" (Suzy Kassem, writer).

Day 241

A man told his friend about a recent dream, "I dreamed that I was gambling on the Lido in Venice and I broke the bank." His friend said, "That's a nice dream. Let me tell you about the one I had last night. I dreamed I was on the Riviera with three stunning women." The first man asked, "Why didn't you call me?" The friend said, "I did. Your answering machine said you were in Venice."

We look forward to countless experiences with anticipation and excitement. Yet, often, these experiences leave us feeling unfulfilled or disappointed. How can we determine which experiences to pursue?

Firstly, the experience should be something you anticipate with joy, a graduation, a wedding, the birth of a child, etc.

Secondly, experiences should make you feel excited and fulfilled while you are experiencing them.

Thirdly, and most importantly, pursue activities where you feel gratified and happy after the fact. It is this criterion that really determines the essence of true happiness. Many things can fulfill the first two criteria—a terrific meal, a big business deal, a new car, a night out, a new job, etc. However, be aware that these things may not prove ultimately satisfying. Now that it is finished, do you feel good or bad? Did the meal leave you feeling satisfied or bloated? Does the deal make you feel proud or ashamed? Do you feel guilty or gratified? Would you tell those closest to you that you took part in this adventure?

The purchase of a fancy new car or big home that is followed by major payments you can't afford, a fun night out with someone inappropriate, a great business deal that has a bad element, or a great feast, that leaves you with stomach pains, each is only temporarily satisfying.

If the experience makes you feel good beyond the moment, for days and weeks and, ideally, for the rest of your life, then you will feel genuine, heartfelt happiness.

Instant gratification cannot produce the reward of genuine satisfaction. Pursue and engage in meaningful rewarding experiences and you will feel real happiness. Be aware that "Temporary happiness isn't worth long-term pain."

Day 242

"Happiness is your dentist telling you it won't hurt and then having him get his hand caught in the drill."— Johnny Carson

"To be wronged is nothing unless you continue to remember it" (Confucius).

People can hurt you. Even loved ones can hurt us. If we focus on this hurt, we can eat ourselves up, aggravate ourselves and engender more self-hurt, anguish and pain. Even when we are hurt, we should focus on all the past positive things that these loved ones did for us, or that others in the past have done for us.

Focus on some specific past positive, happy inducing thing that some person has done for you and you'll instantly feel better. Contemplate the lovely times you still hope to have with that person—the potential to share new experiences and unlimited joy. Forgiving does not erase the bitter past. "A healed memory is not a deleted memory. Instead, forgiving what we cannot forget creates a new way to remember. We change the memory of our past into a hope for the future" (Lewis B. Smedes).

Forgive and forget. Start a new page with new hope.

Day 243

"One time my whole family played hide-and-seek. They found my mother in Pittsburgh."—Roger Dangerfield

Nothing can make a person as happy as making another person happy. I would gladly give my loved ones the gift of happiness, but as much as I may want to, it is not mine to give. Happiness must come through one's own efforts. It is a lifetime work in progress.

Nevertheless, work at your personal relationships. It is up to you to give love. It is up to the other person to accept, appreciate and enjoy that love. Notice the little things that delight your partner and then give them as surprise gifts, not just on anniversaries and special occasions, but at other times and for no reason at all. Think, "What will make my spouse happy? What will make my children happy? What will make my parents and siblings happy?" Strengthen the family unit.

Give time, attention, understanding, direction, encouragement and love to those whom you love.

Make those you love happy. They will love you for it and you will bask in their love.

A person is only so strong but family members give each other the ultimate strength. "Snowflakes are one of nature's most fragile things…but just look at what they can do when they stick together!"

Day 244

An angel interviews Michael, who is trying to enter heaven. "Have you done any good deeds, helped the poor, been good to your neighbor or prayed to G-d?" "Nope", answered Michael. "Think," said the angel, "I am trying to find a way to get you into heaven. Haven't you ever done anything good?" "Well," answered Michael, "there were these Hell's Angels robbing an old lady and I got so mad I ran up to the worst of them, grabbed his arm, kicked him in the knee and spat in his face." "Wow," the angel said, "that's very impressive. How long ago was that?" Michael looked at his watch, "I guess about ten minutes ago!"

According to Stanford Business, a growing body of research has identified one reliable path to finding happiness: doing something rewarding, especially philanthropy. Acts of kindness not only benefit the recipient but also "create a pleasurable 'helper's high' that benefits the giver," says Professor Jennifer Aaker of the Stanford Graduate School of Business, who studied the phenomenon with Melanie Rudd of the University of Houston and Michael Norton of the Harvard Business School.

They found that people whom regularly volunteer report greater happiness than those who don't. They further found that concrete philanthropic goals could boost a giver's happiness more than abstract ones.

In an experimental situation, those who were asked to elicit a smile from others were happier than those who were asked to cheer others. Framing a goal in concrete terms makes a giver more realistic about his/her prospects of success. When expectations are high, it can lead to disappointment. When a goal is framed concretely, you focus on how to achieve it and the standards for success are more discernible. Experimenters found that volunteers who chase amorphous goals, such as changing the lives of others are destined to feel disappointed making a negative rather than positive influence on givers' happiness.

Performing five random acts of kindness a day for six weeks has been shown to boost happiness, as has spending money on others. When one performs good deeds and experience a helper's high, we not only feel greater happiness in the moment, we may also be more likely to give again in the future.

Choose a goal and determine to do five random kindnesses every day. In this way, you will create a feeling of self-worth, of accomplishment and reward, which not only helps others to be happier, it increases your happiness as well.

Day 245

I bought a stock at fifteen. It went down twenty points.

During the course of our lives, we will be burdened by unpleasant experiences and distressing adversities. We will suffer heartbreaking disappointments and disillusionments. Far too often, we will be hurt, inadvertently or even deliberately and with malice, by people we interact or work with or even by those closest to us—people whom we may cherish. Like it or not, devastating external uncontrollable events, as well as or in addition to intentional injurious, irritating and terribly traumatizing actions, will be inflicted upon us and engender wretched pain.

That's reality and that's an unfortunate fact of human existence. The good news, though, is that such conditions only prevail for (hopefully) a small part of our lives.

The most imperative thing is to avoid being a victim. Don't allow yourself to become a prisoner of your own mind and thought processes. It's bad enough that external events and the harmful actions of other people can inflict aggravation, humiliation and distress upon us, but there is absolutely no reason for us to punish ourselves.

Realize for a moment that when you care about others, people you cherish and love and want to make happy, you would do whatever would help them avoid or overcome their trials and tribulations, their pain and suffering. You would do whatever it would take to inspire in them a happy state of mind as well as having others do the same.

So, with sagacious wisdom and kindness, do unto yourself that which you would have others do unto you. Do it by mastering your mind and your thought processes with positive thoughts, instead of what so many of us tend to self-destructively do, punish ourselves by unceasingly imprisoning our minds with the burdensome and hurtful disappointments, imagined impending threats or currently prevalent negative circumstances or conditions.

"The only thing worse than being blind is having sight but no vision" (Helen Keller). Realize the remarkably powerful tool you thankfully possess to instill and impose encouraging, positive, hopeful, happy-inducing thoughts into your head, so that no matter what the present, seemingly hopeless condition, with optimism and hope you have the ability to move ahead.

Day 246

Some days you're the dog, some days you are the hydrant.

Far too often, I have been the instigator and essentially the sole precipitator of the aggravation and distress I have suffered. No one else was around. It was I alone, that by thinking about and focusing upon some negative experiences of the past, present or even some matter I feared might occur in the future, I induced a state of unhappiness and depression and became dejected, discouraged and disheartened. I caused my own gloom, anguish and misery just because I had my mind, my thought process, immerse itself on pessimistic, dispiriting, sad thoughts which, in most cases for no actual valid reason, put me in a state of despair and caused me to feel terribly miserable.

One day, I realized what I was doing to myself and how counterproductive and self-destructive these harmful and hurtful thoughts were. I conjectured that if indeed it was self-induced, I could turn my thoughts around for my own benefit, exploiting this mechanism to produce the opposite result—cheerfulness, optimism, exuberance and, yes, happiness. By having my brain and my thought process focus upon and immerse itself in positive, rewarding, and joyful past, present and, yes hopeful, exciting future experiences, I lifted my spirits, induced a feeling of joy, sparkling sunniness and heartwarming elation. I made myself happy. I learned to be my own best friend instead of my own worse enemy.

Since I am the most involved and critical actor in my own life, it was important that I learn to play a role in that exercise that will maximally enhance the joy and happiness I can produce. The same goes for you.

Become your own best friend. You are indeed the single most important and involved actor in your own life, so it's up to you to learn and to then induce the maximum optimism, joy and happiness you can possibly produce for yourself.

"Happiness is not something ready made. It comes from your own actions" (Dali Lama XIV).

Day 247

The doctor said, "The good news is it's not hypochondria."

We've all heard the expression "You'll worry yourself sick." What are the implications for us of that statement with respect to the advice and prescription in this book? Clearly, what it tells us is what every psychologist knows, our state of mind can and will ruin our physical health, if we allow it to be swamped with worry.

It's that deflated state of mind that apparently produces a certain chemical reaction in the body which negatively impacts and weakens the immune system to the point where we get physically as well as mentally sick. Neither viruses nor bacteria nor noxious germs cause much of the illnesses that plague our society. It is the negative worrisome state of mind and the ensuing stresses that cause many millions of Americans to suffer from a state of depression as well as the ensuing migraine headaches, back pains and ulcers and so many other devastating "psychosomatic" illnesses.

We can readily see that if we control our mind to think positive thoughts, which studies prove promotes good health, we can arouse the uplifting, salutary chemical reactions that engender good health, instead of destructive illness and debilitating depression.

Every moment of your life could be better, but it could be far worse. Use your brain "power" to produce your own miraculous happiness.

Day 248

Before you criticize someone, walk a mile in his shoes. Then, when you criticize that person, you'll be a mile away and have his shoes.

Mrs. Judy Agnew, the wife of Vice President of the United States, Spiro Agnew, told a magazine interviewer that she learned to shrug off criticism of her husband, lest she "be upset every day of the week." Learning to let bothersome things just roll off your back can be enormously helpful. Just "shrug off" any unpleasant experience, which in the long run will probably have little impact on your life.

Developing a "let it go approach" to criticism will go a long way toward your establishing a lifetime of emotional health.

Being careful to watch what you say about others also raises one's own self-esteem. "Slander slays three people: the speaker, the spoken to and the spoken of." There is a terrific story of a woman who approaches her rabbi and asks him for forgiveness for having slandered a friend. The rabbi said that he would first like her to do one thing for him. Take a feather pillow and slit it open and let all the feathers fly in the wind. She did as she was asked to and then returned to the rabbi once again asking for forgiveness. "I will gladly ask G-d to forgive you after you do one more thing," he said. "Anything," cried the woman, "I feel so bad about having slandered my friend." "Now," said the rabbi, "Go retrieve all the feathers!"

Slander, once it leaves your mouth, is as irretrievable as feathers in the wind. Self-respect and self-esteem are generated by controlling both what you allow to leave your mouth and what you allow to enter your ears.

Day 249

Every day, the same old thing: breathe, breathe, breathe…

Sadly, I know of so many people wallowing in sorrow. People with good reason to be depressed; they've experienced a devastating loss, they've missed an unbelievable opportunity, their girlfriend or spouse has left them, they have been financially ruined, their children are rebellious, they've missed the chance to marry and have kids. The list goes on and on. Some just mope all day. Some turn to drinking or substance abuse. Some go so far as to inflict pain on themselves. Some intentionally, or too often unintentionally, commit suicide. Some continue to punish themselves and to hurt those around them, refusing help from others, refusing to help themselves.

Replaying painful memories is a form of self-abuse. Acceptance and moving on is a gift you owe yourself.

"One of the happiest moments ever is when you find the courage to let go of what you can't change." True, you may never be "as happy" again, but you may find a new acceptable level of happiness. Not perfection, but a far cry from misery. Only "you" can decide to make "you" happy.

Day 250

You've heard of the three ages of man; youth, middle age and "you're looking wonderful."

Mrs. Brooke Astor, the philanthropist and socialite who was still alive at 104 years of age, attributed her longevity to the fact that she had a zest for life. She was always reading. She also worked on dieting, exercising, social networking and the ability to handle stress. Most of all, she never let herself become depressed.

In fact, geriatric professionals contend that exceptional longevity, the state of living to one hundred or beyond, does indeed result from factors like diet, exercise, health habits, social support, and the ability to find meaning in life.

The secret to achieving happiness and quality longevity is to have a sense of mission and a positive zest for life, not allowing yourself to become depressed. The two most important days in your life are the day you were born and the day you find out why.

"Your purpose in life is to is to find your purpose and give your whole heart and soul to it" (Gautama Buddha).

Day 251

"Oy, I forgot to exercise again today. Shucks, that makes five years."

Elycia Rubin, co-author of *Frumpy to Foxy in 15 Minutes Flat*, hopes her book "will teach people to feel great about themselves in less time—because we women have so much going on in our lives we don't necessarily have the hours to get ready. However, when we leave the house knowing we look our best, and take a very short time to do it," she says, "it just makes for a more comfortable and confident day.

It is important for both men and women to keep in shape and to be neatly dressed and groomed. This is vital for one's self-respect as well as for the impression one makes on others. "When you look good you feel good."

Besides improving cardiovascular health, building your strength and shaping your body, scientists have found that exercising can boost brain function. It reduces mental stress by increasing concentrations of norepinephrine, a chemical that can moderate the brain's response to stress. It boosts your endorphins, which are your happy chemicals. It helps reduce anxiety and depression. It improves self-confidence by elevating a person's self-perception. Exercise has also been shown to prevent cognitive decline because it boosts hippocampus, the chemicals in the brain that support and prevent degeneration of one's memory and learning ability. Studies further suggest that cardiovascular exercise can create new brain cells, which improve overall performance. It also sharpens your memory. Furthermore, a tough workout increases the brains production of BDNF, a brain-derived protein, believed to help with decision-making, higher thinking and learning.

Exercise causes the brain to release dopamine, the reward chemical, in response to any form of pleasure. Often people use drugs or alcohol to produce this pleasurable feeling, which can be produced more safely by exercising. Exercise is therefore used in addiction control. After exercising, people are found to be more relaxed, sleep better, accomplish more, are better able to tap into their creativity and are even able to inspire others.

Staying in shape makes one feel all around more upbeat. "Movement is a medicine for creating change in a person's physical, emotional and mental states" (Carol Welch).

Day 252

He attended the Cyclathon and remarked, "If they started earlier, they wouldn't have to pedal so hard."

Tour de France champ Lance Armstrong, who battled a near-fatal cancer to win the world's most challenging bike race, calls the disease "the best thing that ever happened to me. There is no question in my mind that I would never have won the Tour if I hadn't gotten cancer," he declares.

"The truth is, it was the best thing that ever happened to me, because it made me a better man and a better rider," he writes in an excerpt from his memoir, *It's Not About the Bike*, in *Vanity Fair* magazine.

In 1996, at age twenty-five, he found out he had testicular cancer that had spread to his lungs and brain. "There are two Lance Armstrongs: pre-cancer and post," he says. "Every boys' favorite question is, 'How did cancer change you?' The real question is, 'How didn't it change me?'"

The athlete underwent brain surgery, removal of a testicle and rigorous chemotherapy treatment during which he lost twenty pounds and "every muscle I ever built up. Everyone assumed I was finished," Armstrong writes. Then, the US Postal Service team picked him up, and he began riding again in 1998.

He became depressed after finishing fourteenth in his first professional race after being diagnosed. Armstrong says he knew he had won the war against cancer, "but I was traumatized by the battle."

He gave up riding and became "a bum." "I played golf every day. I water-skied. I drank beer, and I lay on the sofa and channel-surfed."

It was his fiancée, Kristin Richard, who snapped him out of it by telling him, "You need to decide if you are going to retire for real and be a golf-playing, beer-drinking, Mexican-food-eating slob. If you are, that's fine. I love you, and I'll marry you anyway. But, I just need to know."

"I started riding again a week later," he writes. As he began rigorous training for the 1999 Tour de France, Armstrong noticed "one unforeseen benefit of cancer. It had completely reshaped my body. I was leaner in body and more balanced in spirit."

This was just another bump in his road. We too must learn to survive and overcome life's bumps.

Day 253

An optimist is a ninety-year-old man who gets married and looks for a house near a school!

It always pays off far better to be an optimist than to be a pessimist. A pessimistic approach leads to depression and negative expectations and thus a state of unhappiness even before anything unpleasant or tragic ever occurs and which, in fact, may never ever occur. It causes one to become debilitated and broken down long before any such feared eventuality ever comes about. If, indeed it does come to fruition, one is already so weakened as to be unable to deal with the challenge once it occurs.

Much of what we fear either never actually occurs or in so many cases, the actual result is far less threatening or devastating than one's anticipation. I have talked to people who have been through harrowing trials where they were finally convicted and sent to serve time in prison and in talking about their experience they almost unanimously said (except for maybe one or two that appeared psychotic) that the frightening anticipation of being convicted and jailed was far worse than the actual eventual experience. In some cases, in fact, they said it turned out the actual time served in prison turned out to be a positive experience, so much so that their lives were changed for the better with new learned values and renewed religion and more realistically satisfying expectations and subsequently even new, more challenging and interesting careers.

Mental attitude profoundly affects bodily health for better or worse. Worry weakens one while a good attitude puts you in a far better condition to deal with and even overcome an untoward event.

The optimist retains a positive, uplifting attitude and thus if, indeed, some negative event or even terrible catastrophe actually does come to fruition, he hasn't been paying the price in fear, anxiety and debilitating depression well in advance. He has enjoyed the time up to the actual occurrence and is in a far stronger mental and indeed physical condition to cope and overcome. In fact, people that retain a positive, fighting, winning attitude almost always do better against any and every threat, even cancer, perhaps the worst possible attack of any.

Perhaps the best part for the optimist and the worst part for the pessimist is that so often expectations become self-fulfilling prophesies. Be good to yourself! Choose optimism!

Day 254

"Most of the time, I don't have much fun. The rest of the time, I don't have any fun at all."—Woody Allen

"Life is a shipwreck but we must not forget to sing in the lifeboats" (Voltaire).

Untreated depression, whether it is due to a devastating loss or illness, a break up, a financial setback or a heartbreaking disappointment, often results in social isolation, which only exacerbates the depression.

The classic symptoms of depression are a deep sadness and lack of pleasure in people and activities the sufferer once enjoyed. Irritability and apathy—in fact, a pervasive disinterest in life and what it may have to offer—is another symptom. Other common hallmarks of depression include difficulty concentrating, memory lapses, loss of appetite, diminished energy and a physical slowing down.

Relief of depression can facilitate a person's return to normal functioning. Eliminating depression improves physical functioning, decreases pain, improves the person's outlook and prolongs life.

Mentally healthy people of any age who have chronic physical disabilities or diseases soon learn to adapt to their limitations and get the most out of life that they can. It is not so much that illness causes depression; rather, depression increases the risk of illness, functional decline and even symptoms of dementia. People can cure themselves by changing their mental outlook. This is the best treatment with the most benefit and fewest side effects.

If you are depressed, you can quickly gladden and exhilarate yourself if you "look on the bright side," "pull yourself together" and "be grateful for all the good things." "Caring for yourself is not self-indulgent. It is an act of survival." "From every wound there is a scar, and every scar tells a story. A story that says, 'I have survived.' Turn your wounds into wisdom" (Anonymous).

Day 255

Considering the alternative, life isn't such a bad deal!

In her inspirational book *My Stroke of Insight,* Jill Bolte Taylor, a neuroscientist at Harvard Brain Research Center, describes how her left brain injury that damaged her ability to speak, understand numbers or letters, or even recognize her mother, led her to blissful enlightenment. Dr. Taylor teaches that people can choose to live a more peaceful and spiritual life by sidestepping the use of their left brain, which she says gives us context, ego, time and logic to focus on the use of the right brain, which gives us creativity and empathy.

She has inspired not only stroke victims and their caregivers, but also spiritual seekers, particularly Buddhists and meditation practitioners, who say her experience "confirms that there is an attainable state of joy."

Sharon Salzberg, a founder of the Insight Meditation Society, says because Dr. Taylor uses the language of science, she can demonstrate to the less mystically inclined that this experience of deep contentment "is part of the capacity of the human mind."

It all goes back to the one crucial factor: attitude! For example, she says, "As a child of divorced parents and a mentally ill brother, I was really angry." Now when she feels anger rising, she trumps it with a thought of a person or activity that brings her pleasure.

Even though Dr. Taylor arrives at this "right" attitude approach to attaining a state of joy, a beautiful state of "Nirvana," through a seemingly circuitous scientific approach, she essentially reaches the same conclusion as the prescribed behavior of this book.

Like Dr. Taylor, you can achieve happiness by developing your ability to instantly switch to the "right" uplifting attitude. Always think of the beautiful quote from *The Secret Garden*, "If you look the right way, you can see that the whole world is a garden."

Day 256

Life is a party you join after it has started and leave before it's finished.

"Death: Sometimes when one person is missing, the whole world seems depopulated" (Lamartine, French poet).

Within a couple of years, two different men with whom I play tennis lost a young child to cancer. At the time that these terrible tragedies occurred, I was sure they would be so intensely and permanently devastated that they'd never be able to smile again or be able to enjoy the fun of our tennis games. It's hard to conceive of any more painful hurt or any comparably disheartening adversity. How would they be able to enjoy life ever again?

Yet remarkably, fortunately, each one fought off what I believed would be an inevitably ensuing lifelong depression, commemorating their beloved offspring through the cancer research work each has ardently supported. They have dedicated themselves, so that other parents should not suffer this same terrible ordeal or its grievous agony.

Amazingly, they have bounced back with the most encouraging dispositions—smiling, laughing, playing and being tremendous fun while enjoying renewed, wholesome fun-filled lives. Each man shows that no matter what, "life goes on." Life must go on. Life is what we have been given and which we should learn to make the most of. No matter how terrible, how unfair a particular adversity we may be subjected to and compelled to experience, we can and must bounce back.

There is always the pain of such a loss but we must keep those loved ones within our heart to inspire us and help us grow and help us use the pain in a positive way to make a significant difference. We keep those souls alive by the good we accomplish in their names and in their memories. We make sure that there was a purpose to their having existed in that they helped make our lives better and we in turn help make the lives of others better.

During the course of our lives, it's almost certain that we will have to live through tearful reversals, hurtful hardships, demoralizing misfortunes and even catastrophic disasters. The best way, maybe the only way, to survive, to overcome and live through these horrendously challenging periods is to develop a positive, ever hopeful, ever optimistic attitude which will serve to generate a healthy resiliency, which will in turn reinvigorate and inspire us to ever more satisfactory, rewarding and happiness-providing experiences.

Cry your tears. Dry your eyes and do what you have to do. Then, go on with living!

Day 257

One twin was always optimistic while the other was a pessimist. On their birthday, Dad decided to teach them a lesson. He filled the pessimist's room with loads of toys and filled the optimist's room with loads of manure. When he checked on the pessimist, he found him crying. "Why are you crying?" he asked. The pessimist said, "I know all these great toys are going to break." Going to the optimist, he found him whistling happily while digging through the manure. "Why are you so happy?" "Because," answered the optimist, "with all this manure, I know there must be a pony in here somewhere."

A great lesson in how a positive attitude can inspire a sense of much more than merely passive acceptance comes from someone who has been subjected to one of the most sorrowful experiences any mother can live with. The following is a letter to the *New York Times* from the mother of an autistic child:

"It took almost ten years, two incorrect diagnoses and years of school-recommended counseling before I learned that my son, Christian, had high-functioning autism. The correct diagnosis saved my son's life.

"Today, enrolled in a mainstream middle school, he plays the violin, socializes with a small network of friends and earns As and Bs on his report card—that is, when he remembers to turn in his homework.

"While I have a realistic understanding of the condition, I refuse to allow autism to define this young man. He is more than his condition.

"Each week brings a new round of challenges and the occasional heartbreak, but we have learned to find joy and meaning in every success, no matter how small or routine."

As Christian says, "Everybody's got something." It's true; everybody does have something—some baggage they carry and must deal with through life. During our life we all, at one time or another, experience terribly trying overwhelmingly hurtful, heartbreaking experiences. It is essential that we develop the kind of positive thinking Christian's mother did, so we too can find joy and meaning from even the smallest and most routine successes.

Everyone has baggage. The measure of a man is how he carries and deals with that baggage.

Day 258

Live life one day at a time. After all, isn't that why they were put in consecutive order?

Life is short.
Think about it. Do you think we live more or less than:

30,000 months?
18,000 months?
15,000 months?
10,000 months?
5,000 months?
2,000 months?

Less or more? What is your answer?

    The truth is that very few of us live even one thousand months, which equals eighty-three and one-third years. With life so breathtakingly short, it's incumbent on each of us to make the most of every moment. Train yourself to be positive, upbeat and constructive. Resist wasting any of your precious moments focusing on the negatives, ruminating about what's not right or not perfect, and direct your mind and your thoughts to that which can bring about a feeling of contentment, appreciation and joyfulness.

Day 259

The patient said, "I feel like a new man." The psychologist said, "Can this new guy afford me?"

    Extensive psychiatric sessions, hypnosis, tranquilizers, antidepressants or any combination of drugs or chemicals is not the answer. Self-help is the ideal way to achieving a rapid and ongoing state of happiness. By studying, practicing and implementing the "attitudinal" methods presented and promulgated in this treatise which you have been wise enough to discover and explore, you can effectively and expeditiously help yourself—institute—the "self-help" that will nurture and successfully facilitate your pursuit of happiness and accomplish that fabulously desirable goal.

    Realize on your own the truth of what Shakespeare so wisely said, "There is nothing either good or bad, but thinking makes it so." It is up to you to decide to change the course of your life by altering your attitude. A change in attitude is a catalyst for a change in action. "Men are made stronger on the realization that the helping hand they need is at the end of their own arm" (Sidney Phillips). Anyone can run away, that's easy. Facing your problems and working through them, that's what makes you strong. Once you begin to help yourself, the effort alone gives you strength and happiness becomes reality.

Day 260

Three corpses with big smiles on their faces are lying in a mortuary. The coroner tells a police officer what happened:

"First body: Frenchman, sixty, died of heart failure while with the woman he loved. Hence, the smile, says the Coroner.

"Second body: Scotsman, twenty-five, won a hundred pounds in the lottery, spent it on whiskey and died drinking. Hence the great smile on his face."

The officer asked, "What about the third body?"

"Ah," says the coroner, "this is the most interesting one. That's Billy Bob, the redneck from Alabama, thirty, struck by lightning while bass fishing."

"Why is he smiling then?" asked the officer.

"Thought he was having his picture taken."

"Smiles" is the longest word in the English dictionary because there is a "mile" between the first and last letters. And because that word describes the most inspirational and rewarding action any human being can do to make himself and others feel happier, it deserves to be the longest word in any dictionary.

Smile as much as you can, as enthusiastically as you can, as sincerely as you can and, even, as proudly as you can. It's a really healthy and enormously gratifying exercise. Medical practitioners and psychologists have scientifically determined that smiling is relaxing and salutary for your facial features and brain, while frowning is taxing upon, distorting, and even detrimental to your facial muscles and brain cells. Frowning is depressing. Smiling is uplifting, so smile! Smile! Smile!

"Smiling is the best way to face every problem, to crush every fear, to hide every pain." A smile lets everyone know you are stronger than you were yesterday. As Charlie Chaplin so wisely said, "I have many problems in my life. But, my lips don't know that."—They always smile.

Day 261

He is so poor. All he has is money.

A wealthy man on vacation wandered down to the river where he saw a man relaxing on the shore fishing. "What do you do?" asked the wealthy man. "I lay on the shore all day and enjoy fishing?" "What," cried the wealthy man. "You don't work? You just lie out here lazing around all day?" "Right," said the fisherman. "You see I used to be a big businessman. I worked day and night. I never had time to take a break. I never had time to spend with my wife and my children. I dreamed of taking a vacation. I bought a big house and a big car and was busy earning money to keep them. I never had time to enjoy them. All I wanted to do is earn enough money so I could finally take my wife and kids on a vacation, relax and go fishing. The more money I earned, the more money I believed I needed. The more I worked the more I dreamed of having enough money to live the life I wanted to.

"One day, I just closed up my business, packed up my family and moved to a tiny house in the country where I now take it easy, enjoy my family and laze around fishing."

Don't get so caught up in earning a living that you miss out on living.

Day 262

After examining him, the doctor told the patient he had only six months to live. The patient told the doctor, "Doc, I can't pay you in only six months." So, the doctor told him, "Okay, in that case, I'll give you another six months.

By sharing "battlefield" encouraging and inspiring experiences, cancer patients suffering serious side effects from chemotherapy as well as from the illness itself have entered physical therapy programs that helped them regain a rewarding more normal existence. It helped them regain a revived physically functional life as well as a much-improved emotional outlook and attitude.

In some cases, it helped patients survive longer than others afflicted with the same condition. Even in cases where it didn't prolong life, it did help them to live a better more fulfilling, far "happier" last-years than those that gave in and passively succumbed without putting up that kind of valiant and inspiring fight.

Hardly anything we may face can be worse. Yet, if you determine to make the best of it, it helps enormously. No matter what, don't give in!

It's not how long you live that counts. It's how well you live. Some people have longevity while leading miserable lives. Others live shorter but more enjoyable, genuinely admirable and fulfilling lives. It's all about what you do with whatever time you are allocated. If you do good things, if you maintain a happy spirit, if you are generous with your love and affection, if you stay busy and constructive, if you smile a lot and share your joy and any of your G-d-given assets with others, then you will have lived a truly enviable, happy life.

It's worth recognizing, we all ultimately cross the line to the world hereafter. However, in this most relevant race of all, it's not the one who gets over the line fastest or slowest that wins; it's the one who enjoys the experiences, the scenery, the relationships, the excitement, the thrills and the spills, the achievements and accomplishments along the way and who finally realizes the satisfaction and appreciation of a race well run, that is indeed the winner. So along the way, do all those things that will make you and all those you touch in the course of that exalted race richer and happier for your having been a participant in the challenging but adventurous route to the finish line.

If cancer patients can improve their outlook and make their time on earth more productive, each of us should certainly be able to do the same.

Day 263

Instant gratification takes too long.

In order to be happy, we must train ourselves to be patient. We live in a generation of instant gratification. Our food is microwaved. The Internet immediately answers our questions and we find ourselves angry and frustrated if our needs are not immediately met.

No matter what you are trying to achieve, the best way to succeed is to learn to delay gratification, to make a choice to pass up something now for the pleasure of being able to attain something bigger or better at a later time.

Based on a marshmallow experiment where four- to six-year-old children were given the choice to eat one marshmallow now or wait fifteen minutes and receive two marshmallows. It was found that those who were able to delay their urge to eat the one were, in their adolescent years, psychologically better adjusted, more dependable, more self-motivated and received higher grade scores. These characteristics endured for life.

Learn to save now, so that you can buy something better later. Delay eating something fattening now, in order, that you might make a healthier choice. Decide not to smoke now, so that you may live longer. Study for school now, so that you are able to get a better job.

In order to delay present gratification for future reward, know your values, what is important to you. Know what you want to achieve then create a plan, so that you keep sight of your goal. Prioritize what means the most to you. Because final achievement may take a long time, break down your goals and reward yourself along the way, so

HAPPINESS GUARANTEED OR YOUR MISERY BACK

that you will remind yourself that delaying gratification is leading you to what you want and to attaining the happiness you are after.

Following your impulses is satisfactory now but disappointing in the long run. Mindfulness and awareness will help you delay gratification. "Good things come to those who wait."

Day 264

A doctor called a patient, "Your check came back." The patient said, "So did my bursitis!"

The physical body has what doctors call "homeostasis" working for it. This is the tendency of the body to always move to bring itself back to what we call "normal" or to good health. In fact, that's the best thing we have working for us and that the doctors have working for them. In like manner, you should recognize that what your mind and your psyche have working for you is the "human spirit."

Help your human spirit to reinvigorate your mind to bring it back to positive, "normal" good health, to feeling good. Come to know you can do it. You can make it happen. You can make your internal-self happy despite external, debilitating events. Decide that it's up to you because in the last analysis it truly is. You are more than you think you are. Take advantage of, indeed, exploit the human spirit, your own controllable human spirit. If you do, you will surely become more than you are and thereby determine your own state of happiness, gratification and self-realization.

Develop the latent capacity of the amazing control inherent in you, so that your mind can return your body to a healthy state.

Always be aware that "Beyond each impenetrable expanse of thundercloud obscurity reins a boundless canopy of brilliant sapphire blue" (Cara Fox).

Day 265

"You said you could beat him hands down."
"Yes, dear, but he doesn't want to keep his hands down."

"Life has served that up and I just deal with it" is the response of Freddie Roach to his Parkinson's disease. Freddie lives his life and pursues his career as a leading boxing trainer with a passion, a zest and a dedication that keeps him constantly enthusiastic and excited, so that he does not allow his onerous fateful malady to depress him. In fact, it actually helps him in his drive to aid and encourage his boxer clients, among them world-class champ Oscar De La Hoya, to realize their dreams. In so doing, with this positive constructive approach, this role-model attitude, Roach achieves enormous satisfaction and an admirable happiness despite, and in the face of, a burdensome adversity. That's the kind of functionally adaptive healthy response that will indeed produce a happier life.

I have a friend who is a rabbi, and his son was born with cancer in the eye. The son is blind and probably doesn't have great prospects, but he is so amazingly optimistic. My friend tells me that every day this child lives he appreciates him, he loves him, and he tells all of the kid's brothers and sisters, "Look at your fingers, be aware that they work. You should be happy every minute that they work. Your eyes: think if you couldn't see. Look around. Look at the flowers, look at the sky, look at the moon, look at everything, look at colors and think how lucky you are."

Sadly, most often, it isn't until we lose something that we really appreciate it and recognize its importance. Appreciate what you have before it becomes what you had.

Day 266

"I don't get no respect. I called Suicide Prevention. They tried to talk me into it."—Rodney Dangerfield

Halle Berry, when discussing a magazine article that talked about her suicide attempt ten years earlier, said she wished they hadn't talked about that episode in her life because she was now at the very top of her life. She went on to say, "life is full of ups and downs" and in that respect, despite her current success, fame and popularity, she was indeed like everyone else.

It's tremendously useful and effective to realize and accept the reality that life is full of ups and downs. Once you are cognizant of that truism, you need to use that wisdom to help yourself through the rough, challenging, even through the most discouraging "down" parts of your life, by reassuring yourself that this troublesome aggravating time will pass, as it eventually will, and you will then enjoy exciting new "ups"—maybe even the very top "ups" ever. The challenge is to enjoy the ups and have courage and remain optimistic during the downs.

Stay strong because things will get better. It might be stormy now but it can't rain forever. "Life is like a roller coaster. It has its ups and downs, but it's your choice to scream or to enjoy the ride."

Day 267

A man was spread out over three seats in the second row of a movie theatre. As he lay there breathing heavily, an usher rushed over, "That's very rude of you, sir, taking up three seats. Didn't you learn any manners? Where did you come from?" The man looked up helplessly and said, "The balcony!"

In many instances, you've got to learn to live with or deflect the pain. For example, just as when you first learn to play tennis and your palm gets terribly irritated from the grip, or you learn to stretch furs with your bare hands and it starts to bleed, it hurts. Your physical body develops a callus so that after a while it never hurts again. Likewise, you have to develop a mental callus so as to become immunized from the pain. You've got to fight it off. Once you make up your mind to fight, you mobilize your energies and your body launches its adrenaline and you start to feel invigorated.

When you are very low and just at the point of total hopelessness, you must reassure yourself and believe the time will come again when it will seem to you that "G-d is in heaven and all is right with the world."

Never despair. Realize that G-d will pull you through. "Faith is having a positive attitude about what you can do and not worrying about what you can't do."

In 2015, the most disastrous, unfathomable tragedy happened to Mr. Gabriel Sassoon. He lost seven of his eight children in a freak fire and his wife and one remaining daughter were hospitalized in extremely critical condition. After praising his children, while the eyes and sympathy of the world was on him, he said, "My future depends on complete and utter surrender to G-d." A few days after the tragedy, when questioned as to how he was coping, he said he takes life a minute at a time. Gabriel said, "Now I'm coping. How I will be in five minutes, I cannot tell you. "

Following the burial of his children, who he referred to as his shining stars, Gabriel went to a rabbi to ask for a blessing that he be granted more children.

What an amazing lesson this man has exhibited for us, of acceptance, unwavering reliance on G-d and hope for the future. There is no doubt that, not giving in to everlasting despair, will require an enormous amount of energy and work, but whether it is for himself or his remaining family, he seems willing to work toward that admirable goal.

Day 268

"I read this article. It said the typical symptoms of stress are eating too much, smoking too much, impulse buying and driving too fast. Are they kidding? This is my idea of a great day!"—Monica Piper

Whatever you do, don't allow yourself to suffer from depression. As an article in the *New York Post* entitled "'Sickening Depression" explains, "Depression is more damaging to everyday health than chronic diseases, such as angina, arthritis, asthma and diabetes," according to World Health Organization researchers. They said their findings show that depression impairs health to a state substantially greater than the other diseases and that if people are ill with other conditions, depression makes them far worse.

How often do people feel "I'm so broken that I can feel it. I mean, physically feel it. This is so much more than being sad now. This is affecting my whole body."

There is just no good reason or, in fact, any reason in the world to condone or reconcile oneself to put up with depression. It's only a form of self-inflicted punishment that is terribly harmful and you must and can learn to almost instinctively, kind of automatically, eliminate it from your mind

It is up to you to overcome depression. As Dorothy Rowe said, "Depression is a prison where you are both the suffering prisoner and the cruel jailer."

You have the ability to strengthen yourself. "I am strong, because I've been weak. I am fearless, because I've been afraid. I am wise, because I've been foolish." Conquer your fears, face your issues, and learn from your mistakes. Know that only "you" can convince "you" to move on, to grow from the pain rather than wallow in it.

Depression is like quick sand. If you don't find a way to crawl out of it, you will be dragged under. Self-pity allows you to fall deeper. Decide to accept and overcome your challenge, to pull yourself away from your despairing thoughts and think of all life's positives and all "you" can do to achieve your own personal state of satisfaction.

Pulitzer Prize-winning poet Carolyn Kizer in her collection of poems, *Knock Upon Silence*, wrote a piece of excellent advice, "Submerge your self-pity in disciplined industry." There are innumerable times when we experience what we feel are devastating disappointments that, in addition to overwhelmingly depressing us, causes us to indulge in disabling counterproductive self-pity that only adds to our debilitation and ineffectiveness. The most efficacious and expedient way to address and overcome such a dysfunctional malaise is to indulge in some distracting, useful uplifting work project—some "disciplined industry" that will help raise you and your mood from demoralized and impotent to exuberant and blissfully productive.

Day 269

I was going to look for my missing watch, but I could never find the time.

    King Solomon wisely advised us that in light of all the frustrations, disappointments and challenges that confront each of us in life, we should treasure our time while we have it and use that time to express and experience as much *love* as possible.

    Sadly, it's apparent that for an overwhelming number of us, it isn't until we're on our deathbed, taking our very last breaths, that we come to realize and appreciate how precious and beautiful life—just being alive—is. At that critical moment, we resist with all our might, dying, and wish we could just have a few more years in this world and the opportunity to experiences some of the fascinating possibilities and joys that "life" itself offers—to appreciate the love we have been blessed with.

    Repeatedly tell your spouse and your kids and your precious friends that you love them. This kind of behavior adds immensely to your own personal gratification and will delight them, as well, and add to your happy experience.

    "To love is nothing. To be loved is something. But to love and be loved, that's everything" (T. Tolls).

Day 270

OMG, I have finally discovered what's wrong with my brain. On the left side, there is nothing right. On the right side, there is nothing left.

As I have already urged repeatedly and choose to reiterate once again, because it's so critically important in your portfolio of assets to inspire happiness, it is imperative to smile, smile, smile!

A smile costs nothing and yet can enrich you beyond any material wealth. You can offer it generously, magnanimously to others, to all those around you, to all your friends and loved ones, and yes, to every person with whom you ever come in contact. You will not only not be any poorer for giving it away but also, indeed, be richer in the things that really count—your relationship with others. The more you give it away the richer your life will be.

When you present someone with a warm, joyful smile, you can fill his life with joy, while a frown sends a message like a bad-news letter. It can demoralize, depress and has even been known to emotionally devastate another person. When you frown you even get yourself down.

You, as well as all the rest of the world, will be happier for that simple yet precious, priceless act of sharing a smile.

"To laugh often and much: to win the respect of intelligent people and the affection of children, to leave the world a better place, to know even one life has breathed easier because you have lived, this is to have succeeded" (Ralph Waldo Emerson).

Day 271

He never worries about tomorrow. He knows that everything is going to turn out wrong.

The great German author Thomas Mann pointed out that every critical illness, whether it was tuberculosis back then or cancer today, brings out the dark or the light in individuals. Some people immediately fall apart and crumble, living in misery until their distressing final end, while others respond by getting their adrenaline up, fighting to win their battle for life.

Those who adopt the "fighting" attitude are energized, often to become more alive and activated than they have ever been, and in some cases, in far greater proportion than one would expect. This results in far greater successful outcomes than those that take on a despondent attitude, and for sure, they live their final days out in a much more satisfying manner. They not only die happier, but also, in the preponderance of instances, all of the members of their family, as well as the various other important relations in their lives, experience a much more tolerable, often even uplifting period. The upbeat attitude, the bravery, the courage, and the positive approach all provide an enduring solace to those around the unfortunate.

You can't change the inevitable, but you can make the most of what you have and the time you have. In other words, don't fight what is. Don't eat yourself up. Roll with the punches.

Serenity, effectiveness, and, indeed, success come from accepting and then dealing wisely and appropriately with the challenges you confront.

Day 272

Suicide is the last thing a person should do!

Why does a person choose suicide? He wants to avoid pain. He wants to escape. Often this is not just to avoid physical pain but also to avoid the pain and hardship of facing problems and challenges. Death, or escape from responsibility, is a choice that is available to all of us, every second of every day. Suicide is an extreme and final form of escape. As Phil Donahue said, "It is a permanent solution to a temporary problem."

There are many other ways we may choose to escape. Life is very frustrating, and we need something to ease the pain. Sadly, too many individuals indulge in mind-deadening drugs, alcohol or catatonic denial. Hope is the best medicine, optimism is the best tonic and a positive mental state is the best cure.

Drugs are a form of escaping, resulting in a slow death that's not quite as sudden or traumatic. Killing time is an escape. That's a form of suicide too. If you're turning on the TV just because you're bored, isn't that a kind of suicide? You could be using your time to live and grow. But, you quit because it's too difficult.

We all choose to escape, now and then, from the effort involved in accomplishing the goals and ambitions that we set for ourselves in life. We all want to be great; we all want to contribute to the world. It's just that we don't always feel like putting in the effort. We distract ourselves and escape from whom we really are and what we want to achieve.

HAPPINESS GUARANTEED OR YOUR MISERY BACK

When you are obsessed with unhappy thoughts, which can have the effect of driving you nuts, of overwhelming you, of depressing you, of making you angry, of enraging you, it overcomes you and at its extreme even makes you suicidal. Unhappy thoughts make for an unhappy body. Psychologists know, beyond a shadow of a doubt, that such thoughts cause all sorts of debilitating conditions, from migraine headaches and ulcers to severe backache, to cancer and heart attacks.

Every moment you are alive, use your free will to choose between vibrant life and morbid death, reality or escapism. It's a constant choice. You are either making the choice to take the pain in order to grow or you are quitting. How you resolve that conflict is where your greatness lies.

As Helen Keller said, "A happy life consists not in the absence, but in the mastery of hardships."

Day 273

What excuse did Adam give to his children as to why they were no longer living in Eden? Your mother ate us out of house and home.

When we embrace classical or biblical values and ideals, we insulate our inner selves with diligence and perseverance against the harsh vicissitudes of the intrusive, myopic modern world. The great Hebrew scholars of the Old Testament tell us that G-d put us on this earth, so that we may experience and enjoy—especially enjoy—the fruits of his creation, this amazing, magnificent world.

If you think about it even for just a moment, you will readily realize that there is absolutely nothing we can do for G-d that he can't, of course, do instantly and better for himself. He's like a loving mother with a newborn infant. The infant can give the mother nothing, except perhaps love, which it cannot, of course, express, articulate or demonstrate. The mother gave the infant life and the opportunity to share in its joys, adventures, opportunities and, yes, challenges and disappointments. Is there anything that a loving, caring mother wouldn't do for her totally helpless infant who cannot even say, "thank you"?

Just as a mother loves her child, unconditionally, uncompromisingly, so too you must know that G-d loves you and gave you the ultimate blessing—the blessing of life. He gave you breath. He gave you life. He gives you choice. He gives you opportunity. He gives you challenges and adventure. He gives you the chance for new relationships, new experiences, new knowledge, new observations, insights, visions and dreams.

If you can ingest and build into your mindset, into your operating system, the feeling that "G-d unconditionally loves me and is doing everything for my benefit," then no matter what happens, no matter what disappointment, no matter what adversity you face, you can deal with it.

But why, you may logically ask, do I need to confront and suffer if G-d is so loving? The answer, of course, is complex and elusive to say the least. Wise men and brilliant philosophers through the ages have been perplexed by this question—this dilemma. Talmudists and Torah scholars and all religionists and thinking men since the beginning of time have wrestled with this puzzle. If G-d put us here to enjoy, why doesn't he just let us enjoy? Why must we be burdened, worried, harassed, abused debilitated by all of the maladies, insecurities, human misbehaviors that often cause immense, seemingly irreparable pain, countless calamities, natural catastrophes, and so on, almost ad infinitum?

We have no answers. Life is like a needlepoint; on the wrong side, the threads are all tangled and sloppy. Yet, on the right side, there is a magnificent picture interwoven with spectacular threads. In this world, we can only see the wrong side of the needlepoint picture and we cannot envision the spectacular masterpiece G-d is creating. It is only in the world to come that we will see and understand G-d's beautiful picture.

Right now, our job is to realize that G-d loves us and is doing what is best for us and that He will help us deal with life's tests.

Don't wish for the impossible. Don't wish for miracles. You, yes, you, are a miracle; a miracle that only G-d could produce. Appreciate the miracle that you are. Appreciate the priceless, incalculable wealth you have. In a joyous state, build upon the potential inherent in the unique creation that is you.

"Faith is to believe what you do not see. The reward of this faith is to see what you believe" (St. Augustine).

Day 274

Thanks to you, I have learned that my prayers only get answered if I forward an e-mail to seven of my friends and make a wish within five minutes.

"Prayer does not change G-d, but it changes the one who prays" (Kierkegaard)

Almost all of the world's religions offer us a fascinating and major clue toward accomplishing our most meaningful objective—providing a distinct blueprint for the effective pursuit and achievement of happiness. Universally, they direct that we praise G-d, bless Him, and thank Him for all He has given us. Clearly, G-d has no need for praise or thanks, since He has everything and needs nothing from us mortals. He can have anything he wants. He can create anything he wants. Why then must we praise and thank him for our blessings?

The answer is really quite simple and remarkably elegant. Prayer does not help G-d; it helps us! Each time we pray we are moved to count our blessings, expressing our appreciation for what we have. We are focusing upon all the things in our lives that enhance our sense of good fortune, and consequently, this actually serves to substantially magnify our feeling of happiness.

"The purpose of prayer is not to get you out of trouble. The purpose of trouble is to get us into prayer." Connecting with G-d, appreciating all he has given us, enriches our quality of life.

Day 275

Once there was a clergyman who labeled his files "Sacred" and "Top Sacred"!

Matriarch Rose Kennedy said, "Take my home, take my wealth, but don't take my faith." Keeping your faith and your optimism in the face of all of the turbulence, tragedy and unfathomable misfortune that assaults each of us during the undulating ups and downs of a lifetime is crucial to living a fulfilling, content, predominantly happy life. If you lose hope, if you have no dreams of a finer time, you are doomed to a perennial state of depression and unhappiness.

Conversely, if you can fill your mind with faith, hope and dreams of a future with the promise of achievement, growth and love, you will be assured of a happier, healthier, more energized and gratifying life—the essence of and the very definition of happiness.

Every day, remember to say, "Lord, help me to remember that nothing is going to happen to me today that You and I together can't handle."

Perform spiritually uplifting things such as meditation and prayer to make you feel better emotionally. In a time of stress or crisis, call upon a measure of support from a higher being as well as the perception of a greater meaning and purpose to life. All is in G-d's hands. When problems get too hard for you, throw them up to G-d.

Day 276

Grandpa had a ten-speed bike that Tommy wanted. Grandpa said, "When I want something I pray for it." Tommy replied, "Well, give this one to me and pray yourself up another one."

Don't be reluctant to ask G-d to hear your personal prayers, to pray for yourself. My wife always thought that it is inappropriate to pray on your own behalf. "It's not nice to ask for myself," she would say, and therefore, always prayed for our four daughters and then their kids.

When she told that to Rabbi Noah Weinberg, a prominent rabbi whom she highly respects, he told her that she should first ask for herself. He convinced her to do so by asking her how she would feel if her children needed something, wanted something and didn't come to her and ask for help. She, of course, said that she would feel terribly hurt.

The rabbi said G-d is your father and you are his child, and therefore, he would likewise be hurt if you did not come to Him. So, do pray for yourself.

During trying or tragic times, believe that there is a master plan, an ultimate purpose to your existence, and be consoled by the thought that what you are going though is necessary, useful, even desirable in the scheme of your life. At such times, call on G-d. That's what He's there for.

Day 277

Some people never see the good. I took my wife's family out for tea biscuits. They weren't happy about having to give blood.

"Some people are always grumbling because roses have thorns; I am thankful that thorns have roses" (Alphonse Karr). William Makepeace Thackeray ends his book with this admonishing question: "Ah! Vanitas vanitatum!? Which of us is happy in this world? Which of us has his desire? Or, having it, is satisfied?" Perhaps the most important accomplishment is developing an appreciation for what we have. Then, we can be "satisfied" and, as a consequence, genuinely happy.

When we're living through a painful experience, or actual physical pain itself, we wish desperately to be rid of that condition which causes immense, often unrelenting, suffering. We actually beg that the pain would leave us and we say to ourselves, "If it would only just stop and go away how happy I would be." Therefore, on any day when you wake up without such a hurtful condition, give a great big smile and tell yourself how lucky you are and then really focus upon and appreciate that delightful good fortune. It should make you feel great. If you have kids, perhaps that's the most important message you can give them.

One of the great virtues of Judaism is that we are taught a blessing for things we can all appreciate. We, for example, thank G-d for certain fruits, for the bread that He provides from the ground, for being able to do a simple everyday act like going to the bathroom, and for just getting up in the morning. This kind of appreciation is the smallest, but most meaningful, step you can take towards the biggest and most desirable achievable goal—your own life long happiness.

The Old Testament tells us that G-d put us human beings on this earth to fully experience all the lush "fruits" he provided and for us to enjoy life fully. Life was given to us to live.

It's perhaps no coincidence that if we do not take advantage of this precious opportunity afforded us and live, we are doing the very opposite of what we are meant to be doing—the very reverse of what we are put here for. Interestingly, the reverse of live—or "live" spelled backwards—is "evil." It is evil for us not to live and enjoy.

"If the only prayer we said in life was thank you, that would suffice" (Meister Eckhart).

Day 278

"I miss Al so much."
"Why?"
"Because I married his widow!"

    During a New Orleans funeral, the immediate family and close friends cry tearfully on their way to the cemetery but party and celebrate when they later gather at the house of the deceased. Too often, we stay upset and we forget to heal and get back to the challenges and the fulfilling adventures of living.

    We all inevitably have some downtimes but you must direct yourself to stop mourning! Sit "Shiva"* and then get over it. Cut that time period to the absolute minimum by getting excited about something right now. Move on by making yourself happy, by doing something, by choosing an activity, a goal, which excites you.

    We have the capacity to live with almost any event no matter how terrible, but it's vital that we resolve as expeditiously as possible any condition that stimulates anxiety or depression.

    Mourn and heal.

---

* *Shiva" is a Jewish practice. Upon the death of, G-d forbid, one's parent, spouse sibling or child, the family member sits on a low seat for seven days after the funeral as relatives and friends visit to reminisce about the beloved departed one. It is a time to make the necessary adaptation, to reflect upon and deal with the unhappy situation and then to get up and resume a constructive, meaningful life in tribute to the memory of that lost loved one.*

Day 279

His house was in such bad shape the termites went out to eat.

A man cries to his rabbi, "Rabbi, I don't know what to do. I have a tiny house and nine children. My wife and I are going crazy." The rabbi says, "Don't worry. Here's what you should do: Buy a cow and bring it into your house." The man does as he is told. A week later, he returns, screaming hysterically, "Rabbi, my house is more crowded than ever. Everything is out of control." "Okay", says the rabbi, "buy two horses and bring them into your house." The man does as he is told. The following week he returns to the rabbi. He is beside himself. "Rabbi," he cries, "my house is insane. My wife is having a nervous breakdown. What shall I do?" The rabbi says, "Bring two chickens and three ducks into your house." Once again, the man follows the rabbi's advice. The next week, he returns at wits end. "Rabbi, Rabbi, you must find a solution," the man implores. "Our home is so crowded and so noisy. Everyone is stepping on one another and fighting with each other." The rabbi says, "Alright. Get rid of the cow, the horses, the chickens and the ducks." The next week, the man returns to the rabbi. He is smiling elatedly. "Rabbi!" he cries. "It is wonderful. Thank you so much. My wife and I are so happy. Ever since we got rid of the animals our house is so roomy and quiet."

Put things into proper perspective. Appreciation of one's situation is all a matter of perspective.

Day 280

"I guess I just prefer to see the dark side of things. The glass is always half empty…and cracked. And I just cut my lip on it. And chipped a tooth."—Janeane Garofalo

    In her brilliantly insightful book *So, Stick a Geranium in your Hat and be Happy!*, Barbara Johnson says, "We can choose to pick the flowers instead of the weeds. You have to learn how to release the bubble of joy within you, 'To claim G-d's promise to fill your mouth with laughter and your lips with shouts of joy' (Job 8:21)."

    Life is not easy, perfect, and may not go exactly as you hope, but no matter how it turns out, choose to be happy and grateful. "Happiness is not by chance, but by choice" (Jim Rohn).

    It's your life and your adventure. Take it all in stride. Enjoy it as an interested involved "actor-observer" in this evolving, unique, certainly interesting story as it unfolds each day. This constructive approach will not only make your life more tolerable, it will make it more special and rewarding and greatly enhance the experience and the enjoyment.

    "Pain is inevitable but misery is optional" (Barbara Johnson).

Day 281

I don't like to be interrupted while I'm saying a prayer. There's something about putting G-d on hold...

Alan Pakula, one of the all-time great Hollywood directors and a man who was very incisive with respect to human nature, spoke in interviews about his fascination with psychology and how men deal with their fears. He spoke of a man who is in control, and inside there is a frightened child. Many of us fall into this category.

Elita Saint James, author of *Life Shifts*, wisely advises that fear robs you of energy. By grasping onto hope, dreams and the visualization of a positive outcome you can wipe fear away and replenish and inspire heightened energy and happy emotions.

It is easy to go through life being afraid. Albert Camus said, "Each of us is Sisyphus, condemned to push his or her personal rock up the hill of life and to see it roll back down again. Filled with this certainty, maybe even ennobled by it, we are obligated to be ourselves whether we like it or not."

The Buddha is quoted as saying, "Life is suffering." More accurately, his first truth reads, "There is no lasting satisfaction." And we all know that simply because we were born, we have a rendezvous with destiny.

There is no cure for birth and death, save to enjoy the interval soliloquies. We can live with the fear and put it in perspective if we accept reality. Look for the bright side of life and believe that G-d is here for us and will, whether we understand it or not, deliver what is best for us.

HAPPINESS GUARANTEED OR YOUR MISERY BACK

G-d is with us. We need not be afraid. "Yes, though I walk through the valley of the shadow of death, I will fear no evil; for you are with me" (Psalm 23:4).

Don't live with fear. Live with belief, hope, and optimism.

Day 282

"My one regret in life is that I'm not someone else."—
Woody Allen

A girl hated herself and everyone else because she was blind. She had a loving boyfriend who was always there for her. She told her boyfriend, "If I could only see the world, I will marry you."

One day, someone donated a pair of eyes to her. When the bandages came off, she was able to see everything, including her boyfriend. He asked her, "Now that you can see the world, will you marry me?"

The girl looked at her boyfriend and saw that he was blind. The sight of his closed eyelids shocked her and she refused to marry him. After her boyfriend left her, she saw the note he had written her: "Take good care of your eyes, my dear, for before they were yours, they were mine."

This is how the human brain often works when our circumstances are altered. When our situation changes for the better, very few of us remember what life was like before, and who was by our side during painful situations.

Life is a gift.

Today: Before you say an unkind word—think of someone who can't speak.

Before you complain about the taste of your food—think of someone who has nothing to eat.

Before you complain about your husband or wife—think of someone who's crying out to G-d for a companion.

HAPPINESS GUARANTEED OR YOUR MISERY BACK

Before you complain about life—think of someone who died early.

Before you complain about your children—think of someone who is barren.

Before you argue about your dirty house—think of the people who are living in the streets.

Before you whine about the distance you drive—think of someone who walks the same distance with his feet.

Before you complain about your job—think of the unemployed, the disabled, and those who wish they had your job.

Before you point a condemning finger at another, remember that not one of us is without sin.

And when depressing thoughts get you down, put a smile on your face and thank G-d you're alive and still around.

Day 283

A sewer worker came home for dinner. His wife yelled, "What a life! I'm miserable. I sweat and slave in this hot kitchen while you get to hang around in a cool sewer all day!"

Consider for a moment the most desirable state that all people seek. The American Declaration of Independence hit the nail on the head. Everyone wants "life, liberty and the pursuit of happiness." How is this achieved? Does a lot of money deliver happiness? More often than not, it accomplishes the exact opposite. Does physical gratification deliver genuine happiness? Hardly.

Happiness depends on inner harmony. When a person is at peace with himself and his environment, he is happy. Harmony does not stem from external sources, it emanates from within, from the serenity of the soul. Our senses can be the enemies of harmony. They constantly bombard us with a variety of stimuli to which we are inclined to react, and thus our harmony is disrupted. We cannot be at peace with ourselves if we are at the mercy of a volatile world.

A simple experiment proves this point. Enter a room by yourself. Shut out all sound. Close the lights and sit back in a meditative pose with your eyes closed. In a short while, you will undoubtedly feel a pleasant serenity. Insulated from external influences, your soul naturally gravitates towards harmony; it enters a state of happiness. However, we cannot spend our lives in a dark and silent room and as soon as we step out, we are back into the maelstrom.

HAPPINESS GUARANTEED OR YOUR MISERY BACK

In our own lives, we can also seek to achieve, to the best of our abilities, some semblance of inner harmony. When we embrace real values and ideals, we insulate our inner selves against the vicissitudes of the world around us. With diligence and perseverance, we will then be rewarded with a harmonious and immeasurably enriched life.

Recognize that the source of true happiness is realizing that it does not come from external sources; it comes from within.

Day 284

I'm very lucky. I've been to Europe almost as often as my luggage.

Sometimes, we think we have had good luck, yet the experience proves to be our worst nightmare. And many times, we curse our bad fortune, only to realize later that it was a blessing in disguise.

Dr. Rad, an innovative professor at the Columbia Graduate School of Business, offers his students "mental models" to deal with situations that might confront them. One gem of advice he stresses: "Good things, bad things: who knows?" Difficult events may bring us surprising blessings in the future. And the corollary is likewise often true. Seemingly happy events can have terrible, even tragic, consequences. You pray to marry the most popular girl and subsequently you learn she can't stay loyal to one person. That most popular girl marries someone else, and you are forced to marry your second choice; this girl then blossoms into a comfortable, loving wife.

In 1986, Sharon Christa McAuliffe thought she was the luckiest woman in the world. She was chosen from eleven thousand candidates to be the first schoolteacher to be launched into space. She was an unlucky winner when the Challenger space shuttle exploded, killing her and the rest of its passengers.

It is ironic that we often pursue goals that produce the very reverse—tragedy, depression and tormenting pain. We think if we are successful and reach the top and attain fame that this will engender happiness. But, a quick view of just a few who reached the very top and achieved unbelievable, matchless fame can clearly demonstrate how misguided such a belief is. John Kennedy's fame led to his horrible, vicious death. Similarly, this is true of Bobby Kennedy, Martin Luther King Jr., John Lennon and many others.

Always take the attitude, "This, too, is for the best." Accept what life gives you and pray that what you do get is what is truly best for you.

Day 285

You only live once, but if you do it right, once is enough.

"Happiness is beneficial for the body but it is grief that develops the power of the mind" (Marcel Proust).

Misfortunes, tragedies and major disappointments or failures in life can shock you into a realization that can inspire a change that can launch you on a new, more realistic, healthier—and ultimately more meaningful and happier—life path.

The ideal, if you can work it out, and it's not easy but is immensely desirable, is to take every negative experience and convert it into something positive for yourself.

A Special Olympics athlete whose leg was amputated after years of painful, seemingly never-ending operations proceeded to win all kinds of gold medals. He felt he could excel at anything through incessant, dedicated determination.

Former Los Angeles Dodgers manager Tommy Lasorda's son died at age thirty-three. Lasorda said that had G-d asked him, "If you can have your son for thirty-three years or not at all, what would you choose?" He said he surely would have chosen the thirty-three years with his son happily, thankful for that blessing.

Sooner or later, we must realize there is no station, no one place to arrive at once and for all. The true joy of life is the trip. The station is only a dream. It constantly outdistances us.

Use negative events to make you more cognizant and appreciative of all that is right. Perhaps, prior to the loss, you didn't take

HAPPINESS GUARANTEED OR YOUR MISERY BACK

the time to fully appreciate what you had but use this new insight to enjoy even more what you do still have. It's not how much you have but how much you enjoy what you have, that makes you truly happy.

Day 286

"Since the house is on fire, let us warm ourselves."
—Italian Proverb

The parents, spouses and children of the tragic victims of Pan Am Flight 103 that was blown up by heartless terrorists over Lockerbie, Scotland, responded constructively to that horrific, painfully, devastating tragedy. They mobilized collectively and formed a group, which they named "A Family," and lobbied, pushed and crusaded for greater airline security and safety with the goal of totally eliminating accidents and fatalities of any kind for anyone that is ever a passenger on a commercial flight.

They converted their own terribly painful plight into a cause for the benefit of all humanity and established a worthy memorial to their own lost loved ones. They made a positive contribution causing us all to bless them eternally as they beautifully memorialize those promising, sacrificed lives, which were cut so abruptly and unfairly short. They converted their personal pain into a gift offering and a blessing that will earn them the appreciation, praise and prayers of generations into the infinite future.

Each of us can turn adversity into a positive contribution to a fellow man or even to all society. Use crisis situations as opportunities to advance. "Do you not see how necessary a world of pains and troubles is to school an intelligence and make it a soul?" (John Keats, *Letters of John Keats*).

Day 287

"I got to a traffic light, and it turned red. I said, 'Why me?'"—Geoff Bolt

"I'm never going to complain again," said Barbara Walters on her ABC TV show *20/20*.

Christopher Reeve, the actor who once played Superman on the silver screen, was her guest. Reeve was permanently paralyzed from the neck down in a freak horseback riding accident. Nevertheless, he told Walters how appreciative he was to be alive; he wasn't blind or brain-damaged, and he could see his kids grow up, view the sunrise, and watch the world go on. So, if he, in his hopelessly crippled, tragic condition, could be so appreciative, how can the rest of us complain? How can the rest of us ever be depressed?

Yet, we will soon forget Reeve and start complaining, whining and feeling sorry for ourselves, moping, feeling down, feeling unlucky, feeling depressed all over again.

James Brady, President Reagan's press secretary, who was partially paralyzed, crippled, and left with poor speech, due to a bullet meant for President Reagan, courageously said, "You gotta play the hand that's dealt you. There may be pain in that hand, but you play it. And I've played it."

Don't sit around feeling sorry about your troubles. Get over it! Consider and appreciate how lucky you are.

Once you move on, you will wonder why you remained in and retained your pain. "'Moving on' sounds easy—but I died a thousand times in pain just to appreciate this phrase" (Luna Adriana Ardiansyah).

Day 288

Don't tell G-d how big your problems are. Tell your problems how big G-d is.

Here is some constructive wisdom you should know from an unknown author.

MEMO FROM G-D

To: YOU
Date: TODAY
From: G-D—The Boss!
Subject: YOURSELF
Reference: LIFE

This is G-d. Today I will be handling all your problems for you. I do not need your help. So, have a nice day.
I love you!
Signed: G-D
P.S. And, remember… If life delivers a situation that you cannot handle, do not attempt to resolve it yourself!! Kindly put it in the SFGTD (Something For God To Do) box. I will get to it in MY TIME.

Once the matter is placed into the box, do not hold onto it by worrying about it. Instead, focus on all the wonderful things that are present in your life now.

If you find yourself stuck in traffic, don't despair. There are people in this world for which driving is an unheard of privilege.

HAPPINESS GUARANTEED OR YOUR MISERY BACK

Should you have a bad day at work, think of the man who has been out of work for years.

Should you despair over a relationship gone badly, think of the person who has never known what it's like to love and be loved in return.

Should you grieve the passing of another weekend, think of the woman in dire straits, working twelve hours a day, seven days a week to feed her children.

Should your car break down leaving you miles away from assistance, think of the paraplegic who would love the opportunity to take that walk.

Should you notice a new gray hair in the mirror, think of the cancer patient in chemo who wishes she had hair to examine.

Should you find yourself at a loss, pondering, "What is life all about? What is my purpose?" Be thankful. There are those who didn't live long enough to ask those questions.

Should you find yourself the victim of other people's bitterness, ignorance, smallness or insecurities, remember, things could be worse. You could be one of them!

Love, G-d

Always be aware, G-d is in control and is looking after you.

Day 289

A patient described the pain in his arm. The doctor asked, "Did you ever have this before?" The man said, "Yes." The doctor said, "Well, you've got it again!"

Just as pain may be a special blessing in that it may alert you to go to the doctor and get a treatment that will cure you or which will cause you to change a behavior that is causing the pain, in the same way, you need to use adversity to initiate positive self-enriching actions. Turn every adversity into a learning benefit. Use it as an opportunity to enhance your future, to learn to overcome and then go on to specifically identify, focus upon and enjoy the blessings, which you do possess.

We all have that latent capacity to turn a negative into a positive, the mundane into the beautiful. Witness what Walt Disney so remarkably accomplished—he made out of what most people find unattractive, repugnant and scary, something that is perhaps, arguably, one of the most warm, lovable objects in the whole wide world. He made out of a mouse—which often elicits a frightening, facial-distorting response—a happy-producing, smile-causing, pleasurable experience—the most popular, most beloved, "Mickey Mouse." Look how Sesame Street changed our view of scary, ugly monsters by creating characters like the Cookie Monster. You can transform the ugly into the beautiful. We have the power to alter our perceptions.

"Being happy doesn't mean everything is perfect. It means you have decided to look beyond the imperfections" (Gerard Way).

Day 290

Life is a game, the object of which is to discover the object of the game.

Believe that you shall overcome. It helps enormously during seemingly impossibly tragic, depressing periods. It helps make such times tolerable in that you can project to a time beyond this period of travail when the prevailing troubling condition will no longer dominate and overwhelm your being. Once again, this is a way of thinking that is within your power to control. During periods of well-founded agony and distress, you can change your mood to a happier state of mind.

Believing "We shall overcome" is another helpful approach. With the help and cooperation—the joining with others—you can get beyond your current seemingly hopeless, painful condition. For example, support groups that gather together after the death of a loved one or groups seeking support because they have children that are struck with malignant cancer, etc., help garner a meaningful degree of solace and revitalizing support.

"Overcoming" is not simple. It's a challenge and requires a learned reaction. But, like skiing, swimming or bike riding, happiness can and should be learned. Things don't always go the way we planned, but as Jimmy Dean wrote in his song, "I can't change the direction of the wind, but I can adjust my sails to always reach my destination."

Day 291

All my life I said I wanted to be someone…I can see now that I should have been more specific.

Nelson Mandela, the President of South Africa, said to President Clinton when he was vilified for his inappropriate behavior, "The greatest glory is not never to have fallen, but having fallen to rise up and move on." That is the true glory.

We all fall at one time or another. We demonstrate our unique greatness, and in the process, experience our own admiration and self-respect by bouncing back—by rising up.

As F. Scott Fitzgerald wrote, "Life is essentially a cheat and its conditions are those of defeat: the redeeming things are not happiness and pleasure but the deeper satisfactions that come out of struggle."

Accept and face your challenges. Overcome. Be resilient. It's the right choice. It's the best choice. It's the only choice if you want to live a productive, happy life.

"I've seen better days, but I've seen worse. I don't have everything I want, but I have all I need. I woke up with some aches and pains, but I woke up. My life may not be perfect, but I am blessed" (Anonymous).

Day 292

"The amount of sleep required by the average person is about five minutes more."—Max Kaufmann

Sometimes in life, we get tired, we get exhausted, we get beat up and discouraged. When that happens, we take a break, go to bed, and rest. As G-d advised Abraham, "Get up and go to a new land," setting him off on new challenges, new adventures, and new goals. He became the successful father of a unique, productive people that changed the world and he is esteemed and beloved thousands of years after his life on Earth.

The advice still works. Get up and make your life into a new exciting adventure. Discover your potential and then realize the potentially challenging, adventurous life with which G-d blessed you.

In Hebrew, there is a phrase, "Change your place, change your luck." This change can refer to a physical place or a mental state. Whenever you feel stuck, move yourself out of that place of being or thinking, and new exciting opportunities will unfold before you.

Try this exercise: Lie down on your bed next to a ticking clock. Listen to each tick of the clock. That's your life—your only life—with its precious moments ticking away. Stop wasting time being down or feeling sorry for yourself. Get up and move on toward a new beginning and a different level of happiness.

It's all up to you how you spend the limited ticks allotted to you.

Day 293

"When was the first tennis game?"
"When Moses served in Pharaoh's court!"

I once had the thrill of meeting Jimmy Connors at the tennis courts of the La Costa Hotel and Spa in Carlsbad, California. At the time, he was the number one ranked player in the world. During our conversation, I expressed how lucky he was to be such a fabulous player. Surprisingly, he told me that, in fact, I was the luckier of the two of us. Shocked by that insight, I asked him, "What are you talking about?" He said, "All I can do is play tennis because that's all I totally devoted my life to, but you play tennis plus you're an educated successful investment banker and writer; so, you are way luckier than I am."

We really never know how blessed we are or, indeed, who is most blessed. You may not have developed the conscious awareness or the confidence that there are unique traits or qualities that you possess that others do not have. With whatever knowledge and skills you do posses, though they may be limited, you can develop your latent potential. With a constructive, self-encouraging attitude, optimism and hard work, you can make good things happen for yourself, for those you love, for your community as well as for all humanity.

As Walt Whitman so wisely wrote about 150 years ago, "I celebrate myself and sing myself." He encouraged himself, inspired himself, and made himself feel good. It's what one would do for others if one wanted to make someone feel better and uplifted about themselves. So, do for yourself what you would do for others.

HAPPINESS GUARANTEED OR YOUR MISERY BACK

Tell yourself that you are not an empty vessel. Develop an "inner state" in which you fill yourself with a sense of self-worth, which will, in turn, fill you with an amazing sense of quality happiness.

The more you feel you have self-worth, the more you develop worth.

Day 294

One man said to his friend, "I just had another fight with my wife!" "Oh yeah?" the friend replied. "And how did this one end?" "When it was over," he replied, "she came to me on her hands and knees." His friend looked puzzled, "Really? Now that's a switch! What did she say?" "I think she said something like, 'Come out from under that bed, you gutless weasel.'"

Do you ever stop to think, "What really makes me happy?" At different stages in one's life, one needs, desires and appreciates different things. A baby is happy just to receive nourishment, a calm stomach, a clean change of clothes, sleep and some tender love.

As we progress, our needs increase dramatically. We want many more things. We want physical, spiritual and emotional things.

The common denominator at every age for every race and gender is that everyone wants love, respect and someone to care about his needs.

You have it in your power to help others make you happy by telling them how to meet your needs. A mother can tell her child, "You are a wonderful girl and I would appreciate if you would not raise your voice when you speak to me." A child can tell his parent, "I love you, but I would very much appreciate if you would pressure me less about my school work." A wife can tell her husband, "You are such a terrific husband, but I would love if you brought me flowers every so often." Most people want to make their relative or friend

HAPPINESS GUARANTEED OR YOUR MISERY BACK

happy but don't know how. Most people, if it is asked in a loving manner, will try to the extent they can, to meet the other person's needs.

Don't just remain frustrated with a person, use your wonderful power of speech to communicate and develop a more open, understanding, caring relationship. It will make you, as well as the other person, much happier.

"Take care of your thoughts when you are alone and take care of your words when you are with people." "Watch your thoughts; they become words. Watch your words; they become actions. Watch your actions; they became habits. Watch your habits; they become character. Watch your character; it becomes your destiny" (Lao Tzu).

Day 295

I can handle pain, until it hurts.

The renowned film beauty Charlize Theron, a Best Actress Oscar winner, experienced a frightfully horrible nightmare at the age of fifteen. She witnessed her father, who had arrived home in a drunken rage, shot dead by her mother in self-defense. At age of sixteen, on her own, she left for Europe. She relates that, "When you're at that age and you're trying to get by, it was my survival skills that kicked in—if you roll over, you're going to die." She now asserts, "Whatever happens I can handle it."

She reiterates, "It's all about survival." She tells of her good friend who still lives in South Africa, where she herself was born, and this friend's amazing ability to be adaptive. Her friend worked on a farm, picked corn, rode motorcycles, milked cows and experienced the negatives imposed by apartheid. Theron tells how her friend "deals constructively with the adverse circumstances there every day. She talks to me in this matter-of-fact way about having her handbag robbed or being held at gunpoint in her house."

Incredibly, but certainly most constructively, Theron concludes, "I was raised with the incisive advice that you can feel sorry for yourself, but then get over it, because it doesn't get you anywhere."

Functioning with such a positive attitude has made Charlize Theron capable of achieving her tremendously successful career at such a relatively young age.

If adversity doesn't kill you, it can make you stronger, and, if you handle it well, with a positive, constructive attitude, it can actually serve as an inspirational catalyst to a joyfully fulfilling astonishing success.

"Nobody can change what happened, but you can change what happens next" (Bill Clinton).

Day 296

As the minister started his sermon, a thunderstorm dropped buckets of rain out of the sky. "Isn't that just like the Lord," the minister said. "Here we are relaxing in comfort, and he's out there washing cars."

As we all know, out of the mouth of babes come some of the most incisive inquires, insights and revelations. At one point, when so many natural tragedies were being thrust upon this earth, the tsunami in the far east, the hurricane Katrina in New Orleans, the tornado in Alabama, which took so many lives and destroyed so many families—my little granddaughter, Atara, asked "Zaidy [Grandpa], can't we move to another world?"

I told her the reality is that this is the special world we live in and that we all have to work at making it a better world for ourselves and for our fellow human beings. And that there are certain things over which we have no control and thus have to accept and make the best of. We can and should make ourselves happy despite the untoward events that do occur from time to time. We have to get beyond those adversities and be optimistic about and enjoy the future. We owe it to ourselves to learn, to grow, love and appreciate what lies ahead and make it as exciting, as pleasant and as adventurous as we possibly can.

This is the world, with all its shortcomings, challenges and adversities that is all of ours to enjoy.

Work to make this a happier world for yourself and all your fellow human beings. That very undertaking in itself will enrich your life.

Day 297

Just when I was getting used to yesterday, along came today.

Are you moving in the right direction? Listen for messages from your inner self, and then give yourself time to hear them. Use a planner, as every businessman does. Examine your past and use it to help shape your happier future.

Your personal calendar is your Bible; either you own your time or it owns you. Examine your daily planner. Using a yellow marker, underline those things you can let others do for you. The necessary duties should be underlined in black, while fun things should be underlined in blue. See if you can increase your blue experiences. Highlight the things that are good for your health in red. Use green, which symbolizes the healthy growth of vegetation and plants, for things that contribute to your growth and happiness.

How much time do we spend designing our living room or our office? It's important to us so we invest the effort to decorate these quarters in order to get the most out of them and fully enjoy them. Dedicate at least as much thought and effort to designing your life, so that it will bring you the minimum amount of aggravation or pain and bring you the maximum amount of productivity, success, joy and happiness.

If you plan your life wisely, you will avoid many future pitfalls. Learn now to deal with the inevitable problems that will arise. As John F. Kennedy said, "The time to repair the roof is when the sun is shinning."

Day 298

"My wife's jealousy is getting ridiculous. The other day she looked at my calendar and wanted to know who May was."—Rodney Dangerfield

"The jealous are troublesome to others but a torment to themselves" (William Penn). "Jealousy," says B. C. Forbes, "is a mental cancer."

A child is happy with his toy until he sees that his sibling's toy is somewhat larger. What is a mother to do? The mother must urge the child to be happy with what he has and not look at anyone else's. Comparing only leads to envy and jealousy.

Enjoy and appreciate that which is given to you, that which you have. Don't look at others who may have more or better. Don't look at their wealth, not at their health, nor at their success, nor at their families or any aspect of their lives. You have no idea what adversities they are facing. Only by appreciating your own blessings, without comparing them to others, can you achieve true satisfaction and contentment.

Don't envy others. Realize that others are most probably jealous of you. Look at your own plate and appreciate what you have that others must surely envy. Does anyone ever frustratingly ask, "How come I received bigger or better than someone else? It's not fair."

"Envy is the art of counting the other fellow's blessings instead of your own" (Harold Coffin).

Day 299

"My superiority complex turned out to be an inferiority complex. I said, 'Great, that makes me the least of my problems.'"—Sara B. Sirius

One of the most important lessons is learning to love yourself. No one will ever be closer or spend as much time with you as you. It is highly unlikely that two or three people, if that many, will ever care as much about you as you do. So, learn to love yourself.

If you love yourself, you won't ever knowingly put yourself in harm's way. Consequently, you won't allow yourself to be subjected to, or dominated by, negative, depression-inducing thoughts that rob you of happiness.

If you love yourself, you will treat yourself well instead of abusing yourself. You will guide your mind to positive, joyous, uplifting thoughts.

Learn to love yourself by appreciating that you are special, unique and truly lovable. Treat yourself, at least mentally, as you would treat someone you care for a great deal, someone you really love. Quickly kick out disagreeable, irritable, depressing thoughts and instantly invite and instill enriching, gratifying, cheerful thoughts. Impel these positive, emotionally upbeat and enriching thoughts to drive out the aforementioned negative thoughts.

Six women, aka "The Bombshells," who wrote the best-selling *Dish and Tell: Life, Love and Secrets*, a breezy collection of stories about upper-middle class female anxiety that the *New York Times* described as a "YaYa" of the trophies, advise, "Put yourself first and take care of yourself. No one else will." That advice may sound selfish, but it is nevertheless useful. Be for yourself. Be protective of yourself. Inspire and uplift yourself. Absent a positive feeling about yourself, you will be unable to grow, to achieve, to flourish and to be there for others.

Proverbs says, "If I am not for me, who will be? And if I am only for me, what value have I? And if not now, when?" Right now, begin by looking after yourself. Be the special person, good and productive that you should be. You will like yourself by being someone whose values you yourself respect; most often, this means a person who does for and is there for others. As you become a better individual, you are expanding your "I" to include your spouse, your family, your friends, society, and even the world. "If you are happy, you can give happiness."

Day 300

I am sitting here looking at the most amazing person I have ever seen, smart, funny, caring and absolutely stunning. Yes, I am looking in the mirror!

Through loving and appreciating yourself, you will bring peace, fulfillment, love, satisfaction, maturity, solidity, freedom, wisdom and happiness into your life. To achieve this, you must first know yourself, understand, examine, and be able to express your own values. Get to know yourself honestly and accept yourself, so that you can focus on your strengths rather than your weaknesses.

Concentrate on your good points, so that you build up your self-worth. Recognize the love that is within you, the love you can give yourself and the love you can give to others. Do for others and give to others. Even giving a smile to others makes them, as well as you, feel uplifted.

Get to know your needs, so that you can meet them. Do you need to stop and breathe? Do you need to unwind? Do you need to accomplish? Do you need to talk things out, to meditate or to pray? Do you need to exercise, to sleep or to get up and take action? Meet your needs, not what other people believe you need.

Although it is not good to procrastinate, don't pressure yourself to move too quickly. Step back and watch your actions. Examine how it will affect you. Think, "Would I rather stay overwhelmed or would I rather enjoy my journey as I am completing my tasks?"

Have self-compassion, allow yourself time to figure yourself out. Allow yourself to make mistakes and time to forgive yourself.

Allow yourself time to build your courage and to face challenges. Allow yourself to enjoy life.

Happiness comes from understanding and meeting your own needs, from accepting your pain and from appreciating your blessings. Happiness comes from dealing with your fears, recognizing them and working through them.

Get to know yourself and your needs, so that you can love yourself, appreciate yourself and appropriately direct your life, thereby creating a greater sense of happiness.

"Self-care is never a selfish act—it is simply good stewardship of the only gift I have, the gift I was put on earth to offer to others" (Parker Palmer).

Day 301

A psychiatrist took his patient to the window and said, "Stick out your tongue." The patient asked, "Why?" "Because," said the psychiatrist, "I don't like the psychiatrist across the street."

Freud said, "We can't change the miseries that are inherent in life but we can change the miseries we bring upon ourselves by our behavior and thought processes." Whatever you absolutely must suffer is more than enough. Don't countenance any more than that. Make up your mind you just won't tolerate any more pain and suffering.

If you make up your mind to smile, you can smile. If you make up your mind to be happy, you can be happy. Don't allow yourself to tolerate less. Making yourself happy is a job and a responsibility. When you are happy, you make the people around you happy. It is in fact impossible for someone to make you happy if you're unhappy with yourself. If you are looking for the one person who can make you happy, look in the mirror.

Day 302

Yogi Berra wisely counseled, "If you don't know where you're going, you're likely to get somewhere else."

A philosophy professor stood before his class with some items in front of him. He wordlessly picked up a large empty mayonnaise jar and filled it with rocks. He then asked the students if the jar was full.

When they agreed that it was full, the professor poured a box of pebbles in to the jar. Shaking the jar lightly, he caused the pebbles to roll into the open areas between the rocks. Again, the professor asked his students if the jar was full.

They agreed that it was full, and then the professor poured a box of sand into the jar. Of course, the sand filled the holes, covering everything.

Said the professor, "This is your life. The rocks are the important things—your family, your partner, your health, and your children—anything that is so important to you that if it were lost, you would be nearly destroyed.

"The pebbles are things in life that matter on a smaller scale. The pebbles represent things like your job, your house, and your car.

"The sand is everything else. It is the small stuff. If you put the sand or the pebbles into the jar first, there is no room for the rocks.

"The same is true about your life. If you spend all your energy and time on the small stuff, you will never have room for the things that are truly important.

"Pay attention to the things that are critical in your life. Play with your children. Take your partner out dancing. There will always be time to go to work, clean the house, give a dinner party and fix the disposal." (Laura Bankston).

Know what is important in life. Know where you are heading. Make it important to head toward achieving the right goals and values and pursuing proper objectives and aspirations.

By properly balancing your priorities, it will help you achieve happiness.

Day 303

Living on Earth is expensive, but I appreciate that it does include a free trip around the sun every year.

In her best-selling inspirational book, *Thank You Power*, Deborah Norville incisively preaches what is one of the soundest, most effective and rewarding prescriptions guaranteed to generate the positive, uplifting mental attitude and mindset to achieve a healthy, happy and successful existence—a truly richer, more satisfying happiness-inducing life. She urges that we constantly embrace "an attitude of gratitude." Accordingly, she suggests that each day you write down those things that make you happy, no matter how small—for example, even if you just saw a beautiful flower.

As Edgar Allan Poe wrote, "That pleasure which is at once the most pure, the most elevating and the most intense, is derived, I maintain, from the contemplation of the beautiful."

In fact, there are countless things which G-d created that we can enjoy, marvel at and really appreciate if we only take the time and make the effort to be aware of them: the face of every little baby, the energy and vivacity of every child, the interesting unique features of every human being, the variety of colors and shapes, the movements of the sky and the stars, the constant action and vitality of the ocean waters, the breathtaking beauty of the amazing variety of flowers in the field, the remarkable array of insects and animals that roam the earth, the phenomenal human intellect, the human soul, and, perhaps best of all, love.

HAPPINESS GUARANTEED OR YOUR MISERY BACK

How much more exciting, fulfilling and rewarding our lives would be if we can develop a perennial, emotionally uplifting "attitude of gratitude" for these priceless gifts always available to us!

"Next to excellence is the appreciation of it" (William Makepeace Thackeray).

Day 304

"The only way to avoid being miserable is not to have enough leisure time to wonder whether you are happy or not."—George Bernard Shaw

"Too much of a good thing...can be wonderful" (Mae West).

Anne Frank, living in a hidden attic to hide from the Nazis, said something so poignantly true, "We all live with the objective of being happy; our lives are all different and yet the same."

Deciding to be happy is the first step. Doing things to make yourself happy is the next step. Exercising, getting enough sleep, shortening your commute to work, spending time outdoors, especially in nice weather, meditating, practicing gratitude, such as writing thank you letters, even planning a vacation, whether or not you ever go on it, but giving you something to look forward to, have all been proven to help lower depression.

Hanging out with friends, enjoying family time, following your dreams and doing things you love, as well as helping others, are easy ways that have been tested and guaranteed to enhance your pleasure. Taking note of what you like about yourself, enjoying life's simple pleasures, such as laughing at silly jokes, enjoying warm days, taking walks in the moonlight, listening to music and thinking beautiful, uplifting thoughts are each scientifically verified to help promote happiness.

Think wonderful thoughts. Plan exciting activities. Dream beautiful dreams. Leo Tolstoy said something so simple yet so profoundly true, "If you want to be happy, be."

Day 305

"You wouldn't have won if we had beaten you."—Yogi Berra

When things go bad, you have to say to yourself, "There will be days like this or times like this." When questioned whether she had any regrets about any of the counseling she ever gave, Dr. Laura Schlesinger, a successful radio talk show host, insists that she never second-guesses herself. "I do the best I can at the time and I can't change anything that I already did, so why would I spend the energy to question what I did?" she explains.

From that statement, we can all garner a most insightful lesson in constructive living. If you can't change something you already did, don't beat yourself up regretting what you might have done or should have done. It's done. Move on. Yes, do better next time if you feel there is a better action. Learn from your past behavior. It is appropriate to even invest some time and effort into analyzing what you did and whether there is a better path to take in the future. This can be constructive and can help you to improve and grow. But, don't second-guess yourself. It will only lead to a second-class life. Let go of things you can't change. Focus on things you can. Your mistakes are your past, concentrate on your future dreams.

"We all make mistakes, have struggles and even regret things in our past. But, you are not your mistakes, you are not your struggles, and you are here now, with the power to shape your day and your future" (Steve Maraboli).

Day 306

He asked his caddie, "What do you think of my game?" The caddie answered, "It's okay, but I like golf better."

Tiger Woods, one of the greatest golfers of all time, told an interviewer, "The challenge in life for all of us is to constantly improve, to always strive to be even better than we are, to try to be the best. The only way to do that is to work our butt off every day." With that formula, he became the top pro in the world at a very young age.

If it pays to strive for golf or money, surely it pays to strive for happiness.

Start reaching today for the most meaningful and rewarding of all life's goals—the achievement of personal happiness. Work at it consciously, wisely, and consistently. Follow the recipes, the formulas, the behavior patterns and the positive mental attitude presented in this book. Work hard and consistently at it. It's surely worth it. Remember, if it worked for Tiger Woods, it will work for you.

Strive to be your best, your most gratified, and your happiest. "All life demands struggles. Those who have everything given to them become lazy, selfish and insensitive to the real values of life. The very striving and hard work that we so constantly try to avoid is the major building block in the person we are today" (Pope Paul VI).

Day 307

My wife sat down on the couch next to me as I was flipping channels. She asked, "What's on TV?" I said, "Dust," and then the fight began…

Happiness is not the absence of conflict, but the ability to cope with it. The same holds true for all life's problems. Avoid indulging in self-pity—it's debilitating, depressing, destructive and only adds further to whatever sadness, trial or tribulation we are, at any given moment in time, living through. It does little to remedy either the situation or the negative feelings that derive from it. It doesn't help to whine, cry and mope that it's unfair, that I don't deserve this, why me?

The more salutary, healthier approach for both your mind and body, which limits the damage and the long-lasting pain, is to deal with the reality. No matter how terrible, tragic or irreversible the situation, make the most appropriate adjustment and adaptation that you can, so that you can move beyond whatever this calamity may be. Then, move on with your life. Take control of your life by propelling yourself from having pain to using pain as a catalyst for self-growth. Move from self-pity to self-worth. Realize that you matter, that you make a difference. Accept and deal with the cards you've been dealt.

Give life a chance. Give life a second and third chance. It's your only life. Make the most of it for your loved ones, friends, acquaintances but most of all, for yourself.

"Self-pity is easily the most destructive of non-pharmaceutical narcotics. It is addictive, gives momentary pleasure and separates the victim from reality" (John W Gardener).

Day 308

Three buddies die in a car crash. They go to Heaven, where they are each asked what they would like to hear said about them at their funeral. The first said, "I would like to hear them say I was a good doctor and a good family man." The second said, "I would like to hear them say I was a wonderful husband and a good teacher." The last guy replies, "I'd like to hear them say… look, he's moving!"

Don't second-guess the past. What is, is! Don't look back! Don't say "what if," "if only I had." Accept the reality that you can never change what already happened. If you spend your time feeling sorry for yourself, regretting, hopelessly wishing you could change that one decision that now, in retrospect, proves so critical "if I had only done this" or "if only I had done that" my life could have been different—so much better, etc., you are indulging in the most counterproductive, aggravating, debilitating, activity.

We can never change what was or what is. "I would have." "I could have." "I should have." Intellectually, we are all cognizant of the fact that we no longer "could have, would have, should have." Allowing ourselves to dwell upon such never realizable yearnings and regrets can only lead to terrible frustration and aggravation. "Don't cry over spilt milk."

Dan Rather, the long-term CBS news anchor who held that position for a record twenty-four years, told Larry King when he left

CBS (or was pushed out) that his grandmother Paige told his mother and she in-turn told him, "About yesterday, no tears, about tomorrow, no fears."

Dr. Laura received a call from a thirty-two-year-old woman who complained that her mother was only interested in her own husband and was not devoted to her children. How could she have a mother-daughter relationship? Dr. Laura suggested that trying to fix the past would be a futile effort, but the woman could enjoy a "mother-child" relationship with her own two children by being a nurturing mother to them. This was her second chance to experience a mothering relationship; perhaps, it was a different type, but it was certainly an emotionally rewarding one.

Learn from the past but look to the future.

Day 309

"If a book about failures doesn't sell, is it a success?"— Jerry Seinfeld

    Failure defeats losers and inspires winners. There are so many businessmen, and the companies they started, who became great successes but had a rough start.

    Henry Ford failed and was left broke five times before successfully founding Ford Motor Company. R.H. Macy failed seven times before he achieved success with Macy's New York. Soichiro Honda, being left jobless after being rejected by Toyota for a position as an engineer, began making scooters in his home, eventually leading to his building his company. Akio Morita, founder of Sony, began his electronics with a rice cooker that not only didn't cook, but it burned the rice. This setback didn't stop him as he continued on to build his multi-billion dollar company. Hartland David Sanders, better known as Colonel Sanders of Kentucky Fried Chicken, failed to sell his famous secret recipes 1,009 times before a restaurant accepted it.

    Jack Canfield so brilliantly observed, "Everything you want is on the other side of fear." Don't be afraid to fail. The most valuable thing you can make is a mistake, if you are smart enough to learn from it and move on. As Robert F. Kennedy said, "Only those who dare to fail greatly can ever achieve greatly."

Day 310

"If I had life to live over, I'd live it over a deli."—Soupy Sales

"The Rainbow Fish shared his scales left and right. And the more he gave away, the more delighted he became. When the water around him filled with glimmering scales, he at last felt at home among the fish" (Marcus Pfister).

Figure out what you can do to help another suffering human being and do it. It will lift your own spirits and sense of self-worth and self-esteem.

A smile is the one sure thing you can give away that will make you and the recipient both feel richer. The more you give, the more you have. That is true not only in charity and material possessions, but in friendship, affection and love as well. Giving part of yourself is the one thing in the world that only you can give. It is priceless.

Self-centeredness is counterproductive, as it is undirected, purposeless introspection. Doing good produces ongoing good feelings. It's contagious. It spreads. It ripples across the world and throughout the ages. Best of all, it makes you feel good.

Whoever is happy will make others happy, too! The miracle of love is that love is given to us to give to one another.

Take time to smile, to laugh; it is the music of the soul. Happiness is infectious. Once you learn to grasp it, it spreads within you and to those around you. Remember the classic proverb: "Laugh and the world laughs with you; cry and you cry alone." Laugh it up; it really makes you feel happier. Be friendly; it is the road to happiness. It is incumbent upon us to make ourselves, and those around us, happy.

Share a smile with someone. Lend a bit of humor. Give away a kind word. Like a drop of water on a rock, like a ripple in a stream, it goes, ad infinitum, from one to another.

Your smile will make the world brighter for others when they see it beam. Even more relevant for you, your smile creates a brighter world for you. When you smile, no matter what else is going on in your life, the world feels like a better place.

Day 311

"Don't be afraid to take big steps. You can't cross a chasm in two small jumps."—David Lloyd George

Question: How does a lobster grow?
Answer: It sheds its shell at regular intervals when its body begins feeling cramped. While the shell is off and the pink membrane, which forms the basis for the next shell, is exposed, the lobster is vulnerable. It can be tossed against a coral reef or eaten by a fish. It puts itself at risk in order to grow.

Similarly, we may be locked into a certain way of life that gives us security but can also be stifling. We must step out of our shell for a while, even if we have to make ourselves a little vulnerable. That's the only way we will grow.

To advance in life, you must take risks. You must give up some of what you are and the dull security, which that habit provides, and risk change. Try new things, new approaches. As the saying goes, "You can't steal second base without the risk of removing your foot from first base." Never get discouraged by temporary setbacks. The learning curve is not a straight line up. It has its dips, reversals, backsliding and declines, but ultimately, you will reach a higher plateau, a permanent level of achievement and accomplishment.

Shed your skin and expose yourself to new ideas, unexplored thoughts and magical dreams. "The first step towards getting somewhere is to decide that you are not going to stay where you are" (J.P. Morgan).

Day 312

When you are down in the mouth, just think of Jonah. He came out all right!

No matter how great a challenge you may face, remember that today is the first day of the beginning of your new life, and with the right optimistic attitude, you can make the best of it. You can generate new experiences, new adventures and new fulfillment and joy.

No matter what happens, fight off depression, keep going, keep hope alive, stay upbeat and keep smiling. Follow Winston Churchill's encouraging, succinct but wonderfully invaluable advice, "Don't lose hope, and keep going." You will be amazed how much this simple but incredible advice can help during difficult times.

Stay focused on your targeted goal. Don't allow yourself to become distracted by the mundane, everyday problems and issues. In the long run, they are relatively meaningless, generally pass fairly soon and are quickly forgotten, especially since, in most cases, they have no impact on what really counts in your life, nor do they play any role in your ultimate happiness, except as you may derive useful adaptive lessons, which can help make you deal with events more effectively in the future. "Do not suffer the little stuff." Think about the goal you wish to attain. Once you consciously embrace a mental visualization of your desired destination, you are well on your way to the actual realization of that aspiration. It's self-fulfilling—what we think about we bring about.

Day 313

Two cannibals are eating a clown. One cannibal turns to the other and says, "This taste funny to you?"

Abraham Lincoln, who was under indubitably enormous pressure and who was forced to endure the anguish, the torment and the terribly painful ordeal of a divided nation and of a horrendous civil war that killed tens of thousands of his fellow citizens, proclaimed that "with the strain that is on me night and day, if I did not laugh, I should die."

Learn to avail yourself of this invaluable gambit—to laugh—whenever you're under pressure. Apply it, use it, exploit it for all its worth. And it's really worth a lot—it's priceless—when it comes to lifting your spirits. It will help move you away from unendurable discontentment and ever closer to achieving emotional good spirits and sunniness.

Follow Abraham Lincoln's prescription, "A laugh a day will keep depression away." Laughing is, and will always be, the best form of therapy.

Day 314

He who laughs last probably had it explained to him.

Anytime you feel tense, irritable, aggravated or under stress, force yourself to smile. Instead of the usual response of sulking, frowning and grimacing, which most of us undergo in such situations, which only adds to the foul mood and tends to further exaggerate one's dejection, by smiling you instantly change your mood to pleasantness and hopefulness. It then proceeds to elevate one's spirits and produce a lighthearted gladness. The smile inspires your mind and thought processes to envision and experience enjoyable, optimistic times and places in your life. Sometimes, you smile from the inside out and sometimes you have to smile from the outside in. Either way, your mood will be uplifted.

Secretary of State Colin Powell advised: "It ain't as bad as you think. It will look better in the morning." What this wise, experienced statesman is saying is we tend initially to over react, exaggerate and overestimate the nature of every adversity. We tend to become overly anxious and excessively frightened by what we anticipate as the painful unfolding events that are before us. Once we wake up and start to deal with the situation, as terrible as it may at first seem, or indeed is, it will be something that we can confront and live with and hopefully overcome and then move on and experience new adventures.

"After every storm, the sun will smile; for every problem, there is a solution, and the soul's indefeasible duty is to be of good cheer" (William R. Alger).

Day 315

The general issued a rousing battle cry: "Onward to victory!" Half an hour later, an urgent message reached him: "Need further instructions. Victory not on our maps."

If soldiers lack commitment and devotion, the finest weapons in the world cannot save them. Conversely, many ill-equipped armies have defeated mighty forces because they had the will to succeed. The difference lies in attitude. The will to persevere in the midst of adversity pushes failure aside. If you find it difficult to pick yourself up and brush yourself off when things go wrong, you will lack the strength necessary to reach your goals.

Have an aim. Pick a single target, be intense in the moment and perfect a high-efficiency state. A skeet shooter hit a target 649 out of 650 times by taking this approach.

If you shoot a bow and arrow or a gun without a specific target, you will never hit the bull's-eye. Your shots will be scattered all over the place, and instead of experiencing the satisfaction of hitting the target, you will do serious and irreparable damage.

We are programmed wrong. We are creatures of poor learned behavior habits. We focus on problems instead of solutions that modify behavior. We have to focus on end results. What you can conceive, you can achieve. If you can see it, you can be it.

Being optimistic isn't always being happy. It's taking what the world throws at you and saying, "I'm not going to let this get me down." The goal is not to let life beat you down but rather to shoot for happiness.

Day 316

"My nurse used to drop me a lot." "What did your mother do?" "She got me a shorter nurse!"

Try something interesting and novel. Revert back to babyhood by lopping all your cares. Don't worry beyond the very immediate.

We spend too much time and anxiety concerned about the future and far too much time aggravating over past bad breaks, losses, misfortunes and disappointments. One of the major reasons why babies can so readily smile and have so much bounce and energy is because they are not burdened or debilitated by thoughts of the past or the future. They live in the present, actively and enthusiastically. Worrying is unproductive and debilitating. Worrying is like a rocking chair. It gives you something to do, but it won't get you anywhere.

Baby yourself. Live in and enjoy the present. "Don't worry about tomorrow. Don't think about yesterday. Don't live in the future. Make it through today."

Day 317

"The only thing I regret about my life is the length of it. If I had to do my life again, I'd make all the same mistakes—only sooner."—Tallulah Bankhead

A lecturer was speaking about stress management. Raising a glass of water, he asked, "How heavy is this glass of water?" Answers ranged from twenty grams to five hundred grams. The lecturer replied, "The absolute weight doesn't matter. It depends on how long you try to hold it."

"If I hold it for a minute, that's not a problem. If I hold it for an hour, I'll have an ache in my right arm. If I hold it for a day, you'll have to call an ambulance. In each case, it's the same weight, but the longer I hold it, the heavier it becomes." He continued, "And that's the way it is with stress management. If we carry our burdens all the time, sooner or later, the burden becomes increasingly heavy, and we won't be able to carry on. As with the glass of water, you have to put it down for a while and rest before holding it again. When we're refreshed, we can carry on with the burden." "Before you return home tonight, put down your burden of work. Don't carry it home. You can pick it up tomorrow. Put down all the burdens you're carrying now for a moment. Relax; pick them up later after you've rested. Life is short. Enjoy it!" The lecturer shared some ways of dealing with the burdens of life: 1. Accept that some days you're the pigeon, and some days you're the statue. 2. Always keep your words soft and sweet, just in case you have to eat them. 3. Drive carefully. It's not only cars that can be recalled by their maker. 4. If you can't be kind, at least have the decency to be vague. 5. If you lend someone twenty dollars and never see him again, it was probably worth it. 6. Nobody cares if you can't dance well. Just get up and dance. 7. Since it's the early worm that gets eaten by the bird, sleep late. 8. When everything's coming your way, you're in the wrong lane. 9. You may be only one person in the world, but you may also be the world to one person. 10. Some mistakes are too much fun to make only once. 11. We can learn a lot from crayons. Some are sharp, some are pretty and some are dull. Some have weird names, and all are different colors, but they all live in the same box.

Unfortunately, life has its burdens. They can't all be avoided. But, by developing the right attitude, you can lighten your stress.

Day 318

Out of my mind. Back in five minutes.

We can drive ourselves mad thinking of all of life's disappointments, frustrations and challenges. We all have our highs and lows, our mountains and our valleys. Compare life's mountains/highs with its valleys/lows. I have personally experienced all of them.

Valleys:
Illness of a loved one
The passing of a loved one
Financial losses
Business reversals
Untimely, adverse intrusions
Any kind of bad news
Disappointments and disillusionments
Aggravating situations
Personal failures

Mountains:
Marrying my wife Rozi
The birth of each of my four daughters
Success in my studies
Graduating from Harvard
Getting into Harvard in the first place
My 40th birthday party
Saving up to buy my first house
Business successes

Philanthropic activity
Helping and/or teaching others
Paying off my mortgage.
Writing books
The birth of each of my grandchildren
Transcendental Sabbath dinners
Spa vacations
Enjoying good health and good tennis partners and opponents
Enjoying the graduations, engagements, and marriages of my children and grandchildren

Don't feel bad about the things you didn't do, you don't have or you didn't accomplish. Take pride and feel happy about what you did accomplish—the deep valleys you've raised yourself from, the great mountains you've climbed and the beautiful mountains that lie ahead.

Day 319

Today is an excellent day to find yourself. I suggest you start with the phone book.

Albert Einstein said that significant problems could only be solved if one rises to another level. Try focusing on lifestyle change.

What is the passion of your life? Make it be to cultivate a strong inner motivation. It will enhance your ability and degree of self-control, which will help you achieve almost anything. Successful change happens by design, not by chance. Be a vehicle driven from within. Every champion was once a contender that wouldn't give up. You have to fight through the bad days in order to earn the best days.

Your mind should serve you. Don't let it become a victim of external events. Create an inner reality that is not merely subjected to the inevitable unpleasantness, the tossing, bouncing, banging, and beating of the cruel world outside. Teach your mind to be a faithful servant and develop the firm belief and conviction that you are and must be its master. Teach your mind that you are only limited by your own imagination. You have the power to pull yourself out of depression. Realize that life doesn't have to be perfect, it rarely is, but still life can be wonderful and you are the one who can make it so.

As Henry David Thoreau so brilliantly put it, "As a single footstep will not make a path on the earth, so a single thought will not make a pathway in the mind. To make a deep mental path, we must think over and over the kind of thoughts we wish to dominate our lives."

Day 320

What's Beethoven doing now? Decomposing!

Queen Latifah, a musical superstar who won a Grammy in 1995 and received an Oscar nomination for her 2002 performance in *Chicago*, became both wealthy and famous. Her life was shattered by tragedy when her only brother, who was her best friend all her life and whom she loved more than anyone in the world, was killed while riding a motorcycle she had given him two months before on his 24th birthday. She says, "The foundation of her life was swept away." She'd think about him and cry her heart out. She medicated every day to numb the pain. She said she was getting high and getting drunk every day. And then she "worked compulsively hard," she says. Her career took off but she suffered further tragedy when she and a friend were victims of a carjacking by two gunmen in Harlem that left her friend critically wounded. She says her personal life was spinning out of control.

She was so terribly hurt, she says, she would have given up. But, she claims, and this is crucial as to what helped her to make it through this trying adversity, that the voice inside her kept repeating, "You're going to make it, don't let go."

Then, she says, she met somebody and "sort of fell in love"—not enough to keep him, but enough to realize, "Wow, I can feel again!"

She smiled and said, "I've been hurt since then and I've survived it. I know life isn't always going to be good. There are times you can't really see or even feel how sweet life can be. Hopefully, its mountains will be higher than its valleys are deep. I know things that are broken

HAPPINESS GUARANTEED OR YOUR MISERY BACK

can be fixed. Take the punch if you have to, hit the canvas and then get up again. Life is worth it."

Absorb this sage advice from Latifah, who rose to become a superstar, who has taken the slings and arrows life tends, at some juncture, to assault all of us with and then take the punch—but get up again. Raise yourself up from the lowly valley of pain to the mountainous heights of joy.

Don't give up because things are hard, but work harder when you think of giving up. "Being defeated is often a temporary condition. Giving up is what makes it permanent" (Marilyn Vos Savant).

Day 321

"I think I am, therefore I am...I think."—George Carlin

"I think, what has this day brought me and what have I given it?" (Henry Moore).

Martin Luther King once said, "Everybody can be great, because everybody can serve." This potential that each of us has to serve, to do good, to help someone we love, to do something that improves the lives of others, to do even a simple act that makes another human being feel a little better, can be so rewarding in producing good feelings for yourself—and so ego enhancing—that it can be an inspiration for each of us. You possess enormous and phenomenal personal power to do good. "Carry out a random act of kindness, with no expectation of reward, safe in the knowledge that one day someone might do the same for you" (Princess Diana).

As Helen Keller said, "Many people have a wrong idea of what constitutes happiness. It is not attained through self-gratification but through fidelity to a worthy purpose." By doing good for someone else, you charge your self-esteem and up your self-worth, making you feel fulfilled and exhilarated.

A life isn't significant except for the impact it has on other lives.

Day 322

A waiter approached a table of three Jewish women and asked, "Is anything alright?"

A to Z HAPPINESS

Always be positive. **Attitude** is everything. **Appreciate** all that you have.

Be positive! **Be** optimistic!

Control what you think. You are the **commander** of your own mind so **choose** to eject negative, depressing thoughts that enter your mind and then quickly switch gears and inject positive, uplifting, happy-inducing thoughts.

Determine what you think. Remember, you're the boss. So, be the boss of what you think.

Eject negative, distressing thoughts. **Elicit encouraging**, upbeat, hopeful and cheerful-inducing thoughts.

Focus on exciting past experiences that make you feel good. Even more, **focus** on **future** adventures and experiences that will provide excitement and meaningful rewards and a happy **frame** of mind. And remember, "**faith** and hope" can conquer depression and **foster** happiness.

Govern your mind! Control your thought processes. **Guide** it away from negative thoughts to optimistic uplifting thoughts. **Galvanize** your mindset to achieve the **goal** of ongoing happiness.

Happiness is what you deserve and can achieve if you train yourself to implement the prescriptions in this book.

Invest the necessary effort to learn to induce yourself to think positive, optimistic, inspiring thoughts. **Inculcate** this psychological conditioning, so that it becomes automatic and thereby largely **immunizes** you from debilitating depression and, instead, **impels** encouraging joyous moods.

Jettison, as quickly as humanly possible, any negative or depressing thoughts and instantly redirect and **jolt** your mind and its thoughts to joyful and happy-inducing contemplations and prospects.

Knowledge is power. So, **know** that to induce happiness, you have to learn to **kick** out any thoughts that may create sadness, distress or stress. **Keep** away from pessimism. Be optimistic and **keep** hope alive. And always **keep** busy; it helps to make you feel productive and effective.

Learn to control your mind and what thoughts you allow to inhabit it. **Learn** "that you are the best" and so can determine what you will allow to occupy it. Control your mind, so that you force out any depressing thoughts and force it to exclusively dwell on uplifting, inspiring, and joyous thoughts. **Lighten** up!

Manage your **mind**! **Manipulate** it for your own **maximum** benefit by forcing it to think only the things that will make you feel happy. **Master** your own **mind**!

Negative, depressing thoughts are **not** for you and me and we must learn **not** to tolerate such counterproductive thoughts. We know we can control what we think, so we will only think and allow our mind to become engrossed by cheerful, exhilarating thoughts.

HAPPINESS GUARANTEED OR YOUR MISERY BACK

Optimism is rewarding! So, always be optimistic. It really pays off.

Pursue your goal of achieving happiness by **passionately** devoting yourself, your energies, to implementing the lessons and **prescriptions** that I am conveying to you in this treatise, which you are now imbibing. **Push** yourself, so that these guidelines become automatic habitual behavior. It will distance you and save you from the toxic poison of depression and drive you to **pleasurable** blissful emotions.

Quickly quell troublesome, aggravating, despondent and tormenting thoughts, so that you can progress and succeed in your laudable **quest** for a lifetime of exemplary happiness.

Remember to "accentuate the positive, eliminate the negative and don't mess with Mr. In-between."

Shift gears—whenever you start thinking negative, depressing or distressing thoughts, instantly shift gears and focus your mind on uplifting, inspiring happy thoughts.

Think positively! And you will immediately begin to feel happier. "You are what you think" and what you think you become.

Understand that even in the midst of adversity—painful periods—that if you learn to realize and believe "this too shall pass," you will begin to feel better. Overcoming these challenging episodes will help you to not only survive but to become stronger and successful.

Visualize in your mind's eye experiences, events and times and places that gave you joy and happiness and let your mind dwell on these alluring, encouraging, emotionally inspiring episodes that will infuse you with gladness and heart-warming exhilaration.

Win the challenging battle for happiness by counting your blessings and focusing on what's positive and not what's missing or what's wrong in your life at any specific moment in time.

X-out and learn to discard as quickly as possible distressing, dejecting, troublesome thoughts and experiences from your thought process. **Extricate** these negatives from your mind, as if they are prohibited. **Exercise** your own mind control and e**x**tract, **exaggerate** and **excite** those thoughts which **exhilarate** you and will cause you to **ex**alt instead of **exasperate**.

You are the master of **your** own destiny and you're **your** own happiness. You are in charge of what you think, and as a consequence, you can induce your own happiness (or sadness). Stay in charge—be in control of what you think and think positive optimistic thoughts.

Zealously pursue and practice the happiness lessons herewith offered to you. There is no more worthwhile pursuit or more gratifying achievement. **Zero** in on this phenomenal goal and you will surely realize infinite, priceless success and happiness.

Day 323

If every day is a gift, I'd like a receipt for Monday. I want to exchange it for another Friday.

Focus on what you have, not what you don't have. Focus on what could happen rather than on what didn't happen. When one door closes, another opens, so don't focus on lost opportunities.

Happiness is a mental condition. It is an attitude. Develop an optimistic attitude and you will capture happiness.

Every moment is precious. Appreciate each activity in which you participate, each experience, each event. Appreciate your next breath; contemplate it, enjoy it, savor it. Appreciate mundane daily happenings. Appreciate your next meal, the next time you see daylight and the sun, or the night and the stars and the moon. We spend too little time taking notice of the routine, but it is the accumulation of routine things that make up our happiness.

Aldous Huxley said, "Most human beings have an almost infinite capacity for taking things for granted." We spend too little time taking notice of them because they are routine. Teach yourself to appreciate the little things of every day and every hour, and you cannot help but be happy, because life is made up of the little things.

"It's not happiness that brings us gratitude. It's gratitude that brings us happiness."

Day 324

Happiness is finding two cherries in your martini when you are hungry.

Every morning, repeat these words: "It's a great day to be alive! It's a great day to be alive!"
Then think of all the reasons you have to feel that way:
The sun came up this morning.
Your eyes opened and you can see beauty.
You can hear music, smell flowers, and taste sweets.
Your hand can feel the soft skin of a baby and touch anything you wish.
You can walk and talk and breathe.
Your personal plumbing works.
You can plan, learn, and think.
You can love!
You do not have a stomach swollen from starvation.
You are not suffering intense pain, nor are you dying from cancer, diabetes or heart disease.
You have someone or something you really cherish and love.
You can experience new knowledge and new adventures.
You can still develop new exciting relationships.
You can dream and then pursue the fulfillment of those dreams.
Surely, you can think of many other reasons why it's a great day to be alive. Think about them. Savor them. Cherish them.
"I opened two gifts this morning. They were my eyes."

Day 325

If I could drop dead now, I would be the happiest person alive.

This moment is the beginning of your new life.
Life is too short to waste time being:

- Unproductive
- Uninvolved
- Uninspired
- Unexcited
- Uneducated
- Unloving
- And, especially, unhappy

Comedian George Carlin says, "When you step on the brakes, your life is in your foot's hands." For many, it is easier to drop out of school than to study, to walk out of a relationship than to work on it, to commit suicide than to stay and fight off the depression. It is up to you to decide to be productive, to fight for your happiness. No one can do it for you. Challenges are what G-d gives you, but He also puts in your hands the power to deal with them. Your own gut has to tell you that despite the pain you are experiencing, despite the challenge you must face, you have the ability and the willpower to pull yourself up and attain new reason for joyousness.

Happiness begins with you. It can't be dependent on your relationships, your work, and your finances. It is only dependent on your state of mind. Be cognizant of the fact that "if you are depressed, you are living in the past. If you are anxious, you are living in the future. Only if you are at peace are you living in the present" (Leo Tzu), so keep your mind positive, grateful and optimistic. Happiness is a matter of mindset more than actuality.

Day 326

"I've been doing some extremely abstract paintings…no paint, no canvas; I just think about it."—Steven Wright

A brilliant philosopher had a magnificent array of paintings in his home. His favorite was a canvas that was completely black except for the center. There, a tiny ray of light shown on a key.

He explained that it portrayed that even in the deepest darkness, there is light and it is up to each of us to find the key to open the door to that light. Even in the darkest of situations in the darkest hour, there is something good. Our minds and hearts must search for it.

Steven Kloves said, "We can find a way to be happy in any condition if we remember that we own our happiness." Unfortunately, most of us give away this authority to make us happy or sad, to people and circumstances.

Don't ever allow yourself to remain sad. Live life. Don't let it just pass. When you are feeling down, shift your thoughts to break the pattern of self-pity, sorrow, frustration or low self-esteem. Think of moments that made you happy. If you are unable to find enough of those moments, you are not living enough.

Just because something is not going your way, do not get into a downward spiral. Switch your focus. Don't dwell on it. Pull your "happiness trigger." Walk in the sand. Play music. Read a book. It invigorates you and will make you feel more equipped to deal with the circumstances. Big problems seem smaller given time to digest.

Do whatever pleases you and reminds you that, in the blackest sea, there is a lighthouse, and in the bleakest blackness, there is a key that will open the door to happiness. You just have to want to find it.

Day 327

I work for a good cause, 'cause I need money.

Do you feel incapable or inferior? Do you fear failure? Do you find every excuse not to try, not to move forward? Do you find yourself saying, "I need time, I need to think about it, I haven't decided yet, I'm not sure that's what I want, I'm considering it, I just don't feel up to it, I would, except that...I have other things to deal with first, etc."

In truth, it's best to accept your fear and realize that anyone starting something new, whether it is taking on a job, committing to marriage, having a baby, stepping into any new circumstances or walking into any unfamiliar territory, is frightening.

You can stay and procrastinate, consider, shiver and contemplate. You can strategize and prepare or you can gather your courage and step into the lion's den. Chances are you will realize the lion is not as ferocious as you feared; he wants a companion rather than dinner.

Fear keeps you confined. Yet, fear is a powerful driving force. The fear of doing nothing and of being nobody can spur you to move forward. Think, what passion would you pursue if you overcame your fear?

Day 328

Life is uncertain...eat dessert first.

Arthur Kurzweil, scholar, author, teacher and publisher, relates that he learned the "golden rule" from Rabbi Adin Steinstaltz, lauded by *Time* magazine as a "once-in-a-millennium scholar." Be realistic! Recognize that problems are intrinsic to living. Humans must endure:

- Diseases
- Plagues
- Crimes
- Murders
- Deaths
- Wars
- Depressions
- Accidents
- Family fights
- Envy
- Bad luck
- Hatred
- Divorces
- Cheating
- Losses
- Aging
- Mistakes
- Mutilation
- Religious persecutions

Unfortunately, we can't avoid the maladies life throws our way. The joy we get from living ultimately depends directly on how we view life, how we filter and interpret everyday experience.

Ask yourself, should I feel gratified and happy, or discontented and depressed?

Did I wake up this morning and appreciate my life when I reminded myself of the following:

Can I smile?
Can I see?
Can I hear?
Can I smell and taste?
Can I walk and talk?
Can I see the sun in the sky?
Can I breathe effortlessly?
Am I in pain?
Do I care about a relationship?
Is there a joyous event that I am anticipating?
Is there an activity I enjoy?
Do I have a stomach swollen from starvation?
Do I have AIDS?
Do I have cancer?
Do I have heart disease?
Am I crippled?
Am I homeless?
Am I destitute?
Is there food or drink that I enjoy?
Is there entertainment available for me?
If I suffered a hurtful loss, can I overcome it and find joy in life again?
Do I have sound reason to be angry?
Do I have sound reason to be aggravated? Do I have sound reason to be anxious?
Do I live in an environment that is free from abuse?
Are there exciting adventures that I can look forward to experiencing?

HAPPINESS GUARANTEED OR YOUR MISERY BACK

Is there knowledge I can look forward to acquiring and enjoying?

Are there books I look forward to reading, programs, plays or movies I can enjoy?

Do I appreciate that life equals opportunity?

Can I give love and receive love?

Can I do something nice for someone else?

Can I develop a positive attitude?

Happiness depends not on being able to control life but on the ability to control how we view, accept and deal with life.

Day 329

Attitudes are contagious. Are yours worth catching?

I was waiting for my plane in an airport when I overheard a father and daughter conversing. They had announced her plane's departure and he said to his daughter, "I love you. I wish you enough."

She said, "Daddy, our life together has been more than enough. Your love is all I ever needed. I wish you enough, too, Daddy." They kissed good-bye and she left. He walked over toward the window where I was seated. I did not want to intrude on his privacy, but he welcomed me in by asking, "Did you ever say good-bye to someone knowing it would be forever?"

"Yes, I have," I replied. Memories of expressing my love and appreciation to my dad for all he had done for me flooded my mind. Recognizing that his days were limited, I had wanted to tell him face-to-face how much he meant to me.

"Forgive me for asking, but why is this a forever good-bye?" I asked.

"I am old and she lives much too far away. I have challenges ahead and the reality is, her next trip back will be for my funeral," he answered.

"When you were saying good-bye I heard you say, 'I wish you enough.' May I ask what that means?"

He smiled. "That's a wish that has been handed down from other generations. My parents used to say it to everyone." He paused for a moment, looking up as if trying to remember it in detail, and then he smiled even more. "When we said 'I wish you enough,' we were wishing the other person a life filled with enough good things to sustain them," he added.

Turning toward me, he shared the following as if he were reciting it from memory:

> I wish you enough sun to keep your attitude bright.
> I wish you enough rain to appreciate the sun more.
> I wish you enough happiness to keep your spirit alive.
> I wish you enough pain so that the smallest joys in life appear much bigger.
> I wish you enough gain to satisfy your wanting.
> I wish you enough loss to appreciate all that you possess.
> I wish you enough "hellos" to get you through the final "good-bye."
> He began to cry and walked away.

"I Wish You Enough" (Anonymous)

Day 330

It's so cold your false teeth chattered…and they are still in the glass.

In Crown Heights, there was a Jew, Yankel, who owned a bakery. He survived the concentration camps. He once said, "You know why it is that I'm alive today? I was a kid, just a teenager at the time. We were on the train, in a boxcar, being taken to Auschwitz.

"Night came and it was freezing, deathly cold, in that boxcar. The Germans would leave the cars on the side of the tracks overnight, sometimes for days on end without any food and, of course, no blankets to keeps us warm."

He said, "Sitting next to me was an older Jew—this beloved elderly Jew—from my hometown. I recognized, but I had never seen him like this. He was shivering from head to toe and looked terrible. So, I wrapped my arms around him and began rubbing him to warm him up. I rubbed his arms, his face, his neck. I begged him to hang on.

"All night long, I kept the man warm this way. I was tired. I was freezing cold myself, my fingers were numb but I didn't stop rubbing the heat on to this man's body. Hours and hours went by this way.

"Finally, night passed, morning came, and the sun began to shine. There was some warmth in the cabin, and then I looked around the car to see some of the other Jews in the car. To my horror, all I could see were frozen bodies, and all I could hear was a deathly silence. Nobody else in that cabin made it through the night—they died from the frost.

HAPPINESS GUARANTEED OR YOUR MISERY BACK

"Only two people survived, the old man and me. The old man survived because somebody kept him warm. I survived because I was warming somebody else…"

Let me tell you the secret. When you warm other people's hearts, you remain warm yourself. When you seek to support, encourage and inspire others, then you discover support, encouragement and inspiration in your own life as well.

Day 331

It doesn't matter whether you win or lose—until you lose.

A winner has a program;
    a loser has an excuse

A winner says, "Let me do it for you;"
    a loser says, "That's not my job"

A winner sees an answer for every problem;
    a loser sees a problem in every answer

A winner is part of the answer;
    a loser is part of the problem

A winner says, "It may be difficult, but it's possible;"
    a loser says, "It may be possible, but it's too difficult"

A winner works harder than a loser and has more time;
    a loser is always "too busy" to do what is necessary

A winner makes commitments;
    a loser makes promises (Anonymous)

    The distance to success is measured by your own drive! Do what it takes to become a "winner"!

Day 332

I just let my mind wander and it didn't come back.

We control our personal environment, avoiding snake- or shark-infested areas, hazardous chemicals, life threatening radiation, and overexposure to the sun and cold. Otherwise, we would never survive. We must also protect ourselves from unnecessary self-abuse, from debilitating tension and aggravation and from self-inflicted stress and torture.

We must maximize the time that we enjoy a cheerful, unburdened stress-free, positive mood. You decide what thoughts you allow to enter your mind. This will make for a most rewarding, enhanced existence, and thus a richer happier life.

"There are no constraints on the human mind, no walls around the human spirit, no barriers to our progress except those we ourselves erect" (Ronald Reagan).

We can control what we think, how we think and how we interpret the information, whether we put an optimistic or pessimistic spin on what we are experiencing and whether we remain positive and upbeat or become negative and beaten when processing the facts. We must make the right choice.

Open your mind to joyous, positive thoughts. "Minds are like parachutes. They only function when they are open"(James Dewer).

Day 333

I believe in God's charities. Today a man asked me for a donation for the local swimming pool. I gave him a glass of water.

I asked God to take away my pain.
God said, "No. It is not for me to take away, but for you to give it up."
I asked God to make my handicapped child whole.
God said, "No. Her spirit was whole, her body was only temporary."
I asked God to grant me patience.
God said, "No. Patience is a by-product of tribulations; it isn't granted, it is earned."
I asked God to give me happiness.
God said, "No. I give you blessings. Happiness is up to you."
I asked God to spare me pain. God said, "No. Suffering draws you apart from worldly cares and brings you closer to me."
I asked God to make my spirit grow.
God said, "No. You must grow on your own, but I will prune you to make you fruitful."
I asked for all things that I might enjoy life.
God said, "No. I will give you life, so that you may enjoy all things."
I asked God to help me love others, as much as he loves me.
And God said, "Ah, finally, you have the idea." (Anonymous)

HAPPINESS GUARANTEED OR YOUR MISERY BACK

"G-d didn't promise days without pain, laughter without sorrow, or sun without rain, but He did promise strength for the day, comfort for the tears, and light for the way. If G-d brings you to it, He will bring you through it." "G-d didn't promise a calm passage. He promised a safe landing."

Day 334

The difference between try and triumph is a little "umph."

Always look forward to reaching and working towards inspiring, even thrilling, "dreams." Even as you get older, retain the ability to dream. After you fulfill one dream, dream ahead. Visualize exciting outcomes. Pursue your dreams even during difficult periods.

Exciting, uplifting dreams can fill your brain/your mind to provide happy emotional feelings and a sense of well-being. You can actually experience a less depressing, happier life through focusing on the dream in your head. Setting goals, and dreaming of accomplishing them, can provide a new narrative that actually moves you to a new place. Through "dreams," you can move from a state of morose depression to a place where your mind and your mental spirit are elevated and a lot happier.

We often get swallowed in our life rather than directing and leading it. Taking the time to dream about something, personal or professional, gives you the space to take control of your life and outline your move forward. Dreams allow you to expand your comfort zone, making it less frightening and easier to do things you once found challenging. The dream makes your vision more attainable. As you feel like you are making progress, you can function more effectively, work longer, achieve more and feel better.

We all need to develop the ability to find an activity that will inspire us when we are distressed and depressed. Dreaming about some exciting uplifting future aspiration or achievement is one formula that truly works.

HAPPINESS GUARANTEED OR YOUR MISERY BACK

Dreams should be accompanied by the will and the work to make those dreams come true. Some people only dream of success, while others wake up and work hard at it. Commit to fulfilling your dream by strengthening your "commitment muscle." Exercise this by, one day at a time, doing everything you said you'd do, every expectation, every assignment, every task and everything you would expect of yourself.

Make a list of your dreams then choose one or two to concentrate on first. Clearly define the dream and determine what the minimum requirements are for you to consider your dream fulfilled. Figure out the level of commitment you require to accomplish this dream. The bigger the dream, the more commitment it will take on your part, but a lot of dreams can be achieved if you commit to work on them just fifteen minutes a day, as long as you consistently work on it.

The dream gives you the hope and the positive impetus. The effort brings the success. And if you don't accomplish your original goal, at least the journey was optimistic and enjoyable.

Day 335

Adulthood: If you're not tired, you're not doing it right.

I wish you:
A fresh pot of coffee you didn't have to make yourself.
An unexpected phone call from an old friend.
Green stoplights on your way to work or shop.
A day of little things to rejoice in…
The fastest line at the grocery store.
A good sing-along song on the radio.
Your keys right where you look.

A day of happiness and perfection—little bite-size pieces of perfection that give you the funny feeling that the Lord is smiling on you, holding you so gently because you are someone special and rare.

A day of peace, happiness and joy.

Enjoy, take notice of and appreciate life's little miracles and let them light up your life.

Day 336

I was always complaining about the ruts in the road—until I realized the ruts are the road.

"What is Life?"

Life is a challenge…meet it.

Life is a gift…accept it.

Life is a tragedy…face it.

Life is a duty…perform it.

Life is a game…play it.

Life is a mystery…unfold it.

Life is a song…sing it.

Life is a journey…complete it.

Life is a promise…fulfill it.

Life is a struggle…fight it.

Life is a goal…achieve it.

Life is a puzzle…solve it.

Life is a sorrow...overcome it.

Life is a beauty...praise it.

Life is an adventure...dare it.

Life is an opportunity...take it.

Life is a happening...enjoy it!

Life is a "life"...live it!

Day 337

Sometimes, I wake up grouchy. Sometimes, I let him sleep!

How often do you wake up feeling you need help with work, with school, with making a living, with a business deal, with a health issue, with finding or retaining love, with your relationships, with your spouse, your kids, your parents and/or your friends? You would love to put a pillow over your eyes, turn over and go back to sleep.

You lack energy. You lack motivation. You lack a purpose. You are weighted down by your hurts, your pains, your losses and your fears. Then, the lights blow out and the electricity goes off and suddenly your whole mindset switches. You think, "Why didn't I get up while my lights, my shaver, my hair dryer, my toaster, my phone and my computer were working?"

Then, you realize that only three minutes before, you hadn't even thought about any of these items and their benefits. Suddenly, you have an appreciation of all you have taken for granted. You realize, you had better take stock and value all that you have and all that is going right in your life: at work, at school, at home, within your family and in your relationships. You want to get up, to accomplish, to forge ahead, to live and to enjoy life.

A moment before you receive a call informing you that a family member had as accident, you are just okay—one second after, you are falling apart. What wouldn't you do to turn back time, to appreciate the before?

How come we only appreciate the light after coming through the darkness? Every morning when you open your eyes, imagine the lights have just come on after a blackout. Look at the world with new appreciative eyes and life will feel great.

Every moment should be appreciated and savored. Often, you don't realize the true value of a moment until it becomes a memory.

Day 338

"The best cure for insomnia is to get lots of sleep."

"Inner Peace"

When you take a rest
You're at your best
So devote an hour
To increase your power
Let your mind its worries release
It will thereby produce inner peace
Practice calm meditation
It helps relieve frustration and aggravation
And generates salutary inspiration (Anonymous)

When we are stressed or anxious, we often can't sleep. We under-breathe, creating a need to take in more oxygen and exhale more carbon dioxide in order to relax our heart, mind and overall nervous system. The 4-7-8 is a great breathing trick to put you to sleep. Simply breathe in through your nose for four seconds, hold your breath for seven seconds and exhale through your mouth for eight seconds. This formula has a chemical-like effect on your brain, which slows your heart rate and soothes you to sleep.

If you don't have much time to sleep, another great trick is the 2-4-2. Sleep for two hours at night, then wake up for four hours and do your work, then sleep the last two hours of the night. Your brain thinks you have had a full eight hours sleep. This trick only works for a few nights in a row, then you need real sleep.

John Steinbeck correctly said, "It is a common experience that a problem difficult at night is resolved in the morning after the committee of sleep has worked on it."

Day 339

What is the best way to call your financial consultant these days? "Oh, waiter."

The "collective state of mind of the investing public" is what drives the stock market, rather than a mathematical unemotional scientific analysis. Consequently, it is much more susceptible to psychoanalysis than security analysis. In other words, it's all in the state of mind.

In all aspects of life, whether it is social, environmental, economical, matters relating to family, friends or business, your mind is the decision maker. Your mind is in control and you have the ability to control your mind.

Make up your mind to be happy and optimistic. We must train our minds to notice and cherish the good times. Don't only be aware of the fabulous moments. Be aware of the calm, peaceful, painless, trouble free moments as well.

Author Chuck Palahniuk wrote in his diary, "It's so hard to forget pain, but it's even harder to remember happiness. We have no scars to show for happiness. We learn so little from peace."

Day 340

My uncle gave new meaning to the word love. His dying wish was to have me sitting on his lap. He was in the electric chair.

    Civic leader John Gardner said in a speech, "The things you learn in maturity aren't simple things such as acquiring information and skills. You learn not to engage in self-destructive behavior. You learn not to burn up energy on anxiety. You discover how to manage your tensions. You learn that self-pity and resentment are among the most toxic of drugs.

    "You come to understand that most people are neither for you nor against you; they are thinking about themselves. You learn that no matter how hard you try to please, some people in this world are not going to love you, a lesson that is at first troubling and then really quite relaxing."

    Gardner went on to speak of leading a meaningful life. "Meaning is something you build into your life. You build it out of your own past, out of your affections and loyalties, out of the experience of humankind as it is passed on to you.... You are the only one who can put them together into that unique pattern that will be your life."

    Writer April Lawson explains that the word "'meaning' has become the stand-in concept for everything the soul yearns for and seeks," but life should be about more than material success. The person leading a true meaningful life has found some way of serving others that leads to a feeling of significance.

HAPPINESS GUARANTEED OR YOUR MISERY BACK

Gardner goes on to say that a meaningful life is more satisfying than a merely happy life. Happiness is about enjoying the present: meaning is about dedicating oneself to the future. Happiness is about receiving; meaningfulness is about giving. Happiness is about upbeat moods and nice experiences. People leading meaningful lives experience a deeper sense of satisfaction.

True meaning is an uplifting state of consciousness. It's what you feel when you're serving things beyond self, i.e., G-d, parenthood, a moral system. It is the giving to others and doing for others that gives meaning to one's life.

Day 341

I'm so unlucky—when my ship finally came in, I was waiting at the airport.

Infuse your life every day with positivity—focus on something that you are "lucky" enough to possess whether it's your state of health, the fact that you have a functioning brain, a physical or material asset you possess, a connection—friend or lover or mentor or business partner or child or mother or sibling, or just that you weren't born in Africa, etc., with some horrendous disease like tuberculosis or malaria or hepatitis, etc., or that you're up and alive and can do things that are fun or inspiring or adventurous or just helpful to others.

The circumstances, which you are in, or the opportunities you are now or can in the future experience for which you can feel appreciative, is endless. Of course, you can think of the reasons you're unlucky, but don't. They are insignificant compared to your blessings. Take out a few moments every day and make it a habit to enumerate some of the reasons you are lucky.

"Stop focusing on how stressed you are and focus on how blessed you are."

Day 342

Time is a great teacher, but unfortunately, it kills all its pupils.

Bronnie Ware, a nurse who cared for patients on their deathbed, revealed the five regrets most often expressed by her patients. She realized that people faced with their own mortality grew a lot. These people experienced a variety of emotions such as denial, fear, anger, remorse, more denial and eventually acceptance. Although Bonnie believed that every patient found peace before dying, they still had regrets.

The most common regret was that they wished they'd had the courage to live life true to themselves, rather than the life others expected them to live. Most felt they hadn't fulfilled even half of their dreams and had to die knowing it was due to choices they had or had not made.

Decide your dreams and goals and follow your heart. You control your life. What you think about and work at comes about. "By recording your dreams and goals on paper, you set in motion the process of becoming the person you most want to be. Put your future in good hands—your own" (Mark Victor Hansen).

Day 343

A good outdoor activity to do with kids is trying to find them after you've been looking at your cell phone for three hours.

Right before dying, people, men, in particular, since they are more frequently the breadwinners, said they regretted having worked so hard. They felt they had missed their children's youth and their partner's companionship. On their deathbeds, they finally realized how valuable time with your loved ones truly is.

Harry Chapin wrote a beautiful song, "Cat's in The Cradle," which spoke of a son asking his father to spend time with him. The father says, not now, but continuously promises a future time saying, "We'll have a good time then, son. You know we'll have a good time then." When the boy grows older and the father finally has time for him, the son is then too busy with his own life to make time to spend with his father. In a twist on reality, the son now promises his father to find time to spend with him saying, "We'll have a good time then, dad. You know we'll have a good time then."

In writing this song, Harry Chapin exhibited his understanding of the need to devote time to your children while you have the chance. Ironically, he himself died in a car crash at the young age of thirty-nine. His only child, Jen Chapin, was ten. I imagine he spent lots of time with his little girl while he had the opportunity to. She is now a singer-songwriter like her dad.

HAPPINESS GUARANTEED OR YOUR MISERY BACK

Simplify your life by making conscious choices as to what is possible, what is not needed and what income you can possibly do with out, so that you might create more time and space in your life for the people you love. Life gives us a finite amount of time. Use it wisely.

Day 344

You know that little voice in your head that keeps you from saying all the wrong things? I probably should get one of those!

Interestingly, a common regret of dying individuals, according to Nurse Bronnie Ware, is that they didn't have the courage to express their feelings. Many people believed they had suppressed their feelings in order to keep peace with others. As a result, they felt they had settled for a mediocre existence and never became who they were truly capable of becoming.

Many attributed their sickness to the bitterness and resentment they had carried. Although one has to retain sensitivity when speaking to someone, in the end, being honest raises a relationship to a whole new and healthier level. Either that or it releases the unhealthy relationship from your life. Either way, you feel better.

Strive to have more open, honest conversations, giving deeper connection and meaning to your relationships. But, to feel good about yourself, be cognizant that "the kindest word in all the world is the unkind word unsaid" (Anonymous).

Day 345

A friend is someone who will bail you out of jail. A best friend is one sitting next to you saying, "Wasn't that fun?"

Before a person passes on, in those last few weeks of contemplating their lives, they are often very aware of the mistakes they made. Things they did, that could they live their life over, they believe they would do differently.

A major regret, dying people expressed, was not having stayed in touch with their friends. It seems everyone misses their friends when they are dying. According to Nurse Bronnie Ware, people often do not realize the full value of old friends until their dying weeks, at which point it is not always possible to track them down. Unfortunately, many had become so caught up in their own lives that they do not stay in touch with or devote proper time and energy to people who they cherished.

It is common for anyone, considering that most of us lead a busy lifestyle, to let friendships slip away. But, when one is faced with approaching death, the physical details of life lose their value. People do want to get their finances in order but it is not money or status that is the impetus, but rather, they want to get things in order for their loved ones. Sadly, at this point, they are usually too ill to deal with it. What it comes down to is love and relationships.

When you see a dying person surrounded by his loved ones, family and friends, you know this individual understood what is really important in life. When you forge relationships with others, when you stay close, connect and are there for others, they will be there for you.

Day 346

My parents always thought laughter was the best medicine. I guess that's why a few of us died of tuberculosis.

A surprisingly common regret, mentioned by people in the weeks before their expected death, is "I wish I had allowed myself to be happier." Many people never realized that they had passed up the opportunity to be happy, which they now realize was their choice and their decision.

Most people, fearing change, afraid to take on new challenges, fooled others as well as themselves into believing that they were content, when in truth they would've preferred to live aspects of their lives quite differently. They would've liked to do things that made them laugh more, feel more accomplished and feel more satisfied. They would've liked to add silliness into their lives again.

When people are dying, they realize what they should've done differently. Think about how you would like to live your life, so that when your time is up, you don't have to look back on your life with regret. If you want to laugh more, start now. Always be aware that life is a choice—your choice. "Every day you spend without a smile is a lost day"(Anonymous).

Day 347

I am going to create a Facebook account with the name "Nobody," so when someone posts something stupid, I can say, "Nobody likes this!"

If something makes us unhappy, why do we do it?

According to a *New York Post* October 11, 2015, article, there are eight million photos posted on Instagram per day. 1.49 billion active users go on Facebook per month. Twitter has 316 million active accounts, Tumblr 230 million. Pintrest has 47.66 million visitors from the US alone and is the fastest independent growing site in history.

Studies have shown that this form of communication makes people more vulnerable to depression, loneliness and low self-esteem by creating envy, causing users to feel inadequate and unfulfilled.

A 2003 scientific experiment conducted at two German universities on 584 Facebook users found that one out of three users felt worse after checking what their friends were up to.

Someone else receiving attention for their birthday, their exciting trip or their engagement has been proven to be a spark that ignites one's own feeling of inadequacy and deprivation.

In 1954, Leon Festinger came up with the "social comparison theory," the idea that we measure ourselves in relation to others' failures and successes.

"Seeing Everyone Else's Highlight Reels: How Facebook Usage is Linked to Depressive Symptoms," was published in 2014 in the *Journal of Psychology*. Rather than being happy for others' betterment, users often become sad for themselves. People have claimed to have anxiety attacks, guilt, envy, self-hatred, negative thinking and even suicidal thoughts after connecting to Facebook.

Control your happiness. Decide whether your contacts are making you feel more connected or more alone. Revert back to true face-to-face contact and communication and the old-fashioned concept of phone calling rather than tweeting and texting. Chances are this form of communication will give you more honesty, more personal involvement and greater self-worth.

Day 348

I'm going to change my name on Facebook to "Benefits," so now when you add me, it will say you are now "friends with benefits."

How many of us show one side of ourselves to the outside world while hiding our true self? These days, the gap between the people we are and the people we present to the world have never been wider.

Studies show that young people, no matter how accomplished they are, are the most vulnerable to feel inadequate after comparing themselves to friends on social networks. People feel pressured to present perfect lives and start to feel frustrated and overwhelmed. More and more, people who have shown themselves to have the perfect life, the life that everyone strives for, the perfect relationship, the adoring spouse, the amazing children, the beautiful body, the stunning home, etc., are found to be abusing drugs or alcohol, improperly self-medicating or even committing suicide.

Madison Hollerin, a lovely nineteen-year-old Ivy League student, star athlete and all-around popular girl who posted photos of her fabulous life on Instagram, when told by her mother that she looked so happy in her online photo, Madison answered, "Mom, it's just a photo." An hour after posting a beautiful photo online, Madison leapt to her death. Her family has kept her Instagram account up as a reminder, especially for teens, that a life online may bear no resemblance to one actually lived. One of Madison's favorite quotes posted online was "Even people you think are perfect are going through something difficult."

A 2014 video that went viral, called "What's on your mind?", is about a young man's actual life (broke, dumped, unemployed, drinking and alone) versus his online one (single, carefree, out clubbing, living the dream).

What people claim is not necessarily reality. Pictures are touched up and retouched. People lie at will. People often want to create the illusion of joy, whether in an effort to fool others or to fool themselves.

Know others' realities, so that you are not envious of or competing with lies. Know your own reality, so that you can face it and deal with it and not wait until life crashes down on you.

"The reason we get disappointed is because we compare our behind-the-scenes footage to everyone else's highlight reel."

Day 349

Advertising has really changed our thinking. This morning, my wife put on eye shadow, eyeliner and eyelashes. I said, "What are you doing to your eyes?" She said, "I'm making them look natural."

Advertising is the fine art of making you think you have longed for something all your life that you never heard of before. It is based on creating dissatisfaction, making people want what they don't have or necessarily need, dress differently than they dress, look different than they looked and go places they never knew existed.

Although it has its economic benefits for the economy, advertising makes people feel unsuccessful, incapable and inadequate. No matter how much you do, it is impossible, despite your finances, your drive or your stamina, to keep up with the new products, new vacation spots and new ideas. If you are trying to obtain a certain "status," advertisers continue to move the goalpost and make it unachievable.

Dissatisfaction can be an impetus for improving oneself, but advertising depends on creating dissatisfaction on a material, aesthetic or sexual level. Even if one could purchase it all, advertisers are promoting lies. Do or buy this product and you will be beautiful, popular, admired, envied and satisfied.

We need to recognize the falsity and be able to distinguish truth in advertising and at an early age teach our children to do the same. We need to develop immunity to the wants and needs that are being created by people who don't even know who we are or know or care about our needs.

It has been shown that no one ad is so bad, but the cumulative effect of four hundred ads a day on children gives way to narcissism, entitlement and dissatisfaction.

Considering the abundance of ads everywhere, total avoidance is impossible, but be aware of the pitfall they cause. Don't allow ads to cause you unhappiness.

Day 350

My wife knows exactly what she wants, just as soon as my neighbors get one.

To understand and achieve happiness, we must first realize what makes us unhappy. According to Tiny Buddha, there is only one cause of unhappiness: the false beliefs you have in your head, beliefs so widespread and so commonly accepted that you don't think to question them. Each one of us has our own beliefs about what brings us happiness and we live our life according to it. We define our reality by what we believe.

There are certain common beliefs about happiness that actually make you unhappy, beginning with the need for other people's approval. So much of what we do is to get the approval of others, such as how we dress, whom we are friendly with and even how we speak. The irony is that most people will never give you the approval you seek for more than a brief period because they too are often looking to be accepted by the biggest and the best and will, therefore, move on to get the approval of someone richer, cooler, more popular, or what they consider to be more desirable. At which point, the approval you thought you had will evaporate leaving you once again searching for a way to impress your peers or those you want to be accepted by.

Vincent Van Gogh, one of the greatest artists of all time, only sold one painting, *The Red Vineyard at Arles*, during his lifetime. Despite not making money, Van Gogh painted over nine hundred works of art. His persistence went unnoticed during his lifetime but he proved you don't need external validation to persist in what you believe in.

You have to find security within yourself, accept and love yourself for who you are. The purpose of approval is very different from the pursuit of happiness and we must distinguish between the two. You yourself have to approve of how you present yourself, how you behave, how you act towards others. Feeling good about how you look and act makes a person happy.

Falsely believing that other people's approval will make you happy is a guaranteed way to bring on inevitable disappointment and unhappiness.

Never seek validation from others. Respect yourself by making your own choices. Have confidence in yourself and your worth. "Life is too short to waste time waiting for other people's approval on how you live it" (Dr. Steve Marboli).

Day 351

Baseball can be so confusing to a child. At one game, my coach yelled, "Hold at third," while my mother was yelling, "Come home this instant."

Analyze the relevance of attitude and you'll come up with really incredible insights. A major-league baseball is readily available to anyone at a sporting goods store for ten dollars. Yet, one of these identical baseballs used by Barry Bonds for his record-breaking seventy-sixth home run of the season, sold for $752,467 because people thought this was "The Ball" that set the record. Perception turned a ten-dollar ball into a three-quarter-million-dollar ball! Imagine what perception can do for you!

When a child is brought up feeling loved and secure, he feels capable and empowered. He can deal with challenges. When a child is raised being made to feel inadequate and a failure, he becomes a failure, unable to cope with challenges. His perception of himself shapes his abilities and performance.

With the proper self-training and orientation, you can control what you think and how you feel and positively affect your future success. You can choose to perceive both yourself and whatever experiences, challenges or confrontations life holds for you in a positive light and derive unimaginable benefits from that mindset.

Perception is reality.

Day 352

Some may call me imperfect. I am a dyslexic, atheist insomniac. I stay up all night wondering if there really is a Dog?

You cause yourself unhappiness by believing that you can't be happy unless everything goes right. Too often people miss the forest for the trees. People get stuck on one bothersome issue and miss the total pleasant picture. People lose a piece of luggage on a vacation and can't enjoy being in a magnificent hotel in a spectacular country.

Accept that things can be wonderful even if they are not perfect. Think about it: Are vacations, parties, dates or any other special occasions ever perfect? If something goes wrong, does that mean the entire trip or evening is a failure? It is only a failure if you believe so.

Can't your life be wonderful despite that your spouse, your children, your professor or your friend isn't perfect? In truth, is anything in life ever purely perfect? We have ups and downs every day. Life is imperfect but we have the power to be happy despite the imperfections.

When things go wrong, take a moment to look around and notice all the things that are going right.

Day 353

**Q: Where's Spider-Man's homepage?
A: On the World Wide Web.**

A major misconception that leads us to unhappiness is believing that we are in control. At times, people seem to believe that they are superheroes. They believe that they can control everything and that things will turn out exactly how they planned. The responsibility is overwhelming. The results are often devastating. The disappointment and frustration all falls on their shoulders, leading to guilt and self-loathing.

The reality is that we don't have the ability to control anything, other than our own reactions and our own behavior. We can't control circumstances. We can't control the thinking or actions of others. We can't control the weather or the economy or just about anything else that affects us.

Once you make peace with this, you can start to enjoy the scenery of the journey rather than plotting the impossibility.

Day 354

If anyone is thinking about buying an autobiography, I don't want to ruin the ending for you, but they write a book.

Despite any hardship, in the face of any challenge, with the right attitude, you can live a happy, upbeat life. Aharon Margolin, author of *As Long As I Live*, wrote an autobiography chronicling his unimaginably difficult life.*

At age seven, Aharon suffered a terrible trauma, which rendered him mute, paralyzed by polio and lying in a sanatorium. With unequaled determination, backed by the love of family, he learned to walk and talk and thrive.

Three times following this, he was afflicted with cancer, for which the prognosis was fatal. Each time, he fought the system, the doctors the researchers and the diagnosticians. Each time, he turned to family and friends for a support system. Each time, he fortified and strengthened himself as he moved forward with his life. To complicate this, Aharon bore unbelievable personal tragedies. Each time, he accepted tragedy with smarts, with faith, with courage and with iron determination to fight on.

---

* *After being inspired by the book, I proudly discovered that Aharon Margolin is my first cousin, living in Israel.*

HAPPINESS GUARANTEED OR YOUR MISERY BACK

Aharon's life story gives everyone strength and hope to persist, to remain optimistic no matter what obstacle you might face. We are each stronger than we realize.

"Life's problems wouldn't be called hurdles if there wasn't a way to get over them" (Anonymous).

Day 355

You laugh. I laugh. You cry. I cry. You jump off a really tall cliff. I yell, "Do a flip."

"Sometimes, we expect more from others because we would be willing to do that much for them." Just because you play fair with others, don't expect them to play fear with you. Life doesn't work that way. "It's like expecting the lion not to eat you just because you didn't eat him."

Wouldn't it be a wonderful world if what you did for others they would do for you? If you shared with others, they would reciprocate. If you loved another, they would love you in return. If you treated others with respect, they would treat you in a like manner. But, by expecting this, you are setting yourself up to be disappointed, angry and totally unhappy.

How many people go into marriage with a tit-for-tat attitude? "If I treat you like a king, I expect you to treat me like a queen." But it doesn't always happen. How many people turn to their children and say, "I took care of you, now you take care of me," and the child either can't or won't? How often do you turn to someone and say, "I was there for you, I can't believe you aren't coming through for me"?

Many people are incapable of or unwilling to live up to your standards. Learn to take people as they are and appreciate them for whatever they may add to your life. Do it for yourself. Accepting people for what they are will make you a happier person.

HAPPINESS GUARANTEED OR YOUR MISERY BACK

Decide, to the extent you can, to surround yourself with people who make you feel good, who make you laugh, who are there for you when you need someone, people who value your happiness. They are the ones worth keeping in your life.

Day 356

A man goes into a Zen bookstore and hands the cashier $10 for a book that costs $9.95. He waits and finally says, "Where's my change?"
The cashier says, "Change must come from within."

If you are unhappy with your parents, your spouse, your children, your friends your teacher, or as is only too common, your mother-in-law, learn to accept and deal with it. Retaining this frustration or anger towards others only serves to aggravate you. You can't change the other person. You only have the power to change yourself, your attitude, your responses, your reactions and your feelings toward the other person.

Many people want to be accepted for who they are but have trouble accepting others for who they are. They will make excuses for their own deficiencies in behavior, tardiness, patience, or lack of productivity, but they are unwilling to tolerate or forgive the flaws of others. To be happy, you must learn to be less critical, more focused on other people's positives rather than his/her flaws. Be more understanding, more compassionate and more forgiving.

In *The New Rules of Marriage,* psychologist Terrence Real criticizes couples that are miserable yet have no desire to change. He terms them "comfortable/miserable." If you want a good relationship, you have to get out of your stale comfort zone, working to change yourself and the dynamics of the marriage. This pertains to any relationship.

HAPPINESS GUARANTEED OR YOUR MISERY BACK

Determine which issues result from your own sensitivities and which are the result of your spouse's, your friend's or your relative's sensitivities, and think how you can either accept or change the dynamics.

If you can't change your attitude toward that individual, whether it is their fault or your own, then for your own well-being, to the extent you can, do what you can either to avoid being with or having confrontations with that individual.

"You can not change the people around you, but you can change the people that you choose to be around."

Day 356

A bad attitude is like a flat tire… you can't go anywhere unless you change it.

People who need to feel in control both of situations and of others, or are impatient, intolerant or are always late or those who are overly judgmental or can't control their tempers, not only make others unhappy, they make themselves unhappy. Being or feeling this way is a conscious decision.

Erich Fromm said, "Man's main task in life is to give birth to himself, to become what he potentially is. The most important product of his effort is his own personality."

If you live with a parent, spouse or any person who affects your life, who is controlling, abusive, bipolar, obsessive-compulsive, manic, borderline or even someone who just refuses to respect your boundaries, that person often has the ability to make you feel inefficient, inadequate, insecure, impotent and inconsequential. "The way people treat you is a statement about who they are as a human being. It is not a statement about you" (Anonymous). If that person is not willing to try to change himself, move away from that relationship before it destroys you.

Bad character, whether it be your own or someone close to you, whether it is intentional or not, will only cause you unhappiness. It is up to you to process the implications and change or disconnect, in order to achieve the happiness you deserve.

Day 357

**Patient: Doctor! I have a serious problem. I can never remember what I just said.
Doctor: When did you first notice this problem?
Patient: What problem?**

"Education should prepare our minds to use its own power of reason and conception rather than filling it with the accumulated misconceptions of the past" (Bryant H. McGill).

Our misconceptions only serve to make us sad. For example, elderly individuals often scare themselves, convinced that they are losing their memory, rather than realizing that it's normal to forget where you put your car keys as long as you remember what you need car keys for. Or, occasionally forgetting what you had to do is normal, but the inability to do things you've always been capable of doing is abnormal.

A person with a mark on his body can convince and depress himself, thinking he has cancer rather than a rash, a mosquito bite or just a bump from unconsciously hurting himself.

Other people convince themselves that no one cares about them. Before deciding such a painful thing, determine whether it's your own insecurity that is causing you to feel this way or your own behavior that is truly repelling others or that it is totally untrue.

Some people allow a debilitating fear of what lies ahead, of impending disaster, of going broke or of hopeless poverty, to enmesh their thinking. In the United States, and in most of the developed

Western countries, there is a sufficient security net and support system for the essential necessities that you require in life.

Older people are particularly vulnerable to fears of the future, of going broke, etc., so that it is even more incumbent on them, or on you, if you fall into this category, to impress yourself that you need not be concerned. In America, you'll do all right.

Our minds are a powerful tool. We can convince ourselves of both the wrong and the right things. Find out the facts before you allow your mind to run wild with thoughts that will bring you down. In order to remain calm and happy, rather than freaking out when you experience a situation or notion that frightens you, research the situation or the issue and get the truth before going into crisis mode. Fear causes tunnel vision. Calmly assess a situation and examine the options.

"Only 8 percent of our worry will come to pass" (Mark Gorman). How much of what we imagine and frighten ourselves with is imaginary? Unfortunately, it is easier to misunderstand than to try to understand. Check out your fears and separate fact from fiction and reality from misconceptions before panicking.

Day 358

My wife and I always compromise. I admit I'm wrong and she agrees with me.

Author John Steinbeck wrote, "Try to understand men. If you understand each other, you will be kind to each other. Knowing a man well never leads to hate and almost always leads to love."

Feeling unloved or misunderstood is a major cause of unhappiness. Jumping to conclusions, being unwilling to see someone else's perspective, being too closed-minded, twisting someone else's words or being unable to communicate properly all lead to arguments, irritability and eventual melancholy.

Dr. Sue Johnson, author of *Creating Connections*, says that most couple's arguments are a protest against disconnection. Underneath the anger lies the questions, "Can I count on you? Do you value me?" The anger criticism attacks are cries, "Please be here for me."

Human beings crave love, whether it come from relatives or friends. We have a deep-seated need to love others and to be loved by others, to understand others and to be understood in return. We want connection. We yearn to be cared about and appreciated for who and what we are. When one is missing that connection, he feels alone, lonely and empty.

To be loved, you must let others into your life, open your heart and let them in and be there for others, so that they want to enter.

"People are lonely because they build walls not bridges."

Day 359

Those that forget the pasta are doomed to reheat it.

Dr. Viktor E. Frankl in his outstanding book, *Man's Search For Meaning*, gives an in-depth account of his experiences and the lessons he learned from being in Auschwitz and Dachau Nazi death camps during World War II.

Frankl writes, "In spite of all the enforced physical and mental primitiveness of the life in a concentration camp, it was possible for spiritual life to deepen." Certain intelligent people, despite the torturous circumstances, "were able to retreat from their terrible surroundings to a life of inner riches and spiritual freedom."

Frankl believes that no matter the physical environment, the horrific conditions and the taking away of all human rights, man has the ability to retain his human liberty. "The experience of camp life proves that man does have a choice of thought and action." Frankl feels there were sufficient examples of a heroic nature, men he remembers who walked through the camp comforting others, giving away their last piece of bread, which proved that man can preserve a vestige of spiritual freedom, of independence of mind; apathy could be overcome and irritability suppressed, even in such unimaginable conditions of psychic and physical stress. These men proved that "everything can be taken away from a man but one thing: the last of the human freedoms—to choose one's attitude in any given set of circumstances, to choose one's own way."

Frankl tells how every day, every hour, offered the opportunity to make decisions; a decision whether you would or would not

HAPPINESS GUARANTEED OR YOUR MISERY BACK

submit to those powers which threatened to rob you of your very self, your inner freedom, which determined whether you would rise above or surrender to circumstance, renouncing freedom and dignity to become molded into the form of the typical captive.

It seems clear that the sort of person the prisoner became was not the result of the concentration camp itself but, rather, the result of an inner decision. Frankl is saying that any man, even under such ghastly circumstances, decides what shall mentally and spiritually become of him.

You can choose to take the attitude of hope, of happiness, of meaningfulness, despite any circumstances you find yourself in. "Our greatest freedom is the freedom to choose our attitude" (Viktor Frankl).

Day 360

Oxygen is proven to be a toxic gas. Anyone who inhales oxygen will normally die within ninety years.

A question that occurs to many of us is "How would I myself deal with one of the toughest challenges given to man, receiving a diagnosis which has a fatal prognosis?" Certain individuals, who are told that they have incurable diseases, after the initial shock, are eventually able to accept their fate and all the suffering it entails with a brave, dignified and considerate manner.

A young invalid wrote to a friend that he had just found out he would not live long, that even an operation would be of no help. He wrote further that he remembered a film he had once seen in which a man was portrayed who waited for death with courage and dignity. The boy had thought this a great accomplishment to meet death in such a commendable manner. Now, he wrote—fate was offering him a similar chance.

A young woman, aware that she was dying within a few days, was nevertheless cheerful. She said she was grateful that fate had hit her so hard. She said that previously, she had been spoiled and did not value spiritual accomplishments and she now believed in the eternal life.

In exasperating situations, we can rant and rave, get angry or depressed, or we can chose to embrace life with genuine grace.

If in such painfully dire times, individuals can choose an admirably positive attitude, we too can and should strive, in all circum-

HAPPINESS GUARANTEED OR YOUR MISERY BACK

stances, to face life with a positive disposition that makes life meaningful and purposeful.

Every moment we can choose misery or blissfulness. It's your life. It's your attitude. It's your choice.

Day 361

Artificial intelligence usually beats real stupidity.

"Everybody is a genius but if you judge a fish by its ability to climb a tree, it will live its whole life believing it is stupid" (Albert Einstein).

We all possess signature strengths, the things we like doing, are good at, and are the most essential to who we are. Through the use of exhaustive questionnaires, Martin Seligman, pioneer of positive psychology, found that the most satisfied upbeat people were those who had discovered and exploited their unique combination of signature strengths, such as humanity, temperance, bravery, creativity and persistence.

There are people who wake up in the morning excited to start their day. Others wake up feeling scared, apathetic and wish they could avoid getting up. These reactions are not intrinsic to our personality but rather a function of whether you spend your days using your signature strengths or trying desperately to correct your weaknesses. Marcus Buckingham advanced the idea that we should play to our strengths, especially when it comes to work or career.

People who deliberately exercised their signature strengths on a daily basis became significantly happier for months. A psychological experiment had 577 volunteers choose one of their signature strengths and use it in a new way each day for a week. This group became significantly happier and less depressed than the control groups. These benefits lasted even after the experiment ended and their levels of happiness remained heightened a full month later.

HAPPINESS GUARANTEED OR YOUR MISERY BACK

The more you use your signature strengths in daily life, the less stressed you are the greater your vitality and the higher your self-esteem. These strengths help you make progress toward your goals, maintain social support and meet basic needs for independence, relationship and competence, all leading to you becoming a happier person. Try to discover and consistently use your signature strengths.

"No one is born an expert, but we all have strengths. Always be working to develop your gifts into passion and purpose." Discover which waters are best suited for your strokes and jump in.

Day 362

Remember, half the people are below average.

"Adversity causes some men to break; others to break records" (William Arthur Ward). It is up to you to think positively, to forge ahead despite life's setbacks, hurdles and disappointments. There are innumerable outstanding individuals who could've given up but didn't.

The Beatles were originally told by a recording company, "We don't like your sound, and guitar music is on the way out." Elvis Presley was fired from the Grand Old Opry, being told, "You ain't goin' nowhere, son. You aught to go back to drivin' a truck." Ludwig Van Beethoven's teachers believed he was hopeless and that he would never succeed with the violin or composing. Not only did Beethoven succeed, but he completed five of his symphonies while he was completely deaf.

In the athletic field, Michael Jordan, considered the best basketball player of all time, was cut from his high school basketball team. Jordan says, "I have missed more than nine thousand shots in my career. I have lost almost three hundred games. On twenty-six occasions, I have been entrusted to take the game-winning shot, and I missed. I have failed over and over again in my life. And that is why I succeed."

Babe Ruth had 714 home runs but, for decades, he also held the record for strikes, 1,330. When asked about it, he would say, "Every strike brings me closer to the next home run."

HAPPINESS GUARANTEED OR YOUR MISERY BACK

Tom Landry, coach of the Dallas Cowboys brought the team two Super Bowl victories, five NFC Championship victories and holds the record for the most career wins. He also has the distinction of having one of the worst first seasons on record, winning no games and winning five or fewer over the next four seasons.

Bill Gates, founder of the global empire Microsoft, certainly didn't look like he was headed for success. After dropping out of Harvard and starting a failed first business with Microsoft co-founder Paul Allen called Traf-O-Data, he didn't give up.

People persisted and succeeded in every field from Charles Darwin in science, who himself wrote, "I was considered by all my masters and my father, an ordinary boy, rather below the common standard of intellect," to Socrates in philosophy who was considered, an immoral corruptor of youth and was sentenced to death yet kept teaching up to the time he was forced to poison himself, to Thomas Edison, who was told by his teachers, "He was too stupid to learn anything" and was fired from his first two jobs for being unproductive.

To be happy, you must pursue your dream. Don't ever give up on working towards that dream. As Calvin Coolidge said, "Nothing in this world can take the place of persistence. Talent will not; nothing is more common than unsuccessful men with talent. Genius is not; unrewarded genius is almost a proverb. Education will not; the world is full of educated derelicts. Persistence and determination alone are omnipotent."

Day 363

On their first day of flying, Orville said to Wilbur, "If we only flew three miles, how did our luggage wind up in Paris?"

"Negative thinking patterns can be immensely deceptive and persuasive, and change is rarely easy. But, with patience and persistence, I believe that nearly all individuals suffering from depression can improve and experience a sense of joy and self-esteem once again" (David D. Burns, author of *The Feeling Good Handbook*).

Orville and Wilbur Wright battled depression and family illness before starting their bicycle shop that lead them to experimenting with flight. After numerous attempts at creating flying machines, several years of hard work, and tons of failed prototypes, the brothers finally created a plane that could fly.

Oprah Winfrey, one of the wealthiest and most successful people in the world, endured a rough and abusive childhood. At fourteen, she ran away from home, got pregnant and lost her child. Although Oprah had all the reason and excuses to give in to depression and to give up, her tragic life didn't stop her from becoming what she is today.

Albert Einstein, who is today considered the epitome of a "genius," did not speak until he was four and did not read until he was seven, causing his parents and teachers to think he was mentally handicapped, slow and antisocial. Despite his good grades, his head was always in the clouds. He kept thinking and eventually developed the theory of relativity.

HAPPINESS GUARANTEED OR YOUR MISERY BACK

At age fifteen, the actor Jim Carrey had to drop out of school and was so poor he had to live in a van. This homeless condition didn't stop him from achieving his dream of becoming a comedian.

Benjamin Franklin, due to poverty, had to drop out of school at age ten, so on his own, he became a voracious reader, leading him to inventing the lightning rod and bifocals and becoming one of this America's Founding Fathers.

At age thirteen, Bethany Hamilton, a child surfer, was attacked by a shark, resulting in her losing her left arm. One month later, she was back on her surfboard, and two years later, she won first place in the Explorer' Women's Division of the NSSA National Championship.

Charlize Theron, at age fifteen, witnessed her mother shoot her alcoholic father in an act of self-defense. Instead of allowing the trauma to immobilize her, she channeled her energy into becoming the first South African actress to win an Academy Award.

It is always easiest to throw in the towel, but always be aware that no one and nothing can shatter your dreams unless you allow it.

Day 364

A man recently swam the English Channel. Asked to explain his secret, he said, "Every time I got tired, they threw water in my face!"

Mark Spitz, the famous Olympic athlete who won seven gold medals in swimming, described how to be a champion: "Don't leave it to chance! Work at it!"

Each of us would ideally like to win a championship in the ultimate life battle—the supreme goal—to achieve happiness. While no one is going to present us with a gold medal, you and I really want be "Olympic" champions in the pursuit of happiness. But, as is true in all other pursuits, it just doesn't happen because we want it. It can and does happen if we work at it smartly, constantly and diligently.

To achieve his remarkable feat, Mark Spitz worked at it just about every waking hour of his life for many years, training from the experienced, accomplished champions before him and practicing repetitiously their behaviors and actions, so they became automatic and instinctive.

We must have the same determination, dedication and repetition, so that we develop the positive, optimistic, winning attitude that will make us happiness champions.

The fact that you are now reading this "how-to" book on happiness indicates that you're on the right path to reaching that exalted goal.

In every circumstance, in every situation, from the moment you open your eyes in the morning until you shut them at night, remind

HAPPINESS GUARANTEED OR YOUR MISERY BACK

yourself that you want to be happy and, therefore, you will only do things and think thoughts that will, hopefully, not only not detract from your happiness but increase it.

Now implement, at least at the beginning, with a fanatic fervor the recommendations, the effective formulas and prescriptions herein outlined and you will become an enviable "happiness champion." "If you think you can, you can. And if you think you can't, you're right" (Henry Ford).

Day 365

Don't take life too seriously. It's only temporary.

In a sporting race, there is only one winner, but in the race that is life, there can be countless winners. You surely can be one. The measure is not the winning, but how well you ran the race.

What good did you do? What did you accomplish? Did you make a difference? Is the world a better place for you having lived in it? Did you make a contribution to the human race? What will your friends and family say about you at the end? If you lead a life that is good for you, and for those you encounter along the path, you will achieve serenity and leave behind a lasting legacy of gratification and happiness.

Practice involvement, commitment, caring, giving, helping, contributing and making a difference. Try creating, exerting, resting, dreaming and dream fulfillment.

Enjoy new experiences, travel, discovery, developing one's potential, and being busy with something or someone you love. Never give up. Always look beyond the moment and contemplate an exciting future experience. Believe in the promise that life can forever hold.

Focus your mind on something that will make you feel good: a delicious meal, a warm bath, holding someone you adore, taking a walk in the warm, glowing sunlight, caressing your child.

Use and savor each of your senses; sight to look at beautiful things, sound to hear lovely music, smell to breathe in warming aromas, feel to experience things that delight you, touch to touch someone you love.

HAPPINESS GUARANTEED OR YOUR MISERY BACK

"The greatest challenge in life is discovering who you are. The second greatest is being happy with what you find." Find a new friend in the mirror. Befriend yourself in body, mind and spirit. See the good in yourself. See your potential. Be kind, and listen to your inner voice as it encourages you to turn disappointment into hope, negatives into positives, struggles into victories.

You can't control external events, but you can control your view of what happens. Never forget that your response to what happens, rather than what actually does happen, will determine how happy or unhappy you will allow yourself to become.

Life is what happens to you while you're making other plans, so you must be adaptive. Live the day. Live the moment. Plan, but don't waste time on disappointments or disillusionments. Adjust, renew and design an even better, new plan. Turn your vision into reality. Today is a good day for a beginning. Repackage yourself, and you can become almost anything.

Make your exposure to this book a life-changing experience that inspires you to be optimistic and happy from this moment forward by realizing that happiness is not the absence of problems. It's the ability to deal with them and you have this ability by summoning unprecedented control over your mind.

Know it won't be simple, but as John Kennedy said in 1962, "We choose to go to the moon and do other things not because it's easy but because it's hard." It's never easy; it's life! You may stumble along the way, but if you stick with it, controlling your thoughts and dreams, you will get the results you want. You have the power—develop it, practice it, refine it. Your goal is happiness—achieve it!

Believe in happy endings.

About the Authors

J. MORTON DAVIS has been a Wall Street investment banker, entrepreneur, economist, and venture capitalist for the last six decades. He graduated from Brooklyn College in 1957 and received his MBA with distinction from Harvard Business School in 1959. He is currently chairman and sole owner of D.H. Blair Investment Banking Corp., which specializes in financing emerging growth companies. Davis lives on Long Island, New York, with his wife Rozi.

RUKI D. RENOV (formerly Davidowitz), a native New Yorker, is the author of the very popular books *The Art of the Date, The Art of Marriage* and the children's book, *Don't Burst My Bubble*. She worked on her father's, Morton Davis, book *From Hard Knocks to Hot Stocks* and her mother's, Rosalind Davidowitz Davis, book, *Living, Loving and Laughing and Other Things I Do Before Breakfast*. She directed, conceived and helped arrange three musical CDs performed by her family.

An accomplished and beloved wife, mother and grandmother, Mrs. Renov studied undergraduate psychology and holds a master's degree in finance with honors (Beta Gamma Sigma) from the Bernard Baruch Graduate School of Business.

Mrs. Renov resides with her husband Kal, a private venture capital investor, in Lawrence, New York.